MAJOR & MRS HOLT'S
Battlefield Guide to the
NORMANDY LANDING BEACHES

"Believe me, Lang, the first 24 hours of the invasion will be decisive... for the Allies, as well as for Germany, it will be the longest day."

Field-Marshal Rommel to his aide-de-camp, April 1944.

The American Garden and Pool, Mémorial, Caen.

MAJOR & MRS HOLT'S
Battlefield Guide to the

NORMANDY
LANDING BEACHES

Tonie and Valmai Holt

Leo Cooper

By the same authors:

Picture Postcards of the Golden Age: A Collector's Guide
Till the Boys Come Home: the Picture Postcards of the First World War
The Best of Fragments from France by Capt Bruce Bairnsfather
In Search of the Better 'Ole: The Life, Works and Collectables of Bruce Bairnsfather
Picture Postcard Artists: Landscapes, Animals and Characters
Stanley Gibbons Postcard Catalogue: 1980, 1981, 1982, 1984, 1985, 1987
Germany Awake! The Rise of National Socialism illustrated by Contemporary
Postcards
I'll Be Seeing You: the Picture Postcards of World War II
Holts' Battlefield Guidebooks: Normandy-Overlord/Market-Garden/Somme/Ypres
Battlefields of the First World War: A Traveller's Guide
Major & Mrs Holt's Concise Battlefield Guide to the Ypres Salient
Major & Mrs Holt's Battle Maps: The Somme/The Ypres Salient/
Normandy/Gallipoli
Major & Mrs Holt's Battlefield Guide to the Somme + Battle Map
Major & Mrs Holt's Battlefield Guide to the Ypres Salient + Battle Map
Major & Mrs Holt's Battlefield Guide to Gallipoli + Battle Map
Violets From Oversea: 25 Poets of the First World War, Reprinted as Poets of the
Great War, 1999
My Boy Jack: The Search for Kipling's Only Son

In Preparation:

Major & Mrs Holt's Battlefield Guide to Market-Garden + Battle Map

First published in 1999, Second Edition 2000.
Reprinted by LEO COOPER an imprint of
Pen & Sword Books Ltd
47 Church Street, Barnsley, South Yorkshire S70 2AS

A CIP catalogue record for this book is available from the British Library

ISBN 0 85052 662-0

CONTENTS

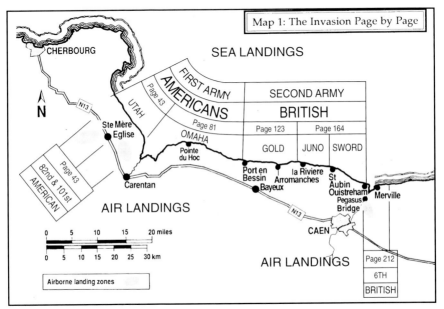

ABBREVIATIONS

Abbreviations used for military units are listed below. At intervals the full name of a unit is repeated in the text in order to aid clarity. Other abbreviations and acronyms are explained where they occur.

AB	Airborne	Fr	French
AEAF	Allied Expeditionary Air Force	GC	George Cross
		Gen	General
Armd	Armoured	Ger	German
Bde	Brigade	Gren	Grenadier
BEF	British Expeditionary Force	Inf	Infantry
		Lt	Lieutenant
Bn	Battalion	LZ	Landing Zone
Brig	Brigadier	Maj	Major
Can	Canadian	Mem	Memorial
Cdo	Commando	MoH	Medal of Honour
Cdr	Commander	Mus	Museum
C-in-C	Commander-in-Chief	OP	Observation Post
Civ	Civilian	Para	Parachute
Col	Colonel	Pfc	Private First Class
Com Deb Mon Sig	Comité du Débarquement Monument Signal	PIR	Para Inf Regit
		Prov	Provisional
		Regt	Regiment
Coy	Company	RM	Royal Marine
Cpl	Corporal	RV	Rendezvous
CWGC	Commonwealth War Graves Commission	Sgt	Sergeant
		SGW	Stained Glass Window
DD	Duplex Drive		
Div	Division	SOP	Standard Operational Procedure
DSC	Distinguished Service Cross		
		Sp	Special
DZ	Dropping Zone	Spt	Support
Eng	Engineer	Sqn	Squadron
FOO	Forward Observation Officer	WN	Wiederstandsnest

INTRODUCTION

Each year, especially since the important 40th anniversary in June 1984, the numbers of visitors to the Landing Beaches, cemeteries and memorials, war museums (some of which prefer to be known as 'peace' museums) in Normandy increases steadily. 1984 was the year that saw the mushrooming of Veterans' organisations, as many of those who participated in the historic events of 1944 reached retirement age and had more time to think back to the experiences of their youth and to the comrades who shared those experiences - some of whom they had to leave behind. Each year new memorials and plaques to divisions, regiments, even to individuals, are dedicated to those who took part in the D-Day Landings and the Battle for Normandy.

The years preceding and following the 50th Anniversary in 1994 saw the inauguration of many new memorials, including the impressive statues to Generals Eisenhower and Montgomery (at Bayeux and Colleville-Mongtomery respectively) and to Stan Hollis VC and the Green Howards at Crépon. They also saw the setting-up of the *Normandie Terre-Liberté* routes and signs by the *Départements* involved in the Landings and the Battle for Normandy (Calvados, La Manche and l'Orne).

The 55th Anniversary inspired another spate of concrete (sometimes literally, but more usually in marble or bronze) expressions of the gratitude of Norman towns for their liberators and homage to their civilian dead and of pride and remembrance of the regiments who took part. Many modest plaques and monuments have been replaced by more impressive memorials - especially along the coastal towns of JUNO and SWORD. The most ambitious projects are the building at UTAH Beach of the American Wall of Remembrance planned, but not executed, at the *Mémorial* of Caen and the rebuilding of a museum at Pegasus Bridge.

Museums range from grandiose and official (like the *Mémorial* Museum at Caen) to private and amateur collections (as at Saint Laurent). Elements of Hitler's Atlantic Wall defences are in some places extraordinarily well-preserved (for example the batteries at Longues, Crisbecq, etc). Shell holes still pock the landscape (as at Pointe du Hoc). Remnants of the brilliantly conceived Mulberry Harbour can still be clearly seen (at Arromanches). The main sites and memorials are well maintained, marked and signed by Departmental and local councils and the *Comité du Débarquement* (qv).

There are, therefore, now more than 300 monuments, memorials, museums, markers and plaques in Normandy to commemorate the Normandy Landings and the Battle for Normandy (a total greater than those of Ypres and the Somme added together). In this book we have selected only those which lie along our five recommended itineraries. For the most part (with notable exceptions like the Headquarters of Generals Patton, Eisenhower and Montgomery) these are confined to the area to the seaward side of the A/N13 road which stretches the length of our area from Cherbourg to Caen and was, to a first approximation, where the Allies hoped to be at the end of D-Day. Another exception is a visit to the site of the little-known but terrible **massacre of American parachutists and French civilians at Graignes** near Carentan, which is recounted in some detail in this book. Also told almost for the first time is the story of the dreadful **crash of British transport aircraft and gliders,** and the subsequent massacre of survivors, at the similarly named village of **Grangues** near Cabourg.

Still, each year, veterans and war widows are welcomed at ceremonies of remembrance and friendly '*Vins d'honneur*' by Normans, faithfully grateful for their liberation. That their liberation was won at the expense of fearfully high civilian casualty lists and ruined towns and villages does not diminish the warmth of these gatherings.

Nowhere more than in Normandy are the *Entente Cordiale* and good Franco-American relations alive and well. Nowhere does the flame of remembrance burn more brightly. The visitor to the areas of the Landing Beaches will be met with a wealth of interesting things to do and see as he or she studies the world-shaping events of June 1944.

It is not only the veterans who visit Normandy. More and more young people (who have perhaps studied the Landings in their history lessons at school) and family groups tour the area, interested to see where dad, or grandad, fought or where history was made.

To add to our own extensive researches, many veterans and local civilians who experienced the events of June 1944 have kindly given us their personal, vivid accounts. Their words will bring those events alive, whether they be heroic, mundane, fearful, amusing, or simply human. Such is warfare.

1998 saw the production of Steven Spielberg's epic film, **Saving Private Ryan,** based on the American policy of attempting to remove the last remaining sons of a family from the danger zone. The story of the 'Pals' Battalion-like 29th Division, whose actions feature in the film, is told in detail in this book, using participants' personal memories recounted to the authors. Hailed as one of the truest representations of modern warfare ever filmed, **Saving Private Ryan** brought the D-Day story to a new generation and rekindled interest in those who lived through it. Visitors to Normandy have grown apace yet again as a result, the American Cemetery having 1.25 million visitors in 1998.

When following the battlefield tours in each chapter, the visitor will be going through one of the most beautiful regions of France - the *Départements* of Calvados and La Manche. To assist you in making the most of their varied attractions and delicious local specialities, some helpful tourist information is given to help you enjoy your visit to Normandy as much as we always do. And if you are an armchair traveller, we hope this book will add to your knowledge of this fascinating campaign.

Tonie and Valmai Holt
Sandwich, Kent. 1999

How To Use This Guide

T his book is designed to guide the visitor around the main sites and features, memorials, museums and cemeteries of the D-Day Landing Beaches, and to provide sufficient information about those places to allow an elementary understanding of what happened where. It makes extensive use of veterans' and participants' memories.

Prior To Your Visit

Read the following sections carefully and mark up the recommended maps (see below). There is no doubt that a better picture of what happened on D-Day, and why it happened, can be obtained from a general understanding of the background to the invasion. Therefore, the traveller is advised to read the Historical Summary below and the brief introductory passages at the beginning of each itinerary before setting out on the tour.

For current information about travelling in France, the reader is highly recommended to obtain a copy of the annual *Reference Guide for the Traveller in France* or *The Essential Guide to Normandy* - see the Tourist Information Section below.

Choosing Your Routes

If You Wish to Visit a Particular Place

Use the index at the back of the book to locate what you wish to visit. If it is a particular grave, find the location from the Commonwealth War Graves Commission/American Battle Monuments Commission (see below) before you set out.

If You Just Want to 'Tour the Beaches'

The beaches landed on by the Americans are covered in Itineraries One and Two and those by the British or Canadians in Itineraries Three, Four and Five.

The Itineraries/Miles Covered/Duration/Rwc/Op

There are five Itineraries, which need not be taken in any particular sequence, nor travelled in the directions given in this book, though it will ease navigation if they are.

The compostion of the itineraries is based upon what the authors, in many years of conducting interested groups around the area, have found to be the places that most people have asked to see.

Each itinerary is preceded by an historical account which should be read before, or concurrently, with setting out. The itineraries cover the five Landing Beaches and the areas of the US and British Airborne Operations. Details of the routes are given at the beginning of each timed and measured itinerary. The times stated do not include stops for refreshments. In the heading for each stop is a running mileage total, a suggested length of stay, a reference for the Holts' Map which accompanies this book and an indication (R/WC) if there are refreshment and toilet facilities. OP indicates an Observation Point from which features of the battlefield may be seen.

Travel instructions are indented and written in italics to make them stand out clearly.

It is absolutely essential to set your mileage trip to zero before starting and to make constant reference to it. Distances in the headings are given in miles because the trip meters on British cars still operate in miles. Distances within the text are sometimes given in kilometers and metres as local signposts use those measures.

EXTRA VISITS

In addition to the itineraries, Extra Visits are described to sites of particular interest which lie near to the recommended routes. They are boxed so that they stand out clearly from the main route. Estimates of the round trip mileage and duration are given.

MAPS/LOCAL ROUTE GUIDES

The guide book has been designed to be used with *Major & Mrs Holt's Battle Map of the Normandy Landing Beaches* and the words 'Map -' in the heading indicate the map reference for that location. Frequent use of this map will also assist you in orientating, give a clear indication of the distances involved in possible walks and show points of interest which are not included in the itineraries or Extra Visits. The map also shows the D-Day objective lines, the line of *Club Route* (the axis of the movement of British forces once the Allies had broken out of Normandy) and *Liberty Highway* (the axis followed by the American forces). A number of clear and simple sketch maps are also provided in the text. The 'Landing Beaches Page By Page' sketch on the Contents page provides a rapid index to the actions on the beaches.

The Michelin Map 231 (1:200,000) which covers the whole Normandy area is also recommended. IGN *(Institut Géographique National)* produce more detailed maps (1:100,000 and 1:50,000) of the Landing Beaches.

Local Route Signs. Normandie Terre-Liberté

The *Départements* of Calvados, La Manche and the Orne have signed eight recommended local routes for what is described as an open-air museum of memory in

Normandy, Land of Liberty. Their white directional signs all carry the logo of a seagull in flight and at important sites well-researched, informative blue signboards (called Normandie Terre-Liberté - **NTL Totems** throughout this guide) describe the other sites in the section and summarise what happened at the site in French and in English. The sections are:-

1. **Overlord - L'Assaut (The Assault)**
   Pegasus Bridge/SWORD/JUNO/GOLD Beaches
2. **D-Day - *Le Choc* (The Onslaught)**
   Bayeux/Port-en-Bessin/OMAHA Beach/Pointe du Hoc/UTAH Beach
3. **Objectif - *un Port* (Objective - a Port)**
   US Airborne/UTAH Beach to Cherbourg
4. ***L'Affrontement* (The Confrontation)**
   The British break-out round Caen/Panzers in the Bocage
5. **Cobra - *Percée* (Operation COBRA/The Breakout)**
   From Cherbourg to Avranches. Patton's tanks on Liberty Highway
6. ***Le Contre-Attaque* (The Counter-Attack)**
   Last German offensive at Mortain. The Panzers Retreat
7. ***L'Encerclement* (The Encirclement)**
   From Alençon to l'Aigle. Gen. Leclerc's tanks progress. 8th German Army encircled.
8. ***Le Dénouement* (The Outcome)**
   From Caen to l'Aigle. The Polish, Canadian and British close the Falaise Gap.
   End of the Battle of Normandy.

A descriptive leaflet, *The D-Day Landings and The Battle of Normandy*, describing the routes, is available from all main tourist offices.

NTL Totem, US Cemetery,
St Laurent.

HISTORICAL SUMMARY

BACKGROUND TO NORMANDY

Pre-1940

The name 'Normandy' derives from the Norsemen who invaded the area in the ninth century. The land they occupied was known as *Neustrie* (Kingdom of the West), one of three Frankish Kingdoms founded by Childeric in 567. It was inhabited by Celtic, Iberian and Gallic tribes who had already been conquered by the Romans in 50BC. The quarrelsome tribes were subdued by Roman rule and an uneasy peace, broken only by the warring Francs and Carolingians, reigned - until the Norman invasion.

The story of the most famous Norman of all, William the Bastard (also known as 'the Conqueror'), is charted in the famous Bayeux Tapestry - a *must* when visiting Normandy (see Bayeux entry below). When William invaded England in 1066 it was with the greatest invasion fleet and force the world had ever known. The fleet and force that invaded, in the opposite direction, in 1944 was also the greatest invasion fleet and force the world had hitherto known. The irony of the conjunction of these two historical landmarks is recorded in the Latin inscription on the Bayeux Memorial: *Nos a Gulielmo victi victoris Patriam liberavimus* ('We, once conquered by William, have now set free the conqueror's native land').

After the Normans it was the English who were to be Normandy's next invaders - during the 100 Years' War. As in 1944, the proximity of Normandy's fine beaches to the English coast attracted invaders, such as Edward III and Henry V. The last battle in Normandy of the 100 Years' War took place in 1450 in Formigny (on what is now the N13 behind OMAHA beach). It is marked by a splendid memorial that was knocked over by a Sherman tank in 1944, but now once more proudly dominates the town's crossroads.

From then until the German Occupation in 1940, the province flourished. Its temperate climate and good soil fostered successful agriculture and dairy farming. Its plentiful seas offered a rich harvest of seafood. The province's reputation for rich gastronomy encouraged tourism, which developed in the 1890s with the rail link to Paris and the burgeoning of smart resorts like Cabourg, Deauville and Trouville. For Normandy it was truly the beginning of the *Belle Epoque,* and royalty, high society and the artistic monde savoured its clear air, beautiful sandy beaches and fine Romanesque and Norman architecture. It was to remain so until the Fall of France in 1940.

The Occupation 1940-44

For the four years until June 1944, the phlegmatic Normans by and large evolved a comfortable *modus vivendi* with their German occupiers. The quality of the German troops during the occupation was generally poor. There was a high percentage of under- or over-age soldiers and convalescents. Many of them were non-German. Most Normans settled for a quiet life with them - glad of the money they could make by supplying much-appreciated dairy produce, cider and Calvados. Underneath the sleepy surface, active members of the Resistance worked by day and, more often, by night. Forbidden radios, tuned to the BBC, picked up the message which was to announce the Allied Invasion.

This message was the first verse of Paul Verlaine's *Chanson d'Automne* (Autumn Song). The first three lines,

> Les sanglots longs
> Des violons
> De l'Automne

(The long sobs of autumn violins)
was broadcast on 1 June. On 5 June, the next three lines,

> Blessent mon coeur
> D'une longueur
> Monotone

(Wound my heart with a monotonous languor)
followed. It signalled that the invasion would take place in 48 hours.

From 6 June 1944

As a reprisal, and in a certain amount of panic, when the Germans realised the scale of the landings, they executed (by shooting) all the male Resistance workers in Caen Prison except two - a youth of only 16 and a man whose name was wrongly recorded by the Germans, who thus did not call him out to be shot. The killings started on the evening of 6 June and continued the next day. Over eighty men were executed.

The Normans certainly paid dearly for their liberation. As well as these Resistance executions, thousands of civilians were killed over the next seventy or so days in Allied bombings and bombardments and in the fierce fighting between the invaders and occupiers.

In Caen alone, starting with an incendiary bomb raid on 6 June and continuing to its liberation on 9 July, at the very lowest count 2,000 (and it could have been as many as 5,000 as records were impossible to keep in those fearsome days) civilians were killed. Thousands more were injured and made homeless.

Lives were lost, homes were destroyed, albeit on a lesser scale, all along the landing beaches. Valuable farm land was scarred and pitted. Livestock was killed in profusion. One of the most vivid memories of many D-Day veterans is the pathetic sight of bloated cows, their legs up-turned, and the dreadful stench of rotting animals. Yet, today the French welcome returning veterans with genuine warmth.

'At one of the wine receptions,' wrote John Slaughter, veteran of the US 29th Division, returning to Normandy in September 1988 for the unveiling of his Divisional

Memorial at Vierville, 'many of the locals would shake hands and say, "Thank you for what you did". This is after we tore hell out of their homes and villages. After three years of living under the Boche iron boot we were their liberators. I now have a different perspective of the French.'

Memorials are on the whole well maintained, ceremonies are well attended, by local people and Resistance workers and Free French standard bearers, often delightfully out of step, standards sometimes less than rigidly held, beret and *Gauloise* both at a jaunty angle, but with hearts in a very correct place.

Although of only small significance, there was another side to the coin. There was an element of collaboration during the occupation. Some British veterans recall being met by fierce sniper fire, which turned out to be from young Frenchmen. After the invasion many female fraternisers had to be ignominiously shaved, tarred and feathered. Returning German veterans are still sometimes greeted with more than cordial enthusiasm in some households - notably, it is reported, when members of 12th SS Panzer attended the burial of Obersturmführer Michael Wittmann in La Cambe German Cemetery in May 1983.

But these were rare cases and the spirit of remembrance and gratitude fostered by the unceasing efforts of the *Comité du Débarquement* (qv) and its chairman, ex-Minister Raymond Triboulet, and by individual French men and women seems as strong as ever.

Great Anglo/American/Canadian-French ceremonies are held every fifth year. But each 6 June and on the successive days into July that mark their liberation, small French *Communes* - like Hermanville with its 'H.M.S.' (*Histoire, Mémoire, Souvenir*) Association and private individuals - like Bernard Saulnier, the Amfréville farmer who for many years held 'open house' for British commandos - welcome returning veterans. *L'Entente Cordiale* is alive and well and manifest along the Normandy battlefields and beaches.

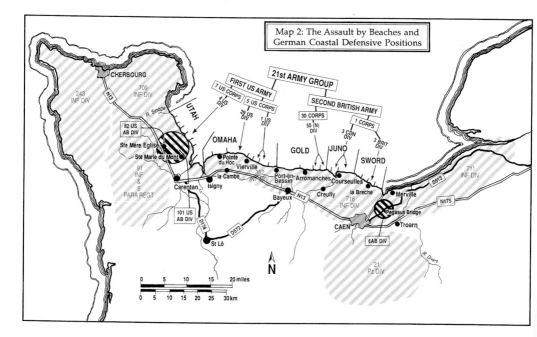

Map 2: The Assault by Beaches and German Coastal Defensive Positions

BACKGROUND TO THE INVASION

Blitzkrieg - War begins - The First Two Years

At dawn on Friday 1 September 1939 Operation WEISS (White) began. Almost fifty German divisions, including six Panzer divisions, supported by over fifteen hundred aircraft, invaded Poland. It was the start of World War II. In Britain general mobilisation was proclaimed. The French went a stage further and instituted martial law.

The German *Blitzkrieg* (lightning war) was overwhelmingly successful. The basic tactic was a close co-operation between tanks and aircraft with a rapid movement deep into enemy territory to sever the defending army from its supplies and communications. The original concept of *Blitzkrieg* has been attributed to both General Hans von Seeckt of the Reichswehr in the 1920s and to Captain Basil Liddell Hart in the 1930s, but its formidable exponents in September 1939 were two German Army Groups: North, commanded by Colonel General Fedor von Bock, and South, commanded by Colonel General Gerd von Rundstedt.

The progress of one formation in particular stood out as a prime example of *Blitzkrieg* at its most formidable - the advance of the XIX Panzer Corps commanded by General Heinz Guderian.

It was all over by 5 October when the last Polish troops surrendered near Warsaw. The Russians too had marched into Poland on 17 September and in accord with their non-aggression pact the Germans and Russians divided Poland between them. Then the Germans and the Russians stopped. The Phoney War began.

The Phoney War

President Roosevelt sent emissaries from America to investigate the possibility of a negotiated settlement. The BEF went to France and the European nations eyed each other across the Franco-Belgian borders and prepared for war. Eight months later, after the period known as the 'Phoney War', or the *Sitzkrieg*, the Germans struck again.

Dunkirk

On Friday 10 May 1940 in Operation GELB (Yellow) seventy-seven German divisions, including ten Panzer divisions and two airborne divisions, invaded Belgium, Holland and Luxembourg. Three Panzer Corps, one of which was Guderian's XIX, struck east through the Ardennes forests outflanking the French in the Maginot Line.

That same day the BEF, strung along the Belgian border, advanced into Belgium to take up positions along the Dyle River under a plan that Field Marshal Montgomery later described as a 'dog's breakfast'. In England the 'Pilgrim of Peace', Neville Chamberlain, resigned, and Winston Churchill became Prime Minister

The German *Blitzkrieg* worked again. Confused by the speed of the German advance, and with no proper liaison between British, Belgian and French commanders, the Allied response was ineffective. The BEF withdrew to the Channel and at Dunkirk between 26 May and 4 June a quarter of a million British soldiers were evacuated - among them the 3rd Division's commander, Major General Bernard Law Montgomery.

Two weeks later General Erwin Rommel's 7th (Ghost) Panzer Division entered the port of Cherbourg in Normandy as British troops were being evacuated under the covering fire of the French cruiser *Courbet*. His division had covered over 140 miles the previous day. At the end of the same week, the French signed an armistice in Marshal Foch's old railway carriage at Compiègne. Adolf Hitler went on a sightseeing tour of Paris. Now he was ready to turn his eyes towards Britain.

Alone

One of the planks of Adolf Hitler's rise to power was his insistence that all he wanted to do was to redress the wrongs inflicted upon Germany by the Treaty of Versailles after World War I. In addition, he claimed, he did not want to go to war with Britain.

At the end of June 1940 various overtures for a negotiated peace were made by Berlin to London. Lord Halifax, the British Foreign Secretary, was 'strictly forbidden to entertain any such suggestion' by Prime Minister Churchill. Hitler had overlooked the fact that Britain's new leader was a descendant of Marlborough and not inclined to give in.

Even before the fall of France, the Prime Minister had told the nation, 'We shall defend our island whatever the cost may be'. The Germans, distrustful of their new ally Russia, planned to attack her, but first, since they would not negotiate, the British had to be dealt with. Southern England had to be invaded.

The Battle of Britain

The German plan for the invasion of Britain, Operation SEALION, could not be implemented until the Royal Air Force had been destroyed.

Hitler's directive for the invasion began, 'The landing operation must be a surprise crossing on a broad front extending approximately from Ramsgate to a point west of the Isle of Wight ...', and, as an essential preparation to the invasion, the directive continued, 'The English Air Force must be eliminated.'

The task fell to the Luftwaffe under Reichsmarschall Hermann Goering and he had little doubt that it could be achieved. The Germans had over three thousand combat aircraft available while the British had less than half that number. Allowing for the fact that the British had to spread their aircraft in anticipation of attacks anywhere in the South of England and the Germans could concentrate theirs, the odds against the RAF were much greater than 2:1.

The Luftwaffe offensive against the Royal Air Force began on 'Eagle Day', 13 August 1940 and by 5 September the RAF, its bases badly damaged and losing pilots and planes faster than they could be replaced, was on the point of collapse. Then, in retaliation for air raids on Berlin, Hitler changed his plans and ordered an all-out offensive on London. The pressure on the RAF eased. Planes and airfields were repaired. Knowing, too that the Germans' target was London, the RAF could now concentrate against their enemy and even up the odds. Radar (Radio Aid to Detection and Ranging) and ULTRA helped too. German air losses increased. Daylight bombing was replaced by less costly night attacks and then, when it became clear that Britain could not be defeated quickly, Operation SEALION was cancelled. It was 17 September 1940.

The Battle of Britain had been won, the Invasion had been stopped. Now came the Blitz.

The Blitz

The bombing of London and other industrial cities and ports in Britain was a night-time terror which lasted from September 1940 until May 1941. During this period 39,600 civilians were killed and 46,100 injured.

On Sunday 22 June 1941, Germany launched her invasion of Russia - operation BARBAROSSA. The Luftwaffe, needing every available aircraft - including bombers - on the Eastern Front for what was expected to be only a 6-month campaign, turned its attention away from Britain. The Blitz was over.

Before the end of the year Winston Churchill spoke in secret to his Combined Operations Staff about another cross-Channel invasion. This one, however, would be going in the opposite direction to SEALION and would eventually be called OVERLORD.

COUNTDOWN TO OVERLORD

1941

March	The Lend-Lease Act was passed in America, and President Roosevelt immediately declared that the defence of Great Britain was vital to the defence of the United States. Thus, every form of support for Britain short of American intervention began.
June	Hitler invaded Russia in Operation BARBAROSSA.
October	Winston Churchill told Lord Louis Mountbatten and his Combined Operations Staff to prepare plans for 'our great counter-invasion of Europe'.
December	On 7 December Japanese aircraft attacked the American naval base at Pearl Harbor in Hawaii and Japan declared war on Britain. The following day the United States declared war on Japan and on Germany on 11 December. Britain and America were allies now in every way. At Christmas, Prime Minister Winston Churchill and President Roosevelt met in Washington to plan Allied strategy. The Americans agreed to concentrate on Europe and 1943 was chosen as the invasion year. Under the code-name BOLERO American forces were to be assembled in Britain in preparation for the assault. During 1941 Hitler ordered the construction of a fortified wall to protect the coastline of occupied Europe from invasion. Known as the Atlantic Wall, it was to stretch from Norway to Spain and incorporate 15,000 strong-points.

1942

June	Eisenhower was sent to Britain to command the build-up of US

Forces. He established his HQ in 20 Grosvenor Gardens and had flats in Claridge's and the Dorchester Hotel. Because of appalling Russian casualties, Soviet dictator Josef Stalin insisted that Churchill and Roosevelt open a second front in order to relieve the pressure on the USSR. The British resisted an early cross-Channel invasion, the Americans supported it. Two plans were considered, called ROUNDUP and SLEDGEHAMMER. The British view prevailed and a European invasion was replaced by an attack on Dieppe and a landing in North Africa.

August
A mainly Canadian force attempted a frontal assault on the Nazi-occupied and defended harbour of Dieppe. It was a disaster. But two major lessons were learned: - 1, that armoured vehicles capable of defeating pill-boxes had to land with the assault troops, and 2, that a frontal assault on a fortified harbour must not be repeated. These lessons led to the development of floating tanks and floating harbours.

October
Montgomery won the 2nd Battle of El Alamein and began the advance which drove Rommel out of North Africa.

November
The Allied landing in North Africa, Operation TORCH, was commanded by General Eisenhower. The landings were successful. It was almost a rehearsal for what would happen in June 1944.

1943

January
The Russians completed the destruction of the German armies at Stalingrad. Coupled with El Alamein the victory marked the Nazis' high-water mark. Hereafter their fortunes declined.
At Casablanca, Churchill and Roosevelt appointed Lieutenant General F.E. Morgan as Chief of Staff to the Supreme Allied Commander (COSSAC) with the task of preparing plans for the invasion of Europe that would:
1. Lead the Germans to believe that the main landing would be in the area of Calais. The general code-name adopted for these deception plans was BODYGUARD.
2. Allow a full-scale assault to be made across the Channel early in 1944. COSSAC HQ was established in Norfolk House in St James's Square, London and today there is a commemorative plaque on the exterior of the building.

June
Lord Louis Mountbatten held a conference with COSSAC, code-named RATTLE, at which Normandy was chosen as the area for the main landings and it was decided that floating harbours, code-named MULBERRY, would be towed across the Channel for use off the beaches.

August
At the QUADRANT conference in Quebec, Churchill and Roosevelt agreed upon a date for the cross-Channel invasion. It was 1 May 1944 and its code-name was OVERLORD.

December	On Tuesday 7 December President Roosevelt told General Eisenhower that he would be the Supreme Commander for OVERLORD. On Sunday 12 December Hitler appointed Rommel to command his Atlantic Wall defences. On Friday 24 December the Allied team that was to command the invasion was announced:

Supreme Commander   General Eisenhower
Deputy Supreme Commander   Air Chief Marshal Tedder
Naval C-in-C   Admiral Sir Bertram Ramsay
Ground Force Commander   General Montgomery

1944

1 January	General Montgomery relinquished command of his beloved 8th Army in Italy and flew to England to set up his invasion HQ at his old school, St Paul's, in Hammersmith.
15 January	General Eisenhower arrived back in London and took up quarters in Hayes Lodge just off Berkeley Square.
21 January	Generals Eisenhower and Montgomery agreed changes to General Morgan's COSSAC invasion plans that set the target date as 31 May, extended the landing area west across the Cotentin Peninsula towards Cherbourg and increased the initial seaborne force from three to five divisions.
5 March	Supreme Headquarters Allied Expeditionary Force (SHAEF) moved from Grosvenor Gardens to an old US 8th Air Force HQ at Bushey Park near Hampton Court. Its code-name was WIDEWING. General Eisenhower lived nearby in Telegraph Cottage, Kingston-upon-Thames.
4 April	Exercise SMASH, a D-Day rehearsal using live ammunition, took place at Studland Bay in Dorset for troops of 50th (British) Division. The DD tanks were launched in the dark, 5,000 yards out. Seven tanks sank and six men were drowned.
6 April	All leave cancelled for troops destined for OVERLORD.
22-9 April	Operation TIGER, a D-Day rehearsal for troops assaulting UTAH beach, took place at Slapton Sands between Plymouth and Dartmouth. Nine German E-boats stumbled upon the force at sea during the night, sinking two landing craft full of men. Some 700 men were killed, three times more than would die on UTAH on D-Day. Fortunately, however, the Germans did not connect the action with an invasion of Normandy.
1 May	General Eisenhower and Admiral Sir Bertram Ramsay, aware that the energetic Rommel was thickening Hitler's Atlantic Wall and covering the beaches with below-the-water obstacles, decided that the landing would be in daylight, and at low tide, so that the obstacles would be visible. Admiral Ramsay was responsible for

NEPTUNE, the sea transportation and landing phase of OVERLORD.

2-6 May   Operation FABIUS, the final rehearsal for OVERLORD, took place at Slapton Sands.

8 May   SHAEF selected 5 June as D-Day - invasion day. The only other totally suitable alternatives that month were the 6th or 7th.

15 May   HM The King, General Eisenhower, Field Marshal Smuts and others attended a conference at General Montgomery's St Paul's HQ to review the final plans for OVERLORD.

18 May   German radio said, 'The invasion will come any day now'.

23 May   The camps containing the soldiers who were to land on 'D-Day' were sealed with barbed wire. Many had armed guards. Senior Commanders were told that D-Day was 5 June, and detailed briefings began.

28 May   The time that the leading troops were to land, 'H-Hour', was settled as, 'a few minutes before 0600 hours and after 0700 hours'. The Americans were to land first on beaches named UTAH and OMAHA. Then, minutes afterwards, to allow for the difference in the time of low tide, the British and Canadians were to land on GOLD, JUNO and SWORD. Generals Eisenhower and Montgomery moved elements of their HQs to HMS *Dryad* at Southwick House near Portsmouth, in order to be near the embarkation ports.

1 June   The first regular morning and evening meetings were begun between senior commanders at Southwick House, principally to discuss the deteriorating weather conditions in the Channel. General Eisenhower, driven by his English driver Kay Summersby (qv), began a daily shuttle between his Forward HQ at Southwick, Bushey Park, his Main HQ, and Stanmore, where SHAEF Air HQ was located. The weather forecast was not good.

4 June   At 0415 General Eisenhower decided that the weather was too bad for the landing to take place and postponed the invasion for twenty-four hours. All the convoys at sea had to reverse their courses. But two British midget submarines, X20 and X23, continued on their way and, just before midnight, took up their positions off the beaches to act as markers for the invasion army when it arrived.

5 June   At 0415 General Eisenhower sought the opinions of his fellow Commanders. Should he postpone again? The weather was still bad, though a brief lull was hoped for during the next 48 hours. Any more delay and the sea-sick army might not be fit to fight. What was worse, the Germans might find out what was going on. 'OK', said Eisenhower, 'we'll go.'

THE INVASION PLANS

The Assault Plan

The plan for the Allied assault on the beaches of Normandy was code-named OVERLORD. The Supreme Commander was General Eisenhower and he appointed General Montgomery to command all British and American land forces.

On 3 January 1944 General Montgomery heard a presentation of the first invasion plan drawn up by COSSAC under General Morgan in July 1943. He criticized the narrow three division front of the assault and insisted that it be extended at each end - to the west across the Carentan estuary to include beaches eventually to be named UTAH and to the east across the River Orne to include the heights above the German gun battery at Merville, the D-Day target of the 6th Airborne Division. The sea landing forces were to increase to five divisions.

The COSSAC plan also included an air lift for two-thirds of an airborne division with a direct assault on Caen. General Montgomery changed this to three airborne divisions - two American ones at the western end of the beaches and one British at the eastern end. He dismissed the idea of a direct assault on Caen.

These and other changes were approved by the Supreme Commander on 21 January 1944 and they formed the basis of the final assault plan. There was, however, a second plan.

The Deception Plan

The deception plan, named FORTITUDE, set out to deceive the Germans as to when and where the invasion would take place.

It was clearly impossible to hide all the preparations for invasion that were going on in England and so, by using camouflage and dummy equipment, the impression was given that things were less advanced than they were, thus suggesting a later invasion date than planned.

Further, by flying twice as many air missions in the Pas de Calais area as in Normandy, by the movement of American and Canadian troops (including General George Patton, whom the Germans considered to be the Allies' best field General) into the Dover-Folkestone area, the picture presented to the enemy was of an impending invasion across the narrowest part of the Channel.

Immediately prior to and during the assault, tactical deceptions were employed - dummy parachutists called Ruperts (one can be seen in the Ste Mère Eglise Museum) were dropped over a wide area to confuse the Germans as to the strength and exact location of the attack. Silver foil called WINDOW was scattered to confuse German radar and naval and air sorties to parts of the coastline other than Normandy were made.

The deception plan did not finish with D-Day. A critical period for an assault landing comes just after the assault troops are ashore when the whole apparatus of supply has to be rewound in order to maintain and reinforce the forces already in position. If the Germans could strike quickly with their armour before the Allies got their second wind, the invasion might fail. Therefore the FORTITUDE plan included misinformation designed to convince the Germans that the Normandy landings were a large- scale diversion and that the main invasion was yet to come - in the Calais area -

and hence they would be unwise to commit all their forces, particularly their armour, to a counter-attack in Normandy. A measure of the success of FORTITUDE prior to the invasion was provided by the double agent Juan Pujol, known as GARBO, who in conjunction with MI5 set up a fictitious network of agents reporting to the Germans. Their appreciation of his efforts (his German controller said that his reports were of 'incalculable value') indicated that FORTITUDE was working.

All three elements of the deception worked. The invasion was not expected in Normandy, but across the Pas de Calais so most of the enemy armour, defensive strength and reserves were concentrated in the north; it was not thought likely to take place in early June (the bad weather helped here) though German intelligence had forecast it for 1944, and even after 6 June enemy armoured reserves were held back in anticipation of a second and larger assault across the Straits of Dover.

THE GERMANS

The Altantic Wall

The successful French defence of Verdun against the single-minded assault of the German army during World War I swung the French military towards defence and in the early 1930s, following meetings held in Verdun, led to the building of the Maginot Line fortifications along the French borders facing Germany.

In response Hitler instituted the West Wall (known as the Siegfried Line to the Allies) in 1938, opposite the Maginot Line in the Saar. Made in depths of up to 3 miles, it consisted of mutually supporting fire positions, pill boxes and dragon's-teeth anti-tank obstacles and was carried out by the Todt Organisation, which had built the *autobahns*.

During the preparations for Operation SEALION, conducted under Führer Directive Number 16, the German Navy was instructed to improve and construct casemated heavy gun batteries capable of firing on England and of controlling the Channel approaches in the Pas de Calais area. At the time that Operation SEALION was called off, following the failure of the Luftwaffe to master the RAF, over seventy offensive emplacements were in position.

In December 1941 the Japanese attacked the US Fleet at Pearl Harbor, and America came into the war. Hitler, realising the impact that American involvement would have immediately decided to turn Europe into *Festung Europa* - Fortress Europe. The German Fifteenth Army of seventeen divisions was given the permanent task of defending Fortress Europe from the Cotentin Peninsula to the Channel.

In March 1942, following Field Marshal von Rundstedt's appointment to command Army Group West, the offensive emplacements in the Calais area were incorporated into a new defensive structure that Hitler decreed should run along the western edge of Fortress Europe, should incorporate 15,000 strong points and be built by the Todt Organisation. It was to be a new West Wall, this time to be named 'The Atlantic Wall'.

The Commanders and the Panzers

Although von Rundstedt, Commander in Chief West, was in command of the German Army in Normandy he did not exercise total control over it. Hitler, the German High

Command (OKW), Field Marshal Rommel and General Guderian, Inspector General of Panzers, all believed that the key to the defeat of an Allied invasion lay with the German armoured divisions - but they did not agree how the divisions were to be used and this aggravated the normally complex commander/subordinate relationship into a strained and inefficient chain of command.

Rommel had taken over Army Group B in February 1944 with responsibility for the defence of an area stretching from Holland to the Atlantic coast of France. He divided his force into two - Seventh Army West of the River Orne and Fifteenth Army East (see Map 2). In his opinion the only place to stop the invasion was on the beaches and he demanded that control of the nine armoured divisions in Panzer Group West be given to him so that an immediate counterstroke could be launched against a landing. To carry out his plan he needed to hold the armour close behind the likely landing areas and with such a long coastline to defend it would use up almost all of the German armour.

Guderian did not like the idea of committing armoured formations to the defence of a particular landing area. In his opinion, it could lead to disaster, because if they guessed wrongly about where the invasion would come it would be difficult to correct their mistake. Von Rundstedt held a quite different opinion. He believed that a landing could not be prevented and that the bulk of the armour should be held well back until the true direction of any landing was clear, when a massive and decisive counterstroke could be made.

Hitler, although he favoured Rommel's belief that the first 48 hours after a landing would be the most critical, compromised, and did not give control of the Panzers to his favourite general. Instead, three of the nine Panzer divisions were placed under Rommel's direct command while the remainder, although technically under von Rundstedt, could not be released without the Führer's authority.

The chain of command was made even more complex because the C-in-C West had no operational authority over the Luftwaffe or the Navy, and formations in Army Group B could, and did, receive orders from three different headquarters - Rommel's, von Rundstedt's and Hitler's.

Ironically, in Führer Directive No 40 of 23 March 1942, which was entitled 'Command Organisation on the Coasts', Hitler had said, 'The preparation and execution of defensive operations must unequivocally and unreservedly be concentrated in the hands of one man.' It was fortunate for the Allies that Hitler did not follow his own orders.

In all, Rommel's command had thirty-nine Infantry Divisions and three Panzer divisions at the time of the landings. 21st Panzer was just south of Caen, moved there from Rennes in April to support the 7th Army. The other two Panzer divisions, one west of Paris, the other near Amiens, were to support the 15th Army in the Pas de Calais. In May 1944 Rommel had asked OKW to move the four reserve Panzer divisions nearer to the coast. Von Rundstedt protested and the request was denied.

When the Allies landed, Rommel had only one Panzer division available in the area, the 21st, and that was at the extreme eastern end of the invasion area, behind Caen and the British beaches.

The Infantry

German divisions were classified into four categories, mainly according to their degree of mobility. These categories were: 'capable of full attack', 'limited attack', 'full defence' or 'limited defence'. But mobility could mean a unit equipped with anything from bicycles via horses to motor transport, and the mobility of Army Group West was very limited.

As an example, 243rd Division was converted to a nominal attack division from being a static division in late 1943 by issuing four of its six battalions with bicycles, but the indigenous artillery regiment and anti-tank battalion never received their planned motor transport.

709th Division alongside and to the east of 243rd Division (see Map 2), and whose area included the small village of Ste Mère Eglise on the N13 Cherbourg to Carentan road, was also to be upgraded from a defence to an attack category. That had not been done by June.

More than half of Army Group West was made up from 'ear-nose-and-throat' soldiers, those who were unfit for anything other than static service, perhaps too old, perhaps recovering from wounds. Some formations were units broken on the eastern front and reformed with a mixture of unreliable conscripts - Poles, Russians and Italians.

Yet, by contrast, there were good and experienced soldiers peppered amongst the pack and one of the most highly trained formations was brought in by Rommel. That was the 6th Parachute Regiment. The average age of its soldiers was $17^1/_2$ years and each one had done at least nine jumps, several in darkness.

Rommel's energetic thickening of the Atlantic Wall defences was not confined to under-water obstacles, mines and concrete. He thickened the defenders too. Reserve infantry was brought forward, sacrificing defence in depth for manpower on the beaches, where he felt it was most needed. Every man in forward units had his own defensive position to go to. In February 1944 he brought the 352nd Division, a 'full attack' formation, from St Lô, and placed it in the area from Arromanches to Carentan. It sat behind the beach the Allies called OMAHA.

Between Rommel's arrival in Normandy in 1943 and 6 June 1944, the German infantry defences, despite all the handicaps imposed by Allied bombing, poor mobility, unfit and unwilling soldiers and differences between commanders, had improved beyond measure. An invasion could not be certain to succeed even though the Allies, thanks to Bletchley Park's breaking of the Enigma codes, which the Germans used to protect all their command radio traffic, knew all of the major German dispositions.

Rommel

In February 1944 Rommel took command of Army Group B under the C-in-C West, von Rundstedt, though he had the right of direct access to Adolf Hitler. His task was to check and progress the Atlantic Wall defences and he rapidly set out on a tour of inspection, beginning in Denmark and then going on to the Scheldt and to the Somme, working south-west across Normandy towards Brest.

To his dismay he discovered that the concrete emplacements that were to form the backbone of the Wall were far from complete and he immediately ordered that other defensive works be instituted on the beaches. These included large wooden stakes with explosive mines or shells attached to them, concrete and metal structures designed to stop landing craft, Czech hedgehogs (large three-dimensional six-pointed stars made by welding or bolting three pieces of angle-iron together), concrete tetrahedrons for anti-tank defence and a variety of other underwater mined obstacles whose purpose was to delay an invading force long enough for it to come under direct fire from the defenders.

Between December 1943 and May 1944, Rommel toured furiously. At first he looked at his whole frontage and then, in February and March 1944, repeated the process, paying particular attention to the area of the Pas de Calais. In April and May he travelled extensively in Normandy, exhorting his men to the utmost effort. Fields that might be used for glider landings were dotted with upright stakes placed sufficiently close together to act as anti-airlanding obstacles - these would become known to the Allies as Rommel's Asparagus.

Rommel's efforts in Normandy immediately before the Allied Invasion may just have been coincidence, or prompted by Hitler's spring inspiration that the Allies would land on the Brittany and Cotentin Peninsulas. On 6 May Hitler insisted that the defences on the Normandy coast and in the area of Cherbourg should be strengthened. Rommel told the 7th Army, and the 91st Division was diverted from Nantes to Normandy with, under command, 6th Para Regiment and other units. Their role was plainly stated - defence against airborne landings.

Thus, barely a month before two US airborne divisions were due to drop on the Cotentin, behind the beach code-named UTAH, it was reinforced by troops whose main role was anti-airlanding.

On 9 May Rommel noted in his daily report, 'Drive to the Cotentin Peninsula which seems to have become the focal point of the invasion'. He drove to Houlgate on the coast to the east of Merville, then to Caen for a briefing by senior officers, including the commander of 21st Panzer Division. After lunch he toured the area covered by 716th Infantry Division whose beaches the Allies called GOLD, JUNO and SWORD. Next he visited the concrete casemated naval battery at Longues and then via Grandcamp and Isigny went on to St Lô for dinner.

On 20 May at his HQ at La Roche Guyon, 30 miles west of Paris, Rommel interviewed two British Commando officers who had been captured in the 15th Army area during a raid exploring beach obstacles. They should have been turned over to the SS but Major General Speidel, Rommel's Chief of Staff, brought them to Rommel who sent them on to a prisoner-of-war camp, which probably saved their lives. What the Field Marshal did not find out was that their names were Lieutenant Roy Woodbridge and Lieutenant George Lane and that their unit was No 10 (Inter-Allied) Commando. Just over 2 weeks later No 10 Commando landed on SWORD Beach near Ouistreham. Forty years later George Lane re-visited La Roche Guyon and stood on the same spot where the Field Marshal had interviewed him.

On 3 June Rommel went to see von Rundstedt to talk over his proposed visit to Germany during 5-8 June, when he intended to ask Hitler for two more armoured divisions to be transferred to Normandy.

At 0600 hours on 4 June, in rain and wind, Rommel left for Germany. He was going home for his wife's birthday.

APPROACH ONE

PORTSMOUTH – CHERBOURG / LE HAVRE / CAEN

Portsmouth

As a prelude to a visit to the Normandy Beaches, an overnight stay in the interesting city of Portsmouth is thoroughly recommended. Known as 'The Flagship City', its 800 years of history are excellently recorded and presented in the city's numerous museums, preserved sites and famous ships.

The Romans, the Normans, Henry VIII, Lord Nelson, Palmerston, Dickens - all made their mark. In 1944 Portsmouth was the area from which Force 'S' and Force 'J' set sail, and in the area beyond Havant, west to Christchurch and including Winchester, was the pre-Invasion assembly area of XXX BR Corps.

The troops were confined in sealed camps and security was, in theory, very tight. Throughout the area vast dumps of supplies, vehicles and ammunitions mushroomed. Local airfields were humming with activity. More than 11,000 aircraft - Typhoons, Mosquitos and Thunderbolts - were massing to provide air cover and undertake bombing raids. Bomber Command was to drop 5,000 tons on coastal batteries in Normandy in 7,500 sorties. Parts of the mysterious caissons which were to make up the revolutionary Mulberry harbours were being assembled. It was all a secret difficult to keep from observant locals.

In 1941 Churchill's advice to Mountbatten was 'The South Coast of England is a bastion of defence against Hitler's invasion; you must turn it into a springboard to launch an attack.' On 5 June 1944 that order became reality. Portsmouth is proud of its vital role in that springboard and today preserves the memory in its many well maintained museums.

Information Centres

The Hard (at the entrance to the Historic Dockyard) Tel: 01705 822693.
Southsea Seafront - during Season only - (next to Sea Life Centre) Tel: 01705 832464
City Centre (by main Portsmouth & Southsea Railway Station) Tel: 01705 838382
They can book hotels, provide information and literature on entertainment, events, sports, museums, harbour trips, tours and guides to historic Portsmouth, Southsea and Gosport, including Season Tickets/All-in Passports/Family Tickets etc to all the museums below.

D-Day Museum with Southsea Castle in background.

D-Day Museum, Clarence Esplanade

This is a *must* before crossing the Channel to Normandy. Housed in a modern, custom built exhibition area, its centrepiece is the impressive Overlord Embroidery. It is comparable to the Bayeux Tapestry in its concept. It was commissioned by Lord Dulverton, designed by Sandra Lawrence and made by the Royal School of Needlework in 1968, who took 5 years to complete the 83m (272ft) long embroidery. It depicts the preparations for Operation OVERLORD, the 6 June Invasion and the Battle

Display in D-Day Museum: 'Preparations for D-Day in a forest near Portsmouth'.

for Normandy. When Bill Millin, Lord Lovat's piper who piped the Commandos over the beaches, first saw the tapestry he pointed out a mistake. He had been pictured wearing a steel helmet - the Commandos wore berets. The picture was changed. There is an audio-visual theatre showing the D-Day Landings, and exhibits using modern techniques.

Open:daily (except 24-26 December) but opening times vary with the seasons. Tel: 01705 827261. Access for the disabled.

Vivien Mallock Statues

In the road in front of the museum are two fine bronze statues, one a 7 foot high figure of Field Marshal Montgomery wearing his field-marshal's uniform with his favourite flying jacket over it, with one thumb tucked informally into the pocket, the other hand holding his army commander's orders for the day. Monty was garrison commander in Portsmouth (1937-38), he planned his D-Day strategy in a house on the outskirts of the city and left Portsmouth to land in Normandy with the British invasion force. The other is a 6 foot 1 inch high figure of a seated, 18 year old boy soldier, called 'Ted' by the sculptress, who symbolises "every mother's son" reading a letter from home. The plinth is inscribed with the poignant quatrain

> Decades of easy peace may go their way
> And tide, and time, may drift us far apart,
> But you who shared our savage yesterday
> Will hold the highest places in our heart.

Commissioned by Portsmouth City Council, they were unveiled by the Duke of Kent on 4 June 1996. Monty cost £15,000 and Ted £18,000. Funds were raised by the Normandy Veterans Association and other veterans' associations, individuals and the business community. The statue of Monty is identical to that in Colleville-Montgomery (qv). The statues were all sculpted by Vivien Mallock (qv), wife of Colonel Russ Mallock, a member of the Airborne Trust which commissioned the fine bronzes which are a striking feature on sites in Normandy. They took three months to research and complete. Vivien's studio adjoins the Thruxton MFH Art Foundry of Mike Fry, who cast the figures of all these personalities of the Normandy Campaign.

Naval Heritage Area, The old Royal Dockyard area.
Recorded Infoline Tel: 01705 861512/Visitor Centre Tel: 01705 861533 - with details of opening times/ticket prices to the following:

  The Royal Naval Museum
  HMS *Victory*
  Mary Rose
  HMS *Warrior*
Old Portsmouth Fortifications
Contact the Tourist Information Centres for details of guided walks.
Portchester Castle
Open:daily (except 24-26 December, 1 January) but opening times vary according to season. Tel: 01705 378291.

Portsmouth Cathedral
D-Day memorial window, unveiled by the Queen Mother on 6 June 1984.
Burma Star Window. Cathedral Book Shop. Tel: 01705 823300. **Open: daily** between
services.
Royal Marines Museum, Eastney
A marvellous museum, with relevance to the Normandy Campaign - over 17,500 Royal
Marines took part in the Landings - on board ship and on land.
Open:daily 1000-1700 (except 22-27 December) Tel: 01705 819385.
Royal Navy Submarine Museum, Gosport
Open:daily 1000 hours (except 24 December-1 January) Tel: 01705 529217.
Southsea Castle (shares car park with D-Day Museum)
Open:daily (except 24-26 December) but opening times vary with the seasons. Tel:
01705 827261.
Southwick House: D-Day Wall Map
Now the Officers' Mess of HMS *Dryad*. The D-Day Map Room may be visited **BY
STRICT APPOINTMENT ONLY.** Tel: 01705 284221, Monday-Friday 0900-1200, 1400-1700.

In 1941 Southwick House was requisitioned as a wartime residence and the
School of Navigation moved there. The Action Information Training Centre was
built in 1943 and the first control room completed in 1944.

On 26 April 1944 Admiral Sir Bertram Ramsay, Naval Commander for
Operation OVERLORD, established his headquarters in Southwick House and by
1 June Montgomery parked his famous caravan in the grounds.

It was from the house at 0415 hours, 5 June, that General Eisenhower said, 'Let's
go' - the signal to commence the mighty invasion. In the run up to D-Day the
Supreme Commander had been making daily shuttles between here and his main
headquarters at Bushey Park via his Air Headquarters at Stanmore. His driver was
the English girl Kay Summersby, the former model for the Worth fashion house,
with whom it was rumoured he was having an affair. In her book, *Past Forgetting*,
written when she was dying of cancer and when one might imagine she would
have no motivation to hide the truth, Kay asserts that they were indeed lovers.
Whatever the truth of the matter she paints a picture of a charming and very
human Commander-in-Chief and gives an insight into the overwhelming
pressures that lay on the shoulders of just one man. These pressures led to
Eisenhower writing in his own hand a note accepting full responsibility for the
failure of the invasion. Oddly he dated it July 5, an indication perhaps of the inner
turmoil he must have been undergoing. The note said -

> 'Our landings in the Cherbourg - Havre area have failed to gain a satisfactory foothold
> and I have withdrawn the troops. My decision to attack at this time and place was
> based upon the best information available. The troops, the air and the Navy did all that
> Bravery and devotion to duty could do.
>
> If any blame or fault attaches to the attempt it is mine alone.'

The great D-Day Wall Map, on which the progress of the Invasion was to be charted,
was made of plywood by the Midlands toy company, Chad Valley, in May. The two
men who installed the map were not allowed to go home after they had completed their

work, despite the fact that the area displayed ranged from Norway to Spain, but were held there without access to the outside world until the invasion was under way! It can still be seen, with the D-Day weather maps, in the Map Room here, together with a painting by war artist Norman Wilkinson of the assault forces going into GOLD Beach and other action scenes. The map and the room fell into disuse after D-Day and it was not until the war was over that the operations room was restored. One of the best impressions of the atmosphere of the room during its heyday can be obtained from the painting *Headquarters Room* by the official war artist Barnett Freedman.

Spitbank Fort Visit by ferry from Gosport Pontoon or Clarence Pier.
Open: Easter-mid-September. Tel: 01329 664286.

THE CHANNEL CROSSING

P & O FERRIES. From P & O Ferry Terminal, Portsmouth.
Reservations/Prices/Sailing Times - Tel: 0730 2230/0990 980 555/0870 600 3300.
Portsmouth-Cherbourg.
SuperStar Express. Catamaran. March - October. Crossing Time 2 hours 45 minutes. Reclining Seats available.
Conventional Ferry. Crossing Time 5 hours daytime, 7 hours 30 minutes overnight. Cabins/Reclining Seats/Club Class available.
Portsmouth-Le Havre - Timings/Facilities as per Conventional Ferry, Portsmouth-Cherbourg.

 Then take the spectacular Pont de Normandie (qv), the A29 and follow signs to the A13-E46 Autoroute de Normandie, direction Caen, approximately 45 minutes.

BRITTANY FERRIES
Reservations/Prices/Sailing Times - Tel: 0990 360 360.
Portsmouth-Caen. From Continental Ferryport off the M27 Motorway.
Crossing Time 6 hours daytime, approx 6 hours 30 minutes overnight. Cabins/Commodore Class/ Reclining Seats available.
The ferry actually arrives at the Port of Ouistreham (qv). Then take the D514 to Caen (approximately 10 minutes).
Poole-Cherbourg. From the Terminal off B3068 from the A35 (avoiding the lifting bridge).
Crossing Time 4 hours 15 minutes daytime, approx 5 hours 30 minutes overnight. Cabins/Club Class Reclining Seats available.

CHERBOURG
Cherbourg is not included in any of the Itineraries as it did not figure in the D-Day Landings on 6 June. However, it was a vital factor in the invasion planning and is therefore briefly described here. Cherbourg is at the tip of the Cotentin Peninsula. It can be visited at the end of the Channel crossing to Cherbourg in Approach One or as an Extra Visit from Valognes in Itinerary One.

 That a major port should be included in the landing beaches area was always a vital factor. The beaches of Normandy were particularly suitable as they included two - Cherbourg and le Havre - although following the lessons of Dieppe neither was in the initial assault area. Both were considered vital to the success of OVERLORD, as Cherbourg alone was not considered capable of supporting the twenty-nine combat divisions to be put in the lodgement area. At first it was thought that Cherbourg should be taken by the eighth day by the Americans who had landed by sea at OMAHA and UTAH, and those who were due to drop behind UTAH. The US 1st Army's main task was 'to capture Cherbourg as quickly as possible'.

That Cherbourg and le Havre were spared from heavy Allied air attacks in the spring of 1944 was a clue to the Germans that the invasion might take place on the beaches between them. Hitler ordered strong defences in this area, envisaging some 40 strongpoints facing the sea and 80 covering the land approach, and this was enthusiastically implemented by Rommel although neither port received the two heavy gun batteries that German Navy plans had specified they should have. Troops were ordered into the Cotentin in May, but few defensive positions in the area were completed, especially the *Zweite Stellung* (Second positions) due to be constructed as a further defensive line a few kilometers in from the coast, which Rommel ordered to be abandoned in May in order to concentrate on defences further forward.

When the strength of German reinforcement of the Cotentin was appreciated, probably from information supplied from Bletchley Park, the date for taking the port was revised to D+15, i.e. 21 June.

Following the invasion, the Americans reached Valognes, on the N13 road, a bare 13 miles from Cherbourg, on 19 June. Hitler had flown from Berchtesgaden to meet von Rundstedt and Rommel on 17 June at Soissons. Sensing defeat, a furious Hitler pronounced that 'Cherbourg be held at all cost'.

Between 25,000 and 40,000 Germans, including Todt Organisation and naval personnel, were locked in the peninsula as the US V11 Corps swung around from Barneville on the west coast of the peninsula, to which they had fought after landing at UTAH, and headed directly north for Cherbourg. During 20 June, the Germans hastily reformed their 'Landfront' into four regimental *Kampfgruppen*'. All were understrength and weary, their combat efficiency low.

On 21 June the US 8th and 12th Infantry Regiments had fought their way into the edges of the main Cherbourg defences. One of their first missions was to flush out a suspected V1 weapon launching site near Bois de Rondou (to the right of the N13 on the D56 at le Mesnil au Val). Remnants of the installation can still be seen today.

On the evening of 21 June US VII Corps was ready for the final assault. Cherbourg's capture had become even more vital because of a heavy four-day storm in the Channel which blew up on 19 June and which seriously disrupted troop and supply landings on the captured beaches. The artificial harbour at OMAHA was completely destroyed and Admiral Hall, the naval commander at OMAHA, decided not to attempt to rebuild it. General Collins ordered a renewed attack on Cherbourg, which should be 'the major effort of the American army', with 'air pulverization'. The air attack with four squadrons of RAF Typhoons, followed by six squadrons of Mustangs plus twelve groups of US 9th Air Force fighter bombers, went in at 1240 on 22 June, their object to demoralise the enemy. The bombing went on continuously for an hour and involved 375 aeroplanes. The previous night General J. Lawton Collins commanding V11 Corps broadcast a message demanding the surrender of Cherbourg by 0900 hours the following morning. General von Schlieben, commanding the mixed force *Gruppe von Schlieben* defending Cherbourg, ignored the 0900 hours 22 June ultimatum. The assault went in.

The US 9th Division with the 60th Infantry and the 47th Infantry attacked on the right. The 79th Division attacked along the axis of the N13 up to the Fort du Roule. The 4th Division was to seal off the city from the east.

General Schlieben's command post was in a vast underground command bunker in the rue Saint Sauveur. On 22 June he received a message from Hitler, 'It is your duty to defend the last bunker and leave to the enemy not a harbour but a field of ruins'. 'Reinforcement is absolutely necessary,' replied the unimpressed General to Rommel.

The fighting nevertheless continued through 23 June, when the outer ring of fortresses was penetrated. On 24 June US VII Corps entered the city itself. Losses were heavy. Lieutenant-Colonels Conrad Simmons (Commander 1st Bn 8th Infantry) and John W. Merrill (Commander 1st Bn 22nd Infantry) were killed, together with many of their men. On 25th June, General Omar N. Bradley brought down a naval bombardment on the Cherbourg batteries from three battleships, four cruisers and screening destroyers. The ships did not escape damage, and during a three-hour duel the battleship *Texas* and the cruiser *Glasgow* were hit with a total of 52 naval casualties.

Schlieben radioed, 'Loss of the City is unavoidable... 2,000 wounded without a possibility of being moved... Directive urgently requested.' Rommel replied, 'You will continue to fight until the last cartridge in accordance with the order from the Führer.'

That day Corporal John D. Kelly, who after three attempts took an enemy pill box, and Lieutenant Carlos C. Ogden, who destroyed an 88mm enemy gun, were both awarded the Medal of Honour. The fort was finally reduced on 26 June. That day too, General Schlieben's underground bunker was discovered in Saint Sauveur. A German prisoner was sent in to ask for surrender. Schlieben declined, but a few rounds from a tank destroyer into the tunnel entrance brought out not only General Schlieben but Admiral Hennecke, Naval Commander Normandy, and some 800 Germans. The next day Schlieben's deputy, General Sattler, formally surrendered the fortress of Cherbourg to Colonel Smythe, Commander of the 47th Infantry Regiment.

The last of the outlying gun batteries fell on 30 June and work on clearing the harbour began immediately with over 100 mines being found in about two weeks, for the loss of three minesweepers and seven other small vessels.

A D-DAY MEMORY

Lt J.J. Whitmeyer. 9th US Infantry Division. Participated in the capture of Cherbourg.

"I was at that time a lieutenant in the Infantry. We had a schedule about a week or so to go from UTAH Beach to Cherbourg. I think it was due to fall ... in about a week and actually Cherbourg was emptied on the 26th of June and I think the history records may even show that it was captured on the 27th. There was a sergeant in the 314th Infantry, who at that time was a private, who was the first man accredited for mounting the steps of the City Hall in Cherbourg, and this was like 8pm on the 26th June. As I recall his name was Finlay. We had in my own organisation only three Medal of Honour winners and two of those people were awarded the Medal of Honour, the nation's highest award as you are aware, for combat in an operation to take Fort du Roule.

Fort du Roule commanded completely Cherbourg and the success of ever utilising Cherbourg as a harbour. It took a little bit more time to do than the Regimental Commander desired. It took a day and a half, because of an underground bunker as big as a small city - railroad tracks, a number of terraced 88 guns as well as weaponry that the German used, and it required a sergeant - Hurst was his last name - from E company of my battalion to lower charges by way of a rope into the apertures to silence the gun that was firing onto the main railroad terminal area. My own particular part in that operation:-

I was on, I believe, the Avénue de Paris - it is or was the main street that leads on down on the railroad terminal and to the docks for the steam ships. This was a major harbour of course, and the Germans on the 23rd of June, as I understand it, were expecting the fort to be captured and knowing the importance to the United States or the Allied armies and navies, decided to make it impossible or to render it useless. They took all of the heavy equipment they could - box cars, locomotives, cranes - whatever heavy equipment they could find - strung it across the entrance into the main terminal, and then dynamited or exploded it in some manner. They also - the ships that were in the harbour - they scuttled them. I can vividly recall crawling across this tangle of steel, and on the outer edge there was a dog tank trap which, as you know, is just a large ditch, in order to get to the beaches. Truthfully, the last pill box as far as I was concerned and when I say the last, it's not the last to fall, but the furthest point on the Cherbourg Peninsula that a pill box was placed, fell to 3rd Platoon of G Company which I commanded. I was unfortunate enough to have one of the privates who was in my unit go on top side in order to lower as a remembrance the Swastika flag that the Germans had flown. It was just a short period of time. I did not have with me what we refer to as a 'walkie talkie' - they weren't any good. They weren't as good as those you can buy for $4 or $6 now in a toy store. If you got anyone on it would be some tank outfit and we really didn't have communications. I can recall sitting down to clean my rifle when some fire was directed on the pill

A D-Day Memory continued

box. I thought it was a counter-attack. The gentleman who had gone top side - this soldier - he came stumbling down the steps. He was shot four times by the 4th Division who was attacking the pill box while we were in it. That is just one of the, you know, mistakes or lack of communication. We did not know and nor did they, who they were and they didn't know who we were. A sergeant by the name of Lepley, about the best soldier I've ever known. He fought in three wars. He climbed through the aperture in which a gun was placed facing the sea and tried to make his way back through that tangle of metal to say, 'Hey quit shooting. You know you're shooting at American troops.' But he didn't come back and so another fellow and myself we did the same thing and that time the fire lifted and we were able to get out this American soldier who had been wounded. And as I understand it with regard to Cherbourg, it took about two weeks for the British engineers, the American engineers - whoever were responsible - not necessarily to clear the scuttled ships but to clear the port and that shortly thereafter in landing the American troops without putting them on landing craft, and were able to dock at one time something like twenty-five vessels and numerous landing craft, and it was a tremendous job on the part of those people who had to make the clearance."

TOURIST OFFICE. 2 Quai Alexandre III, near the Avant Port.
Tel: (0)2 33 93 52 02, Fax: (0)2 33 53 66 97.
They will supply a list of events (there are often sailing, windsurfing and other nautical competitions in the summer) and make hotel bookings.
   Conveniently placed by the Gare Maritime is the ***Hotel Mercure. Tel: (0)2 33 44 01 11. On the way out of Cherbourg, en route for Itinerary One, is the **Hotel Campanile, la Glacerie.Tel: (0)2 33 43 43 43.

MUSEUM & MEMORIALS
Fort du Roule Museum of War and Liberation/Map Ch3. Tel: (0)2 33 20 14 12
Set on the 112m high Montagne du Roule, with panoramic views over Cherbourg, this museum underwent extensive renovation and improvement for 1994, with access by lift from the town (look out for signs from the Thémis roundabout area, entering the town on the N13).
Original maps, posters, photographs, record of Free French forces, well-documented story of the Battle for Cherbourg.
Open:daily 1 April-30 Sept 1000-1800. 1 Oct-31 March (closed Mondays) 0930-1200, 1400-1730. Entrance fee payable. Reduction for veterans, children and groups.
Memorial and Plaque, Hotel de Ville/Map Ch1,2.
On the town hall, Place de la République, Cherbourg, there is a memorial plaque to Sergeant William F. Finlay 39th Regiment, US 9th Division, who was the first US soldier to enter the town hall on 26 June 1944 and who died in action in Germany on 1 April 1945, aged 20. Also in the square is a memorial to civilians who were deported or shot by the Germans, surrounded by a rose called 'Resurrection'.

Cherbourg town hall with Sergeant Finlay plaque.

Remnants of Atlantic Wall Defensive Bunkers

In the harbour area, and near the Hotel Mercure, there are many examples still to be seen of massive German bunkers. For details of the Atlantic Wall remains in and around Cherbourg, see *Cherbourg Sous l'Occupation* by André Picquenot, published by Ouest, France.

PLUTO

PLUTO (the Pipeline Under The Ocean, qv) was laid from the Isle of Wight to Cherbourg (in four pipe-lines), and connected to underground pipes across the UK to Ellesmere Port. On French soil the lines ran for hundreds of miles close behind the advancing armies with interspersed pumping stations to keep the petrol flowing with more lines being laid later, including fourteen across the Channel to Boulogne.

APPROACH TWO

DOVER-CALAIS-CAEN

P & O/Stena Line. From Eastern Docks, Dover
Reservations/Prices/Sailing Times - Tel: 0990 980980
Crossing Time - 75 minutes.   Club Class available.

SeaFrance Ltd. From Eastern Docks, Dover
Reservations/Prices/Sailing Times - Tel: 0990 711711
Crossing Time - 90 minutes. Club Class available.

Hoverspeed Ltd. From Western Docks, Dover
Reservations/Prices/Sailing Times - Tel: 0990 240 241. Fax: 01304 240088
Hovercraft Crossing Time - 35 minutes
SeaCat Crossing Time - 50 minutes.
Club Class available on both.

Eurotunnel. From Eurotunnel Passenger Terminus, Folkestone-Cheriton
Reservations/Prices/Sailing Times - Tel: 0990 353535
Crossing Time - 35 minutes.   Club Class available.

The Ferry Travel Club offers good prices on Cross-Channel fares
Tel: 01304 213533.

As the complete journey from Calais can now be made on the Autoroute system, this is
the quickest method of reaching Caen for those living in the south-east of England.
   Approximate time, without stopping for refreshments, and taking the most clearly
signed route to Caen (over the Pont de Normandie): 3 hours 30 minutes.
   N.B. This route is quite expensive in **motorway tolls** (in 1999 the journey cost 129
francs in tolls, the Pont de Normandie toll alone being 33 francs.)
   The alternative routes are via Rouen or Pont de Tancarville (see Michelin Map 231).
*From the Ferry Port, follow blue motorway signs A16/A26, direction Paris/Reims.
After 5 miles Boulogne and Rouen are also signed (A16 E15-E40/E402). After 9
miles, the entrance to the Channel Tunnel is signed.* **If arriving via the tunnel,
deduct 9 miles from the following mileages.** *By-pass Boulogne and continue
direction Rouen-Amiens A16-E402.*
At 57 miles the Département of the Somme is entered.
At 66 miles the Battlefield of Crécy is signed.
   At 73 miles the motorway forks. Follow the Rouen/Le Havre A28-E402 signs. At

116 miles Caen is signed. At 120 miles the motorway forks. Take the Caen A29-E44 signs. At 130 miles the motorway forks. Continue towards Le Havre/Caen A29-E44 and at 176 miles the Pont de Normandie is reached.

The spectacular **Pont de Normandie** was opened in January 1995. Its design by architects C. Lavigne, F. Doyelle and M. Lechevalier, and designer M. Virlogeux, was a technological leap, its 184 staying cables providing incredible wind stability (able to withstand gusts of over 300 kph). Until the Tatara Bridge in Japan comes into service, its 856m central span is the longest in the world. The towers are 215m high and weigh 20,000 metric tons. It cost 2 billion French francs and 1,600 people were involved in its construction. Their names are engraved on the bridge pier. At night this stunning bridge becomes magical, lit up with blue and white lights designed by Yann Kersali who also lit the Champs Elysées and the Golden Gate Bridge.

There is access for walking across the bridge for the wonderful view over the Seine Estuary and the River towards Rouen [**it is absolutely forbidden to stop your car on the bridge to take photos**] from both the Calais and Caen directions. There is an exhibition room on the Calais side which has boards telling the story of the bridge, photos, a model and a film about the building of the bridge.

Open: daily 0900-1900. No entrance free. Tel: (0)2 35 19 24 50.

Guided visits are available by appointment. Fee payable. Tel: (0)2 35 24 64 90.

There is also a bar, restaurant and cafeteria, l'Armada. **Open daily**. Tel: (0)2 35 53 28 02.

Next to it is a souvenir shop with films, books, posters, postcards etc about the bridge.

Near the toll building is The Engineers' Garden, with a 8.5m model of the bridge. The names of famous visitors to the bridge, other great bridges and places of interest in Normandy are featured here.

Extra Visit to 6th Airlanding Brigade Memorial, Berville-sur-Mer. Round trip: 10 miles. Approximate time: 25 minutes

On crossing the bridge, exit from the motorway and take the D312 direction Berville. Pass through Fiquefleur and continue to the centre of Berville. The memorial is on the lawn in front of the school (next to the Mairie).

The commemorative plaque, mounted on a rock, was unveiled on 7 June 1997 during an impressive ceremony attended by Veterans of the 1944 6th Airborne Brigade and of the Piron Brigade, members of today's 6th Airborne, and many local dignitaries. Elements of 6th Airborne liberated the town in their progression from Bénouville to Ranville and on to the mouth of the Seine.

Return to the bridge and rejoin the Approach Route.

Follow signs to Caen on the A13-E46.

You are now passing through the picturesque *Pays d'Auge* (see Tourist Information at the end of the book).

At 223 miles Caen Centre is signed.

At 225 miles the *Mémorial* Museum is signed.

CAEN

Caen was the ambitious D-Day objective of the 185th Infantry Brigade Group of the 3rd British Division, which was not achieved on 6 June. It was not taken by the Allies until 9 July. It was a fearsome and costly period for the citizens of Caen.

Air raids continued spasmodically throughout the month of June and into the next, until the dreadful climax of Operation CHARNWOOD 7-9 July. It was the final battle for Caen, preceded by a literally murderous attack on the night of 7 July by Lancaster and Halifax bombers.

Monsieur Poirier, the deputy mayor whose D-Day memory appears below, estimated that there were more than a thousand planes and that the raid lasted 45 crushing minutes. The dead and wounded reached unbearable and untreatable proportions, and many were buried, alive and dead, in the shattered buildings.

During 8 and 9 July the Germans withdrew and in the afternoon of 9 July the French-speaking Canadians of the 3rd Canadian Division entered Caen from the west and the British 59th and 3rd Divisions from the north. They offered cigarettes and chocolates to the citizens, who came out of their ruins, waving their battered *Tricolores*. 'The women kissed them, the men saluted them, but with dignity, without mad exaggeration. We have all suffered too much for our dearest ones to acclaim excessively those who have been forced by the necessity of war to do us so much harm,' commented an exhausted Monsieur Poirier.

Many Allied 'liberators' were appalled at the carnage and destruction as they entered the shattered city. Some seemed oblivious to the extent of the damage.

Monsieur Poirier, who had received the first German officer to enter the town on 18 June 1940, was now greeted by a British officer. They shook hands at length, both had tears in their eyes, and they had a long conversation about the basic needs of the Caennais. Finally, the officer asked if Monsieur Poirier could direct him to a good hotel where he could get a hot bath. 'Brave Major H', commented the deputy mayor, and explained that three-quarters of the city was razed to the ground. Although the worst was past, the fighting raged around the city until, on 15 August, after sixty-five days, the bloody battle for Caen was over.

What to See and Do In and Around Caen

Caen is a thriving city with many cultural and commercial events - notably the annual *Foire de Caen* in September at the *Parc des Expositions*. In the centre is a variety of theatres, cinemas, department stores and speciality shops, bars, restaurants and hotels, e.g:

***Mercure, near Bassin St Pierre, rue de Courtonne. Attractive design. Tel: (0)2 31 47 24 24

***Moderne, Blvd Maréchal Leclerc. Centrally located. Tel: (0)2 31 86 04 23

***Holiday Inn, Place Foch. Centrally located. Tel: (0)2 31 27 57 57

There are also several conveniently sited hotels off the *Périphérique* (N13 ring road), e.g:

***Novotel, Ave. Côte du Nacre. Smart, well-run, with outdoor swimming pool. Very popular business and tourist hotel. Tel: (0)2 31 93 05 88.

*** Friendly, 2 Place Boston. Indoor pool. Tel: (0)2 31 44 05 05

**Campanile, Hérouville. Small, but well-equipped rooms. Family run. Tel: (0)2 31 34 02 04

Interior of the Mémorial, Caen.

**Ibis, Hérouville. Small rooms but attractive décor. Tel: (0)2 31 95 60 00.

Many memorials exist today as a tragic reminder of the civilian suffering - Caen is known as a 'Martyr Town'. The Caennais are faithful in their memory to their own dead and to their liberators. Each 6 June and 9 July ceremonies of remembrance and thanksgiving are held, when allied veterans and war widows are warmly welcomed. Memorials include:

Mémorial: Un Musée Pour la Paix (A museum for peace)/**Map H17.**

Esplanade Dwight-Eisenhower. Off the *Périphérique*, to the north in the new la Folie Couvrechef district. It is well signed.

Not surprisingly, after their June and July 1944 suffering, the Caennais [the citizens of Caen] wished

IN HONOR AND MEMORY OF OUR BRAVE AND GALLANT ALABAMIANS WHO FOUGHT AND SACRIFICED THEIR LIVES FOR THE CAUSE OF HUMAN LIBERTY IN THE NAME OF FREEDOM AT NORMANDY.

The Alabama plaque, 'Waterfall' State Wall, Mémorial, Caen.

their magnificent new museum to be a symbol for peace. It was opened on 6 June 1988 by President Mittérand, in the presence of French and Allied veterans, 150 children of Caen, ten from the USSR, ten from Hiroshima and ten from each of the thirteen countries who fought in Normandy in 1944, whose official representatives laid thirteen symbolic memorial stones in the forecourt. The countries involved were Britain, USA, Canada, Belgium, Greece, Czechoslovakia, Poland, Holland, Norway, Luxembourg, East and West Germany and France. Outside the museum there are two **Normandie Terre-Liberté (NTL) Totems**, describing the martyrdom of the town and its citizens during the bombardment and bombing that preceded their liberation. The latest research puts the civilian casualties at some 3,000.

The vast building (70m (230ft) long, 55M (180ft) wide, 12m (40ft) high) is on three levels and as well as a cinema to seat 170 houses the following: *The Main Hall.* Reception area, well-stocked shop, ticket office, cloak rooms, rest area, telex which constantly records any acts of war throughout the world, a World War II Typhoon.

First Floor. Historical journey with milestones of history on a huge cylinder, from ancient times to the present day, with particular emphasis on the pre-war years, the occupation, World War II, the landings, the resistance and the reconstruction. There are several films, including original World War II material and finally a film whose subject is 'Hope' for freedom and human rights.

There are also cafeteria, restaurant, *bureau de change*, children's play area and ample parking facilities. The museum uses the most up-to-date audio-visual and computer technology and was funded by fund-raising committees, notably in the USA, and in Britain, Canada, Norway, Germany, and France, supported by the City of Caen and the *Comité du Débarquement.*

Around it is a Memorial Valley, which is approached over a Bailey Bridge, at the end of which is a lift or stairs leading to the Memorial Gardens. The American Garden has a pool and waterfall, below which is a wall with commemorative stones to the States/Units which took part in the Landings. There is also a Canadian Garden and a Gingko Biloba tree planted by the Dalai Lama on 17 April 1997 and the unique Nobel Peace Prize Gallery which also features the Red Cross, the League of Nations and the United Nations.

This impressive, highly technical museum is a must, but requires at least two hours for a thorough visit.

Open:daily 0900-2100 (except 1 Jan). Tel: (0)2 31 06 06 44.

A D-DAY MEMORY

Monsieur Poirier, *Maire-Adjoint,* responsible for the passive defence of Caen and the efforts of the citizens to survive June-July 1944.

(Permission to reproduce extracts from his moving and graphic account, (reprinted with other, anonymous memories by the *Mairie* of Caen in 1984) has been given by the Documentation Centre of the *Mémorial* Museum of Caen.)

"6 June I was woken up at about two in the morning by the dull, distant yet deafening sound of a bombardment. What is it? There's no doubt whatsoever.

A D-Day Memory continued

Something's up on the coast. Is it the coastal batteries firing? Are they far off bombs? Could it be the landings? Aeroplanes prowl and sirens sound the alert. It is the 1,020th alert. It's never going to end ... I get up and report to my Passive Defence Command Post in the Central Commissariat's shelter. I call up the sectors, who in turn call their outposts. Everyone's at their post. The wakening population besieges the bakers ... It's the landings we've all been waiting for!

The Boches are taking off. Already! Really one has to smile - we're imagining that it's all going to happen without any pain. About 7 o'clock some bombs drop beside the station. I'm informed of one killed and two wounded. The morning passes calmly, but in the distance is still the bombardment of hundreds of artillery pieces from allied war ships. I lunch hurriedly, because I sense that something new is about to happen.

English planes prowl ceaselessly above the town and at 1300 a large formation of bombers release their bombs on the centre of the town. It is the first air raid of such unprecedented violence. The Caennais are stunned. An unbelievable number of bombs fall ... my sectors report to me on my special telephone, but already three lines are cut ... Red Cross emergency teams rush to the stricken regions. There are many dead and wounded, and general consternation at the suddenness of the attack. A crowd of terrified people flock into the Command Post and the shelters in the Town Hall cellars. They bring in the wounded and I send them to Bon-Sauveur [a convent], and already atrociously mutilated bodies are brought in... The raid only lasted about ten minutes but the damage is enormous. The Monoprix shop is in flames and there are more than ten homes on fire in the centre.

At 1625 another short raid, but as violent as the 1300 one. Bombs fall in the rue de Caumont, annihilating the annexe to the *Préfecture* ... old St Etienne is hit ... rue de Carel, the bus depôt for Courriers Normand, and all the coaches in it ... the undertakers where we had stored 500 coffins 'our supply for serious emergencies' - reduced to ashes. We won't have a single coffin to bury the dead. Two wards receive fifteen or so one- and two-ton bombs, burying eight nuns and thirty patients under the debris: one of the Sisters and five patients are killed outright. The St Jean Hospice is destroyed. An ambulance driving over the Vaucelles bridge is hit by a bomb, the young Red Cross driver killed and her body thrown into the Orne. Our No 1 first aid post takes a bomb which totally destroys it. Dead and wounded everywhere. Already the Red Cross and other voluntary workers are insufficient for the task. There aren't enough ambulances, not enough stretchers, two first aid posts are out of action. In spite of prodigious acts of devotion, the medical corps cannot look after or operate quickly enough on the wounded that are being constantly brought in.

The fires multiply, a quarter of the town is in flames... During the entire evening we hear the roar of aeroplanes. Doubtless they are observers who are coming to take stock of the results of the raids. The teams of helpers work relentlessly in the rubble to pull out buried survivers who are calling out.

There are so many sad victims that we won't be able to save because of lack of adequate tools and lack of enough helpers."

To visit the following memorials, pick up a town plan from the **TOURIST OFFICE** at Place Saint-Pierre (near the Castle) Tel: (0)2 31 27 14 10. (See Holts' **Map H3,4,5,6,7,8,9,10,11,12,13,16,31** for the following and other memorials in and around Caen.)

Boulevard Bertrand
Plaque to the first Canadian soldier (called Hill) killed in Caen on the wall of the *Préfecture* garden.

Place de la Résistance
Monument to the Déportés (French deported by the Germans during the war).

Rue de la Délivrande
On the left-hand side, opposite the 'LTE' building, a calvary remembering those who died in the liberation.

Fosses St Julien
Ruins of the famous church, destroyed in the bombardment, with a great modern wooden cross marking the site.

Place de la Gare
At the railway station is a plaque to the railway workers killed during the occupation, the landings and the bombardment.

Crossroads of Pont de Vaucelles (over the Orne) and Quai Meslin
Monument describing the collaboration of the Resistance workers with the Regina Rifle Regiment.

Place Monseigneur des Hameaux
Plaque commemorating the raising of the *Tricolore* and the Cross of Lorraine on 9 July, beside the Abbaye aux Hommes, in which 10,000 people took refuge during the battle for Caen.

Chapel of St George, in the Château
Memorial to the civilians, killed on 8 July, whose ashes are sealed in the wall.

3rd British Division
The memorial was erected by the City of Caen and designed by the Portsmouth architect Ken Norrish. It stands about 13 feet high and consists of columns of Caen stone rising out of the symbolic ruins of the city. Above the columns rises a metal representation of the 3rd Division badge with other brigade and regimental badges on the columns themselves. It recognises the liberation of Caen on 9 July by the '3rd British Infantry Division'. It was dedicated on 7 June 1988 and stands just below the battlements of Caen Château.

Itinerary One

- **Itinerary One** starts at Ste Mère Eglise, looks at the 82nd and 101st Airborne Divisions' drop zones and the US 4th Infantry Division's landing at UTAH Beach. See Map 4 below.
- **The Route:** Ste Mère Eglise - Airborne Museum and Plaques, Church and Stained Glass Memorials, *Comité du Débarquement* and Mayor Renaud Memorials, Pump, Plaque rue de la Cayenne, Town Hall - Memorials and Kilometer Zero, US Cemetery

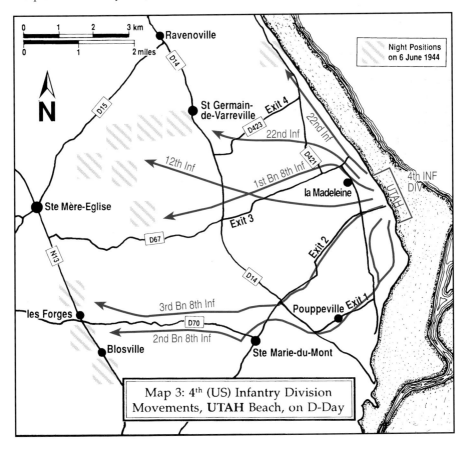

Map 3: 4th (US) Infantry Division Movements, **UTAH** Beach, on D-Day

Marker No 1; 'Iron Mike' Statue; US Cemetery Marker No 2; 508th Parachute Infantry Memorial; US Cemetery Marker No 3; General Pratt Memorial; Ste Marie du Mont - Signs, Stained Glass Window; Exit 2; Danish Memorial, UTAH Beach - Museum, US Memorials; Chapelle de la Madeleine; Leclerc and *Comité du Débarquement* Monuments; Batterie de Crisbecq; Batterie d'Azeville; 365th Fighter Group Memorial; Liberty Museum, Quinéville.
• **Extra Visits** are suggested to Montebourg; German Cemetery, Orglandes; Gen Patton's HQ, Néhou; Valognes; Cherbourg.
• **Planned duration,** without stops for refreshments or Extra Visits: **4 hours, 30 minutes**
• **Total distance: 37.2 miles.**

BACKGROUND TO THE AMERICAN AIRBORNE OPERATIONS AND UTAH BEACH

The American air and sea landings north of Carentan on the Cotentin Peninsula are so interdependent that the memorials, drop zones and beaches can be seen on one comprehensive Itinerary and therefore the background information for the 4th Division landing on UTAH, and the 82nd and 101st Divisions' airborne landings, precedes the tour.

THE AMERICAN AIRBORNE OPERATIONS

Drop Time:	0130 hours
Divisional Commanders	82nd: Major General Matthew B. Ridgway
	101st: Major General Maxwell Taylor
Defenders:	91st Division
	709th Division
	6th Parachute Regiment
91st Division Commander:	Lieutenant General Wilhem Falley
709th Division Commander:	Lieutenant General Karl W. von Schlieben
6th Parachute Regiment Commander:	Major Friedrich-August von der Heydte

The Plan - The American Airborne Operations

The American airborne assault on D-Day was in its own right the largest ever to have been attempted. The two divisions, the 82nd 'All American' and the 101st 'Screaming Eagles', comprised six parachute infantry regiments (PIR), a total of over 13,000 men, including attached arms and services. The parachute assault alone needed 822 transport planes.

It adds greatly to the general understanding of what happened if the Holts' map included with this volume is consulted in conjunction with the explanation. The D-Day objective line and the area taken by the end of D-Day are shown on the Holts' Map.

The broad plan was that the parachute divisions would secure exits from UTAH Beach (the four main ones are shown on the map in squares Q and S), gain control of the crossings over the rivers Merderet and Douve (particularly at la Fière, Map Square R, and at Chef du Pont, Map Square R), prevent German movement along the N13 from Carentan or Valognes, and gain and secure landing grounds for reinforcement by glider at dawn and dusk. Ahead of the main bodies of the parachute troops pathfinders were to jump to mark the drop zones.

In particular the 82nd, landing slightly north and to the west of the 101st, charged its 505st Regiment with taking the town of Ste Mère Eglise and the bridges at la Fière and at Chef du Pont. The 507th was to capture remaining bridges over the Merderet River and the 508th was to establish a defensive line west of the river in anticipation of counter-attacks. Less than two weeks before D-Day the drop zones and landing areas were moved some 10 miles further east in response to the German reinforcements that had been brought into the area, which meant that the 82nd had to begin again to familiarise itself with the ground via air photos, and that the division would be dropped astride the Merderet River and into the flooded fields.

The 101st Division had been created in August 1942 from the 82nd and was commanded by General Maxwell D. Taylor. Three drop zones were allocated to the paratroop forces with the tasks of securing the four exits from the beach that the seaborne force would need and of taking and protecting the landing zone which was to be used by the division's gliders. Following these tasks the division was to seize the town of Carentan and take up positions to meet German attacks from the south. Thus, if all went well, exits would be secured for the forces arriving on the UTAH beach and the flanks of the invasion force would be protected by the airborne forces.

Not all the Allied senior commanders liked the airborne idea. Air Chief Marshal Trafford Leigh Mallory, Commander in Chief of the Allied Expeditionary Air Forces, had opposed the plan from the time that General Montgomery first altered the COSSAC drop on Caen to a three-division airborne assault behind the beaches. Leigh Mallory maintained that flak defences were so strong, and that the terrain was so unsuitable for parachutists or gliders, that losses in men and machines could be as high as 75 per cent or more. Montgomery, supported by General Omar Bradley, persisted with his plan. However, the day after the new drop zones for the 82nd were announced Leigh Mallory went to see Eisenhower and expressed his fears that troop carriers and tugs flying in a straight line at 1,000ft would be easy targets for flak guns, and that the flooded and swampy ground in and around the rivers was unsuitable for landing airborne forces. Eisenhower overruled him but not until he had gone to his tent to wrestle alone with what he called a 'soul-racking problem'.

On 5 June the Supreme Commander said to his British driver, Kay Summersby, 'I hope to God I know what I'm doing', and that evening they drove to Newbury where the General visited four airfields. He talked to General Maxwell Taylor and men of the 101st Airborne Division, going from group to group, shaking hands and talking briefly to each man. 'It's very hard really to look a soldier in the eye,' he told Kay, 'when you fear that you are sending him to his death'.

What Happened on D-Day - The American Airborne Operations

The thick cloud and bad weather made it difficult to navigate and some of the pathfinders missed the drop zones and set up their homing beacons in the wrong places. Although the enemy flak was not as deadly as Leigh Mallory had forecast, there was enough of it to cause the relatively inexperienced troop carrier pilots to take avoiding action. They therefore weaved and flew higher and faster than they should have done so that when the paratroopers jumped they were not only too high and moving too quickly, but they were probably also in the wrong place. (See Map 4.)

The 82nd Airborne Division, dropping west of Ste Mère Eglise and astride the River Merderet, was more fortunate than the 101st. The 505th PIR, the first 82nd regiment to jump, landed pretty well on its drop zone, Zone 'O', and within three hours had taken Ste Mère Eglise one mile to the east, thus controlling any movement by the Germans from Valognes down the N13. The division's other two regiments, the 507th and 508th, were scattered west of the River Merderet which resembled less of a river and more of a broad ribbon of swamp. Thus the division was divided by the water, and the bridges

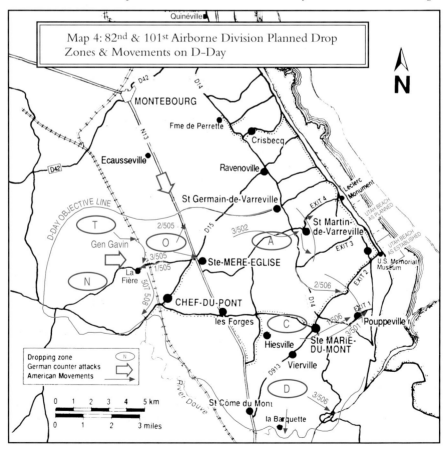

Map 4: 82nd & 101st Airborne Division Planned Drop Zones & Movements on D-Day

at Chef de Pont and at la Fière, by which the 82nd could communicate, and which formed the only links by which the Germans might be able to bring up reinforcements, became of critical importance.

The 101st Airborne Division was distributed over an area of almost 400 square miles. By dawn only 1,100 men of the division's 6,600 had reached their reporting points and only a further 1,400 assembled by the end of the day. The countryside added to their confusion. Small fields bordered with strong hedges were typical. They all looked the same. It was difficult to know which way to go. Yet by 0600, $4^1/_2$ hours after the main landing, the division had secured the western ends of the causeways leading from UTAH. Without those exits the 4th Division could not get off the beach because the ground around them was flooded and marshy. Thus, before the infantry had arrived, the 'Screaming Eagles' had virtually guaranteed the success of the UTAH landing.

UTAH BEACH LANDINGS

Assault time:	0630 hours
Leading Formations:	8th Regimental Combat Team of the US 4th Infantry Division
US 4th Division Commander:	Major General Raymond O. Barton
Bombarding Force A:	Battleship: USS *Nevada*
	Monitor: HMS *Erebus*
	Cruisers: USS *Tuscaloosa* (flagship)
	USS *Quincy*
	HMS *Hawkins*
	HMS *Enterprise*
	HMS *Black Prince*
	Gunboat: HNMS *Soemba* (Dutch)
	Eight destroyers
German Defenders:	709th Infantry Division and elements of 352nd Infantry Division
709th Division Commander:	Lieutenant General Karl W. von Schlieben
352nd Division Commander:	Lieutenant General Dietrich Kraiss

The Plan- UTAH Beach Landings

Before the landings, high-altitude heavy bombers followed by lower altitude medium bombers were scheduled to soften up the Atlantic Wall. Then, as the troops headed for the beaches, Allied warships were to shoot them in, keeping the defenders' heads down so that the assault troops could establish a bridgehead ashore.

General Barton, commanding the 4th Division, planned to land in a column two battalions wide with a frontage of just over 2,000 yards.

Leading the assault was the 8th Infantry Regiment with attached to it the 3rd Battalion of the 22nd Infantry Regiment. The regiment's first task was to open the route inland by getting to the high ground in the area of Ste Marie du Mont (Exit 2)/les Forges (the D70 road) and then to push on to make contact with the 82nd Airborne Division to their north in the direction of Ste Mère Eglise. Ultimately the division was charged with driving on to take the port of Cherbourg.

What Happened on D-Day - UTAH Beach Landings

The weather was not good. Waves of five to six feet and winds of fifteen knots or more in mid-Channel made life uncomfortable for the men on the ships. The skies were overcast and the heavy bombers, who were to bomb the Atlantic Wall, could not see their targets and had to bomb by instruments alone. This fact, coupled with the 8th Air Force decision that there should be a delay of several seconds in releasing the bombs to avoid dropping any on the assault craft, meant that most of their 13,000 bombs fell too far inland. Sixty-seven of the 360 bombers of IX Bomber Command sent to UTAH failed to release their bombs at all because of poor visibility.

The medium bombers at a lower altitude fared better, but a third of their payload fell into the sea and many of their selected targets were not found. Thus the pre-landing aerial bombardment did little towards overcoming the coastal defences.

At about 0300 hours, some thirteen miles out to sea, the 4th Division began unloading from their transport ships into their LCVPs (Landing Craft, Vehicle & Personnel). It was a $3^1/_2$-hour journey to the beach and before that began many men, overloaded with heavy equipment, fell or jumped from the rigging on the sides of the transports into their assault craft, breaking their legs on impact. Others, as the boats rose and fell in the choppy sea, missed the LCVPs altogether and fell into the water.

As the craft, each with about thirty men on board, headed for the shore, many soldiers were violently sea-sick. Yet they had much to be grateful for. The sea crossing had been unopposed and as the craft neared the shore the expected hail of German fire did not materialise.

At 0550 hours the heavy Allied naval bombardment began, concentrating upon locations where major German gun batteries were known to exist. Then, closer in, the cruisers opened fire upon coastal defences such as pill boxes and machine-gun posts. Finally, just before the LCVPs touched shore, the 'drenching fire' began. This was a torrent of high explosive fire by shallow draft vessels close in to shore, such as destroyers and LCVGs (Landing Craft, Vehicle & Gun). Then as the troops prepared to land, the fire lifted to the first vegetation line. It was the naval equivalent of the army's creeping barrage.

The LCVPs of the two assault battalions of the 8th Infantry Regiment hit the sand on time. It was 0630 hours. The ramps went down and out came the GIs, relieved to be ashore but with a hundred yards of open beach to cross before reaching the shelter of the dunes and a low concrete wall on their seaward side. There was no opposition as they crossed the sand, but Brigadier General Theodore Roosevelt, the assistant divisional commander who accompanied the first wave, quickly realised that the Division had landed in the wrong place - 2,000 yards south of where they should have been.

An instant decision was needed: whether to try to correct the mistake by somehow signalling to the following waves out at sea or to accept the situation and continue the operation right there. Roosevelt chose the latter. Cane in hand he strode up and down, exhorting men to get up and off the beach and to move inland. It was a wise decision and one which won him the Medal of Honour. The intended landing place was far more heavily defended than the spot where they had actually landed and though German artillery and small arms fire did sporadically harass the 4th Division as they poured ashore, casualties were very light. Because the landing troops had no need to attempt to find shelter behind beach obstacles, as their comrades were having to do 15 miles to the east on OMAHA, the assault engineers were able to get to work on clearing the shore which they had completed by 0930.

It is unwise to be dogmatic about casualty figures since they are frequently manipulated for propaganda purposes by both sides in a conflict. However, by the end of the day, best estimates suggest that some 23,250 troops had come ashore and only 210 were killed, wounded or missing.

THE TOUR

- ### *Ste Mère Eglise/0 miles/60 minutes/RWC/Map R 1-14*
  The approach from the N13 is the same whether coming from direction Caen or Cherbourg. After taking the Ste Mère exit follow the road signed to the town.

It leads to a large sign on the left which proclaims '6 Juin 1944. D.Day. 505th Airborne. H Minus. General J.M. Gavin' and a crest. Before the board is a plaque which summarises the story of the 505th's action on D-Day. Behind it are 5 fir trees.

Follow the road into the town along Rue Général de Gaulle. On reaching the main square, Place 6 Juin, turn right. On the corner as you turn is the

TOURIST OFFICE. Tel: (0)2 33 21 00 33

Continue along Rue du Général Eisenhower and park in front of the church.

The sights in Ste Mère Eglise are best visited by walking. There is a variety of restaurants, snack bars and souvenir/book shops in the town. The local speciality is the cheese *Petite Sainte Mère Eglise.*

Ste Mère owes much of its fame to an American called John Steele. Steele was a paratrooper of the 505th PIR of the 82nd Airborne Division and shortly after 0130 hours on the morning of 6 June he, and some thirteen thousand other airborne soldiers, jumped out of over 880 transport planes flying over Normandy. Steele fell onto the church steeple in Ste Mère Eglise, slid down it and then with his parachute caught on a flying buttress hung there for all to see. His story was told in the film, *The Longest Day.* But there is more to the story of Ste Mère Eglise than the adventures of John Steele.

The Germans arrived in the town on 18 June 1940. There was no fighting and over the next four years, despite the occupation of their houses and the huge swastika flag that flew outside the town hall, the inhabitants learned to live with their invaders. As 1943 wore on the number of soldiers billeted in the area began to decrease and there was little other than high prices to remind citizens that there was a war on. Sometimes an occasional Allied aircraft would drop leaflets.

Early in 1944 German anti-aircraft gunners - Austrian and mostly old - moved in, parking their wood-burning trucks in the square but behaving well and without any apparent enthusiasm for fighting. Lieutenant Zitt was put in charge of the town and through the mayor, Alexandre Renaud, requisitioned stores and labour to build field defences.

On 17 April the Germans turned their attention to putting up anti-airborne landing poles and ordered that all radios be handed in to the town hall. There were to be severe penalties for listening to the BBC. Lieutenant Zitt began to demand more co-operation from Monsieur Renaud, which the mayor stoutly resisted and then on 10 May all the Germans, except the anti-aircraft gunners, left. They had been moved to the Cherbourg Peninsula.

Everywhere, though, there was activity, and there were always soldiers passing through the town, including Georgians and Mongols of very Asiatic appearance. At the end of May the town was briefly fortified and then, once again, became quiet. Following Rommel's inspection of the Cotentin Peninsula all the weapons and fighting soldiers had been moved forward towards the beaches. Only the Austrians remained, quite at home and causing no trouble.

On the evening of 5 June yet another of the frequent Allied air-raids began, and a large house in La Haule park, opposite the church, caught fire. The mayor and the villagers formed a long line from the village pump, passing buckets of water from hand to hand to throw upon the flames. As they struggled to pass the buckets quickly enough, paratroopers began to fall like human confetti amongst them. At least one paratrooper fell into the burning house.

The Germans shot at the Americans as they fell and ordered the French to go back into their houses. The Austrians, having no stomach for a fight, remained for about half an hour and then departed, leaving a few active soldiers here and there with only the machine gun on top of the church still firing. Just a few yards from the gun John Steele hung from the corner of the steeple pretending to be dead so that no one would shoot at him. After two hours he was cut down and taken prisoner, probably the last prisoner taken before active resistance in the town ceased at 0430 hours. The town had been liberated, the first town in France to be so. As the paratroopers gathered in the square and the sun began to rise, silence reigned.

The task of taking the town had been that of the 3rd Battalion of the 505th PIR commanded by Lieutenant-Colonel Edward C. Krause. Following a good drop on and around their planned dropping zone, DZ'O', the colonel ordered his own men to enter Ste Mère Eglise by stealth, using knives and bayonets and, where necessary, grenades. The tactic worked. The Germans were taken by surprise. At 0930 hours the enemy counter-attacked from the south with two companies of infantry and some armour. Most of the 2nd Battalion under Lieutenant-Colonel Benjamin H. Vandervoort, which had established a defence line north of the town, moved back to help. The colonel broke an ankle in the drop but, using a stick as support, continued to command his battalion. The Germans then launched a simultaneous attack from the north onto the remnants of the 2nd Battalion which numbered forty-two men. When the attack and counter-attack sequence finally ended, some eight hours later, only sixteen of the forty-two men had survived. Both colonels were awarded the DSC for their conduct during the capture of Ste Mère Eglise, the medals being pinned on them in July by General Bradley himself. General Gavin was awarded the DSC at the same ceremony.

Soon after midday German artillery fire started to fall on the centre of the town and it continued sporadically all day and into the night. It began to look as if Liberation would exact a heavy price in civilian casualties and damage to property - a higher price than Occupation.

Intense local fighting continued in the Communes around Ste Mère Eglise, but on the afternoon of 7 June American tanks arrived from UTAH Beach. The beachhead was truly secure and the link-up between air and ground forces was complete.

Start your walking tour at the Museum, opposite the church on Rue Général Eisenhower.

• US Airborne Museum/Douglas C47/Commemorative Plaques/WC/Map R7

Outside the museum is a **NTL Totem**. Begun on 6 June 1961 when General James Gavin laid the foundation stone, and housed in a parachute-shaped building, the museum was designed by architect, François Carpentier, who had designed the successful museum at Arromanches.

Since then there have been many additions and improvements, including an audio-visual show in 4 languages, touch screen information on the Battle of Normandy and films depicting the paratroopers' equipment and the C47. Veterans are asked to sign the Book of Honour. The most important addition has been that of the C47 aircraft Argonia, in a hangar shaped like a delta parachute, beside the museum, almost exactly where the burning house stood.

After its chequered career, including taking part in

Plaque to William H. Tucker, museum grounds.

The entrance to the Airborne Museum, Ste Mère Eglise.

A D-DAY MEMORY

Technical Sergeant John J. Ginter Jr of the 92nd Troopcarrier Squadron. Flew paratroopers over Ste Mère Eglise in the Argonia.

"I was the Flight Engineer and part-time co-pilot of this aircraft, 4100825 Squadron Markings J8 Taylor E. I got this aircraft at Fort Wayne, Indiana. We left America on February 13, 1944. From there we flew to Morrison Fields in Florida. From Florida the next day we departed for Puerto Rico. From there the next day we flew to Trinidad. The next day we flew to Brazil. The next day we went to Natal, Brazil. The next day we went to Fernando Island. The next day to Dakar, Africa, where, as I left America with a cold, the aircraft was grounded. And then weather conditions there permitted us to go over the Sahara Desert into Marrakesh, French Morocco. We were delayed for three days because of weather conditions over the Atlantic. Then we departed French Morocco and landed in Valley, Wales, England (sic). This flight time took 11 hours and 35 minutes. We had fuel tanks installed in this aircraft, added fuel tanks - 400 gallons. There were 804 gallons in the wing tanks, total of 1,204 gallons of gasoline.

We departed Valley, Wales and our final destination was an airfield, which is located in Newark-in-the-Trent in Nottinghamshire. Well we constantly trained in England, simulating paradrops, glider tows, and we moved our base to near Exeter.

We constantly trained there, then on 4 June in the afternoon we were alerted for the Normandy Invasion to breach Hitler's Europa - his fortress. I and my ground crew - two other people - had painted the stripes on this aircraft. Alternate white, black, white, black and the reason for that was to not shoot us down as our aircraft were shot down in Sicily. For in the Sicily invasion our own Navy had shot us down - I believe, though I'm not sure of that, and this was the reason for it. The fuselage was marked and each wing was marked, and the way I did it was I had put a piece of string around and marked with crayon and filled it in with a flat white and flat black paint. And that was the reason for the stripes.

Now we were taken back into interrogation (briefing). When we were ready to go we got orders from SHAPE (sic) High Command to postpone the Invasion for 24 hours because of the bad weather conditions across the Channel. We were then put into barracks and an MP - I mean Military Police - each set apart by 10 feet with a Thompson sub machine gun and had orders to shoot to kill if we attempted to flee from the area. And this was because of the fact it was extremely great secret information that we contained.

On the 5th we got the 'GO' and I came out at preflight of the aircraft, checking the para racks. The paratroopers were sitting, standing, constantly relieving themselves - nervous, very nervous, and as I'm under the aircraft checking the pararacks which I found later on contained mines I knew the reason. We boarded up and set up, took off - an extremely heavy load. We took every inch of the runway and we did get airborne and we formed up and we came out over the Channel. I'm up in the cockpit with the pilot and the co-pilot, checking the instruments, making sure that everything is OK and from there we found the pilot marker and made a turn going in towards the Islands - Guernsey and Jersey and,

A D-Day Memory continued

of course, the Cherbourg Cotentin Peninsula. As we were going in I see tracer bullets, but they looked just like Roman candles for sure and as we approached them they were more intensive. We seemed to have been out of range. But the second Island, as we turned, all hell started to break loose. You know ... [John Ginter felt unable to continue with this part of his recollections].

After the war we were getting new aircraft an improved version known as a C46 and I believe this aircraft (the Argonia) was sold by the United States Government to the French Government Naval defence. The last time I saw this aircraft was in Châteaudun."

Operation MARKET GARDEN and working as a civilian aircraft, the Douglas C47 returned to Normandy, lovingly restored, by Yves Tariel, President of the Parachutists' League of Friendship and his associates. It was unveiled in its custom-built museum here in June 1983.

In June 1994 a **marker to the 505th Parachute Infantry Regiment** was unveiled in the grounds and on a tree is a plaque to **Private William H. Tucker** who landed in it on 6 June 1944. Tucker later became Vice-President of one of America's largest railways.

Open: daily 1 Feb-31 March and 1 Oct-15 Nov 1000-1200 and 1400-1800; 1 April-30 April 0900-1200 and 1400-1845; 1 May-30 September 0900-1845. Open Sat/Sun 18 Nov-30 Nov 1000-1200 and 1400-1800. Closed 16 Dec-31 January. Tel: (0)2 33 41 41 35. WC in grounds.

Entrance fee payable. Reductions for children, senior citizens and groups.

Beside the museum is a café, then a house at whose entrance is a sign with a crest and the name *La Haule*. It was to here on D-Day that the residents of Ste Mère carried buckets of water from the pump in an attempt to save the burning house. The small cul de sac beside it is named after **Robert (Bob) Murphy**, who landed there on 6 June. He survived the war and was a frequent visitor to Ste Mère.

Walk over to the Church.

• Stained Glass Windows, Church/Map R13

There are two fine stained glass windows commemorating the US paratroopers. Over the portal is the predominantly blue window, designed by Paul Renaud, son of the 1944 mayor, and made by the glassmaker Loire. It shows the Virgin Mary surrounded by paratroopers. On the 25th anniversary of the drop, in 1969, the veterans of the 82nd Airborne donated another stained glass window, which was dedicated on 4 June 1972. It shows St Michael, patron saint of the parachutists, and incorporates the Cross of Lorraine and various military insignia. Traces of machine-gun bullet marks can still be seen near the pulpit, and it was on the tower of this church that US paratrooper John Steele hung, playing dead throughout the night of 5/6 June - and an effigy of Steele normally hangs from the steeple during the summer months. There is an hotel/restaurant named 'The John Steele' (who died in Kentucky in May 1969) around the corner from the Place du 6 juin along rue du Cap-de-Laine.

On leaving the church, walk left to

The church, Ste Mère Eglise, with an effigy of John Steele on the steeple.

Stained glass window to 82nd AB Division in the church.

Kilometer Zero, the Mairie.

The famous pump

• Pump (Map R12)

It was from here that the line of villagers passed buckets of water to the burning house.
At the opposite side of the square are

• Comité du Débarquement Monument and Alexandre Renaud Memorial/Map R10,11

The *Comité du Débarquement Monument Signal* is one of ten set up to commemorate the landings/liberation. Alexandre Renaud, mayor at the time of the Liberation, died in 1966. Monsieur Renaud was a distinguished author of books and novels about World War I (in which he was an officer), the Hundred Years' War and a futuristic account of World War III. He also wrote the most vivid and accurate contemporary account of the June 1944 drop: *Ste Mère Eglise: First American Bridgehead in France.*

Turn left along Rue Général de Gaulle back in the direction you drove into the town and turn first right. Continue almost to the end of the road to No 8 on the left.

• Plaque, Rue de la Cayenne/Map R26

Erected on the house where four parachutists of the 505th were killed on 6 June 1944: 'Sgt Stanley Smith, Pfc William C. Walter, Pvt Robert L. Herrin and Pvt Robert E. Holtzmann.' The first three are buried in the American Cemetery at St Laurent.

Return to the square and walk past the memorials up rue Cap du Laine to

Plaque to 505th PIR, rue de la Cayenne.

• Town Hall Memorials/Flag/Kilometer Zero/Map R1,2,3,4,5

Outside the town hall is the pink marker stone of Kilometer Zero. The Kilometer Zero marker stones were erected by General de Gaulle's Government in 1946. They follow the path of General Leclerc's Free French 2nd Armoured Division and can be seen on roads 'from Chad to the Rhine'. One famous stretch leads to Bastogne, another traces an historic path through Reims, Verdun and Metz on the N44 towards Strasbourg. The 'Flame of Freedom' emblem, which decorates the markers, was also used on Free French postage stamps. Behind Kilometer Zero is the memorial to the twenty-two civilians of Ste Mère Eglise (including a World War I veteran) who died in the battle of June 1944, and to the left and right are small plaques commemorating the liberation of the first town in France. To the right and rear of the marker stone is a stone erected in tribute to Generals Gavin and Ridgway and 'all the gallant liberators of the town'. Inside the town hall is the great Stars and Stripes, the first US flag to be raised in liberated France. It was also the first to fly over Naples in October 1943. In addition there is a painting by a German soldier portraying the parachute drop of 4/5 June.

KILOMETER 0/KILOMETER 00/"FIRST TO BE LIBERATED"

The visitor may be somewhat confused by rival claims along the Landing Beaches.

For instance, which is the historical beginning of Liberty Highway - Kilometer 0 outside the town hall at Ste Mère Eglise, or Kilometer 00 at UTAH Beach? Both *Communes* proudly claim that their marker (known as a *borne* in French) is the rightful monument, and countless discussions and newspaper articles have argued their respective cases for many years.

Both have a case. Chronologically Ste Mère Eglise was the first town to be liberated - by the Americans - when Lieutenant-Colonel Krause, commanding 3rd Battalion of the 505th PIR 82nd US Airborne Division, hoisted the Stars and Stripes there at 0430 hours.

Geographically UTAH Beach, between Exits 2 and 3, was the first section of French soil to be occupied by the Americans landing from the English Channel.

Bayeux (14 June) claims to be the first city to be liberated, Courseulles (6 June) the first port. The café at Pegasus Bridge (qv) makes the earliest claim of all - to have been liberated on 5 June, before midnight. However, John Howard's watch, broken on landing in his glider, firmly fixes the time as 0016 hours on 6 June.

As visitors drive into the small seaside resorts along GOLD, JUNO and SWORD beaches, they will be greeted many times by a 'Welcome' sign that proudly claims 'First town/village to be liberated, 6 June 1944'. You will often be driving along 'Avénue de la Libération' or a street named after the individual Allied commander who led the invasion force in that area.

The rivalry indicates the pride and joy of the occupied French people on being liberated, plus a certain amount of Gallic exuberance, and should be accepted as such by the somewhat puzzled visitor.

Return to the Square. Follow signs to D17/Camping/College of St Exupéry along Rue du 505 Airborne. Pass the Hotel du 6 Juin on the left and fork right. After some 300 metres on the right is

• US Cemetery Marker Number One/Map R6

The commemorative stone is one of three marking the first three US cemeteries, all of which will be visited on this tour. There were some 3,000 soldiers buried here. By 10 June there were eight battlefield cemeteries in the American sectors, but shortly afterwards the graves registration organisation began to concentrate the burials in five places - St Laurent, Blosville, Ste Mère Eglise, La Cambe and Orglandes. In March 1948 they were either re-interred into the one National Cemetery at St Laurent or sent home to America. The sports field behind the marker was where a set was built for making the film *The Longest Day* and actor Red Buttons played the part of John Steele on a recreated steeple.

Return to the Square and your car. Drive out of Ste Mère Eglise by returning to Rue Général de Gaulle. Turn right in the direction of the Town Hall and then left on D67 direction Chef du Pont. Just after the bypass bridge, fork to the right on the D15 and continue direction Pont-l'Abbé signed Mémorial des Parachutistes crossing the Carentan-Cherbourg railway line, to the River Merderet. Stop in the large parking area to the right.

• *'Iron Mike' US Parachutist Monument, la Fière/2.4 miles/10 minutes/Map R27*

The Merderet is very wide here and it was flooded in June 1944 (as it still can be in times of heavy winter rains - as in January 1999). From the bridge ahead a 500-yard-long causeway crossed the flooded area. The Americans actually seized this causeway - one of their prime objectives - on D-Day, with a mixed group of 400 paratroopers from the eastern side led by Colonel Roy Lindquist of the 508th and a patrol of the 2nd Battalion of the 507th from the west. But German opposition was so strong they had to let it go at the end of the day. General Ridgway ordered it to be retaken and on the morning of D+3, following a massive artillery bombardment, the Americans attacked again. Despite intense German resistance, and a Sherman tank being stuck on the causeway, the Americans, urged on at the very front by Generals Gavin and Ridgway, and supported by artillery support and direct fire from a platoon of tanks, secured the crossing. A signboard in the parking area describes the action.

General Ridgway believed in leading from the front. His view was that 'the place of a commander is where he anticipates the crisis of action is going to be, and it was obvious to me that these causeway crossings were the spots of greatest hazard'. In his opinion it was the presence of divisional and battalion commanders urging their men on that ensured the capture of the causeway. So intense was the fighting at la Fière that it was, he said, 'the hottest sector I saw throughout the war'.

The handsome bronze statue of an American paratrooper, known as 'Iron Mike' (after St Michael, the patron Saint of the Airborne) was unveiled on 7 June 1997 by Major-General Kellogg, Commander of the 82nd Airborne, who jumped with his men in the commemorative drop that day. It bears the legend (in English on the front and in French on the back) 'A grateful tribute to the American Airborne Forces of D-Day 6 June 1944.' The statue is a replica of one that stands in the US Army Infantry School at Fort Benning in the U.S.A.

Charles N. Deglopper, Private 1st Class, C Company 325th Glider Infantry, 82nd Airborne Division was awarded the Medal of Honour for his actions here on 9 June when he volunteered to support his comrades by fire from his automatic rifle while they attempted to withdraw through a break in the hedgerow, 'scorning a concentration of enemy automatic weapons and rifle fire, he walked from the ditch into the road in full view of the Germans and sprayed the hostile positions with assault fire'. Although soon wounded, he continued to fire whilst his comrades reached a more advantageous position and established the first bridgehead over the Merderet. When his body was later found it was surrounded by dead Germans and the machine guns that he had knocked out.

On the bridge is a blue and white sign *Voie Marcus Heim.*

'Iron Mike', la Fière   General Gavin's fox hole, la Fière.

Marcus Heim. Major commemorative ceremonies were held in Normandy on the 40th and 50th anniversaries of the landings. In 1984 the Germans were not invited to attend and after much discussion with its former allies the French government decided that they would not be invited to the 50th anniversary either. Nevertheless, a Bundeswehr platoon commanded by Major Heim held a small ceremony of remembrance at the German cemetery at la Cambe on 4 June. It was not an official occasion, explained Major Heim, 'We are here on our holidays'.

Return towards the bypass bridge. Some 100 metres on from Iron Mike in the bank on the right is a sign denoting **General Gavin's Fox Hole in June 1944.**

Doubtless the reconstructed fox hole owes a lot to the Gallic exuberance that accompanies the various claims of towns and villages to have been the 'first' to have been liberated. However, General Gavin was most certainly at the la Fière action and if he was not in a fox hole at this exact spot he would have been in one not very far away.

Continue towards the bypass bridge. Turn right just before it on the D67 to Chef du Pont and 100 metres on there is a memorial marker on the left. Stop.

• *US Cemetery Marker Number Two/4.6 miles/ 5 minutes/Map R14*

5,000 American soldiers were originally buried here, including Brigadier General Theodore Roosevelt, Junior, who led the 4th Infantry Division ashore at UTAH Beach. As with the other markers, the main formations represented in the cemetery are listed - 82nd Airborne Division, 101st Airborne Division, 4th Infantry Division, 9th Infantry Division, 79th Infantry Division, 1st Engineer Amphibious Brigade, 70th Tank

Battalion, 746th Tank Battalion and the 90th Infantry Division.
Continue on the D67 through Chef du Pont to where that road crosses the River Merderet. Stop on the east bank.

• 508th Parachute Infantry Memorial/7.1 miles/ 10 minutes/Map R15,16

There is a memorial stone on the right and a memorial garden and plaque opposite on the left, donated by the 508th. The bridge is 100 metres further on and there is a blue **NTL Totem** signboard on the left describing the action and a further sign, *Marais du Grand Fossé.*

There were three drop zones for the 82nd Airborne Division all just west of Ste Mère Eglise (see the in-text map number 4 above). Zone 'O', immediately alongside and to the west of the N13 as it leaves Ste Mère Eglise towards Cherbourg, was the one where the first and most accurate drops occurred. The 505th Parachute Infantry Regiment and the 82nd's Divisional HQ came down in that area.

Zone 'N', the drop zone for 508th PIR, is about 2 miles north-west across the river from here, but the sticks were scattered along a 6-mile elongated path in that direction, with extreme elements fifteen miles away due north.

Drop Zone 'T', two miles north of Zone 'N', was almost empty, though 507th PIR, who were due to land there, achieved probably the best grouping of the division, but one mile due east of where they should have been. Their extreme elements were the farthest flung of all, from fifteen miles north of here to twenty-three miles south.

Causeway over the River Merderet in flood as it may have looked in June 1944.

Memorial to the 508th PIR, Chef du Pont.

As part of their defensive measures the Germans had flooded the Cotentin area. The river here looked more like a shallow lake than the small stream you may well be looking at. Two of the division's three regiments, 507th and 508th, were across the other side of the water. Their task was to control the lateral routes into the Cotentin by establishing a defensive line three miles west of the bridges over the Merderet. This was one of the bridges and it was supposed to be taken and secured by 505th PIR, the third divisional regiment which had landed pretty well on target three miles north of here alongside Ste Mère Eglise.

Unfortunately for the 82nd Airborne Division, particularly for the men west of the Merderet, they had dropped into the area defended by the German 91st Division which had been especially trained in anti-airlanding operations. In addition many men had fallen into the swamp lands caused by the flooding and under the weight of their equipment were drowned.

A D-DAY MEMORY

Trooper Howard ('Goody') Goodson. I Coy 3rd Bn 82nd Airborne Division. 505th Parachute Infantry Regiment. Dropped near Ste Mère Eglise.

"It was a very secret mission and at one time we were prepared to board the aircraft on 5 June and then they sent us back because of the weather and then on 6 June ... sometime around midnight of 5 June, we boarded the aircraft and took off for Normandy.... It was a full moon night when we left England. You could see the fighter aircraft all around the plane until we finally hit the coast of Normandy and all of a sudden it was just black. I thought it was cloud but it was smoke from German ack ack fire and I believe our plane was hit two or three times, it was shaking all over and I was scared to death.

We were wearing the authorised American jump suit which consisted of a jacket and a pair of pants with many many large pockets ... and we had a main chute and a reserve chute and about everything else you can imagine we carried into battle. We even carried land mines in on our persons, grenades ... the only place we could find to put our gas mask was the bottom part of a leg and it was the first thing we got rid of when we hit the ground. We were so heavily loaded that the crew chief on the plane had to come around individually and pull each man up. He couldn't rise up by himself. We had twelve men on each side I believe and we had a cable going through the aircraft and we used static line. When the red light came on it meant stand up and hook up and then we would wait for the green light to go on and when that went on the first in line on the door side went out. Each person should check the man in front but on the Normandy jump I don't think anyone checked anything we were all so ... in a big hurry to get out of the plane.

After I hit the ground and got my chute off ... on this jump everyone decided that we would get a piece of our parachute and that's the first thing I did ... I entered a very quiet area, I could hear battle going on in other places but where I was it was very quiet, no-one around me, so I ripped off a piece of my camouflaged parachute, put my gun together - we carried a bren/rifle that went in three pieces

---

A D-Day Memory continued

and was zipped up in a cloth bag ... and eventually I heard movement and I used my little cricket and it turned out to be a friend from my company called Pat and he was also the first person I saw in Sicily after I jumped. A group of us got together and advanced into Ste Mère Eglise where there was fighting going on and we were eventually taken over by our battalion commander, Colonel Krause. He set us up in a defence of the town."

Opposition to the paratroopers was considerable, yet the dispersion that made it impossible for them to gather in enough strength to achieve their objectives also made it difficult for the Germans to work out what was going on and thus to concentrate in order to take effective offensive action. In addition, there was confusion within the German command because two of the divisional commanders were away playing war games at Rennes when the invasion began. What is more, Lieutenant General Wilhelm Falley, commanding the 91st Division, was killed by paratroopers as he made his way back to his headquarters. Falley was in his staff car with two of his officers when he bumped into Lieutenant Malcolm Brannen and four men of the 508th. Oddly it was an encounter which would be paralleled by a similar incident on the opening day of the battle of Arnhem on 17 September 1944, when General Kussin, the town commander, speeding back to town to organise its defence, bumped into a patrol of 3 Para and was shot and killed by them. After Brannen had left, Corporal Jack Schlegel, one of Brannen's men, came upon the car and found a large swastika flag in it which he took away. In 1974 he presented the flag to the museum at Ste Mère Eglise.

The Americans headed for the obvious dry ground offered by the railway embankment (you crossed the line from Ste Mère Eglise and will cross it again on leaving here) and by mid-morning some 500 men had gathered near the bridge at la Fière 1^1/$_2$ miles due north of here which the itinerary visited earlier. Several attempts were made at that time by elements of 505th and 507th PIR to take the la Fière bridge, but these failed, and when General Gavin, the Assistant Divisional Commander, arrived he took seventy-five men and set off down the road you drove along, heading for this bridge.

Unfortunately a number of enemy soldiers had dug themselves in along the causeway in front of you, and on the west bank, and Gavin's force could not move them. Rumour had it that two enemy soldiers who had stood up intending to surrender had been shot, but it is not clear who shot them - their own side or Americans.

Meanwhile, the Divisional Commander, General Ridgway, had arrived at la Fière and decided upon another attack on the bridge there. Most of the men here were withdrawn, leaving a platoon to hold the ground. By good fortune a glider containing an anti-tank gun came down nearby and Captain Roy Creek, commanding the platoon, used the gun to hold off an enemy counter-attack but he could do no more than hold tenuously on to this eastern bank.

Over to the west, elements of the German 1057th Regiment were moving steadily towards the river and the bridges, here and at la Fière, with orders to destroy all paratroopers in the area.

To the right, in a north-easterly direction along the line of the river, there is some high ground about 1¹/₂ miles away known to the paratroopers as Hill 30. There Lieutenant-Colonel Shanley commanding a group of about two companies of men of the 508th PIR took up position and broke up repeated German attacks in this direction, thus saving Captain Creek's small force and denying the Germans use of this bridge as well as making a substantial contribution to the security of the men at la Fière. That is why the 508th memorial is here. Three of Shanley's men who stayed in isolated posts while Shanley was establishing his position, Corporal Ernest Roberts, Private Otto Zwingman and Private John Lockwood were all taken prisoner. Each was awarded the DSC. Zwingman was killed in December 1944 while still a prisoner.

Return to Chef du Pont along rue du Capitaine Rex Combs (signed 100 yards on the first building on the left hand side) and take the D70 east towards the N13 and Carentan. 100 yards before the D70 passes under the N13 there is a memorial marker on the right beside the road. Stop.

• US Cemetery Marker Number Three, les Forges/ 10 miles/ 5 minutes/Map R17

This is les Forges, the site of US Cemetery Number 3, the third of three large burial grounds established in Normandy by the Americans. It was opened in June 1944 and remained a cemetery until 1948. Then the men buried here were repatriated or re-interred in the National Cemetery at St Laurent above OMAHA Beach. There were 6,000 burials of soldiers from 9th Infantry Division, 79th Infantry Division, 1st Engineer Amphibious Brigade, 101st Airborne Division, 82nd Airborne Division, 746th Tank Battalion, 4th Infantry Division and 70th Tank Battalion. The memorial was erected on 21 January 1958.

Around this area was Landing Zone 'W' for the 82nd. The in-text map number 4 shows the drop zones for the two divisions. Drop zones were areas allocated to parachute troops and Landing Zones areas for gliders. Paratroop forces were generally given the task of landing in advance of glider-borne forces and of securing the landing zones in order to allow the gliders 'safe' landings. The Americans were using both Waco and Horsa gliders. The latter had a tendency to break up on hard landings and the US pilots christened it 'The Flying Morgue'.

By the evening of 6 June 1944 elements of the 8th Infantry from UTAH Beach had reached this point and established overnight positions here.

The tour now effectively leaves the area of the 82nd Airborne Division assault and enters into that of the 101st Airborne Division.

Continue on the D70 under N13 dual carriageway, direction Ste Marie du Mont to the crossroads with the D129. Turn right direction Hiesville. At the first junction continue on the D129 direction La Croix Pan. At the next crossroads stop at memorial on the left.

• General Pratt Memorial, Hiesville/12.4 miles/ 5 minutes/MapR18

Brigadier General Don F. Pratt was the first American general officer to be killed in the Liberation of France. The area to the right of the D129 down which you have driven was LZ'E' which had been secured by the 3rd Battalion of 501st PIR. The division, the

101st, was due to be reinforced here and on other LZs by two glider landings on D-Day, the first one at 0400 hours. There were fifty-three Waco gliders in all, carrying 148 men, and in the dawn light many aircraft crashed or ran into hedges. Five men were killed here, including General Pratt. He was the Assistant Divisional Commander of the 101st Airborne Division and ironically had originally been scheduled to cross to France by sea. It had pleased him greatly to hear that he would be going by glider. Unfortunately he sat in his jeep with a parachute underneath him and when the glider crash-landed he hit his head on an overhead strut and broke his neck. Sitting behind him was Captain Gueymard who marked the fatal spot and was instrumental in organising and funding the memorial. General Pratt is now buried in Arlington National Cemetery in Washington.

In the village of Hiesville are memorial **plaques to General Taylor and the headquarters of the 101st Airborne Division,** established there at 9 o' clock on 6 June, on a farm gateposts (one in English and one in French). The General had selected the site for his HQ from a map before leaving England. He reached his HQ late in the afternoon having organised the securing of Exit 1 and having struggled across country dotted with paratroops of both divisions. He found it hard going, he said, 'not because of the enemy but because of the condition of my legs as the result of the pre D-Day squash game'.

Turn round and return along the D129 to the D70. Turn right towards Ste Marie du Mont and UTAH Beach.

The fields to the right were DZ'C' for the 101st Airborne Division. Owing to the scattered drop there was a mixture of men from 502nd PIR, who should have been on DZ'A' three miles to the north and 501st and 506th PIR who were at the right place. The latter, however, dropped in and around the village as well. The parachute landings in the fields that are passed on the right were probably the most concentrated of the whole American operation.

Stop outside the church in the village.

* Ste Marie du Mont/15.7 miles/10 minutes/Map R19

This small village is at the end of Exit 2 from UTAH Beach, which is about $3^1/_2$ miles ahead. The church was probably the first thing that the Americans who dropped in this area recognised as the sky lightened. It enabled them to deduce where they were.

The drop had been in darkness and very badly scattered, and, as the men of the 'Screaming Eagles' landed among the hedgerows and small fields, or fell into the flood water, they suddenly felt alone. The noise of the aeroplanes and the crack of the flak explosions had gone. Now everything was unfamiliar and in the moonlight every shadow a threat. Each man had been given a small metal click-clack device which made a noise like a cricket and in a staccato avalanche of snapping noises men gradually came together.

The story of the two American airborne divisions on D-Day is one of countless acts of leadership at very junior levels. Private soldiers displayed initiative worthy of high commissioned rank and commanders showed dogged determination to get on with their appointed tasks no matter how few men they had or how far astray they had been dropped.

General Maxwell Taylor, commanding the 101st Division, dropped just south of the village. As the divisional history puts it, 'The commander of 14,000 men found himself on a battlefield without a single one of those men within sight or hearing, any order he might have given would have been received only by a circle of curious Normandy cows.' General Taylor had dropped by parachute and like so many of his men had no idea precisely where he was when he hit the ground. As the sky lightened he recognised the distinctive shape of St Marie's church steeple and knocked on the door of a nearby farmhouse to ask where the nearest Germans were. The farmer confirmed that they were in the village and then handed the General a clip of First World War rifle ammunition. *'Allez me tuer un Boche'*, (Go kill me a German) he said.

The General knew that it was vital to secure the causeways and to do so quickly before the sea armada arrived. As officers and men slowly gathered, he ordered Colonel Ewell, who commanded the 3rd Battalion of the 501st PIR, to take a group of about a hundred men to secure Exit 1 and, on seeing that the party was very heavy on officers rather than soldiers, commented, 'Never were so few led by so many'. Moving from the area of DZ'C' and around the southern side of Ste Marie du Mont the Americans had a short fire-fight with some Germans in a dug-out, killing six. It was their first contact with the enemy. They moved on, accompanied by General Taylor, to the village of Pouppeville, 1¹/₂ miles north-east of here and at the end of Exit 1 from UTAH Beach. There the General left the securing of the causeway to Colonel Ewell who, with his men, engaged in a house-to-house struggle with grenadiers of the 1058th Regiment of 91st Division. After some hours the Germans surrendered with twenty-five dead and wounded out of a force of sixty-three.

The *Commune* of Ste Marie du Mont has placed a dozen signs around the village which describe the actions in the area. A booklet about them can be bought in the Boutique du Holdy which also houses a small collection of historical items and souvenirs. In the church are modern commemorative stained glass windows, replacements for those destroyed during the fighting, and opposite is the *Hotel /Restaurant 'Estaminet'* which provides a variety of menus. Tel: (0)2 33 71 57 01.

Some five minutes away to the south on the D424E1 is **the memorial to US 36th Fighter Group, ALG16** at Brucheville (Map R29).

Continue through the village on the D913 along Voie Gen Eisenhower signed to UTAH Beach.

This is Exit 2.

Exit 2

Exit, or causeway, 2 is typical of the four exits that were the only routes by which the seaborne invasion force would be able to get off the beach (there were three other possible routes but these were not felt to be suitable). The whole area had been flooded and nowadays it is difficult to imagine how it must have looked and how vital it was to secure the causeways, which were in effect pathways across a swamp. The task of controlling Exit 2 was that of 506th PIR, but their transport planes only managed to put ten loads out of eighty-four in the right place. However, Lieutenant-Colonel Strayer, who commanded the 2nd Battalion, and who had dropped four miles north of here, gathered elements of his battalion, plus some men of the 82nd Division who had dropped even further off target, and fought his way south. By 1330 he had Exit 2 under control.

Along the roadside are markers naming part of the road after non-commissioned American soldiers. There are forty-three of them marked by seventy-six signs. The first one here is Sonnier Road. At the first crossroads, to the left along Collins Road, the D115, is the village of Audouville la Hubert, site of the largest POW camp in Normandy. Before the village is a junction with the D14 and just after it on the right-hand side of the D115 before it crosses Exit 3 is a farmhouse. Here is yet another 'first'. General Eugene Landrum set up on D-Day an advance HQ for V11 Corps in the farmhouse. On the gateposts, **plaques** in English and in French claim that at 1000 hours on D-Day General J. Lawton Collins established **'The first Command Post of the American Army in France'**. In fact General Collins did not come ashore until the following day and 'what', you might ask, 'is a Command Post?'

The road you are travelling along, the D913, then becomes Bryant and then Jones Road. At this point there is an information board at Aire des Sources, and Liberty Highway kilometer marker 10. The road becomes Hinkel Road and, as it reaches the beach, Danel Road.

At the point where Jones Road becomes Hinkel Road, by a bridge over a small stream, La Petite Cricque Bau, is a memorial statue on the right. Stop.

• UTAH Danish Memorial/18 miles/5 minutes/Map S11

This memorial, raised in 1984 and designed by Danish architect Svend Lindhardt, commemorates the 800 Danes who took part in the landings. The Danes, mostly serving on board ships, were those who had escaped from Denmark and were attached as individuals to British units. A number joined SOE and in April 1945 Major Anders Lassen, attached to the SAS Special Boat Service, won a posthumous VC in Italy.

Continue down Exit 2 to the museum where Danel Road exits from the beach. Park.

• UTAH Beach Museum / US Memorials / 19.4 miles / 45 minutes / RWC / Map S2,3,4,5,6,7,8, 9,10,16,17

It is helpful to walk down to the beach and to consider the basic story of what happened here before going into the museum - which has been built around German blockhouse W5. The area had been visited by Rommel early in May in line with Hitler's premonition about Normandy being a likely invasion target. When Rommel was pleased with what he found he often gave a concertina or mouth-organ to one of the soldiers putting up obstacles, in the hope that the soldier would play and encourage his comrades to sing, thus building morale. When he came here, however, he was not pleased.

He inspected the beach and the obstacles, and then demanded that Lieutenant Arthur Jahnke, in charge of blockhouse W5, take off his gloves and show his palms, Jahnke did so and, on seeing the weals and scratches on the young officer's hands, which had clearly come from helping to put up beach obstacles, Rommel relented and told him that the blood he had spilled in putting up obstacles was as important as any he would spill in combat.

Memorial to Brigadier General Don F. Pratt, 101st AB Division, Hiesville.

One of the informative plaques, Ste Marie du Mont.

Memorial to US 36th Fighter Group ALG 16, Brucheville.

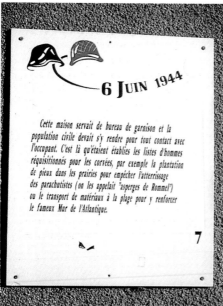

Just a week before the invasion General Marcks, LXXIVth Corps Commander, held a small parade in front of W5 during which Jahnke was awarded the Iron Cross for service in Russia.

Early on the morning of 6 June Jahnke was in W5, woken by the noise of aeroplanes and puzzled by the sound of gun fire coming from the direction of Ste Marie du Mont. He despatched a patrol to find out what was going on and to his surprise they returned in half an hour with seventeen American prisoners. The Americans told him nothing.

Then the air and naval bombardment began. Huge spouts of sand, pieces of concrete and clouds of dust filled the air. In little more than half an hour W5 was ineffective. Their weapons, 50mm, 75mm and 88mm guns, were all out of action. Those men who had not been killed were dazed and shocked by the noise and brutality of the explosions.

Jahnke was wounded. As the noise lessened and the disorientated defenders looked out to sea they saw the approaching armada and, in the leading waves, floating tanks. The lieutenant tried to activate his own tanks, small wire-controlled tractors carrying explosives, called GOLIATHS, but they would not start. The devices, almost 5,000 of which were built altogether, were driven by a 703cc motor cycle engine and could move at 12 km per hour. Although in theory they had a range measured in kilometers the fact that they were wire-controlled limited their use - even if they started.

The Americans, encouraged by a 57-year-old General called Roosevelt, charged up the beach, engineers blew a hole in the sea wall and then, supported by their armour, they rushed W5. Jahnke and his men surrendered. UTAH beach belonged to 4th Division. Roosevelt, who had once commanded the 1st Infantry Division, had been removed from active command and given a desk job. After much lobbying, he had got himself the appointment as second in command of 4th Infantry Division and, at 57, was the oldest officer to land with the assault troops. Sadly, he died of a heart attack on 12 July, in an orchard near Carentan. He never learned that he had redeemed himself and had been given command of 90th Division.

In 1987 Arthur Jahnke returned to W5 and shook hands with another veteran of that 6 June - an American of the 8th Infantry Regiment who had led the charge ashore.

Force U for UTAH had launched its thirty-two DD tanks only 2 miles from shore, instead of the planned 4 miles, because of the bad weather. It was a fortunate decision and twenty-eight tanks made it to the beaches providing direct fire support to the infantry and helping the assault engineers to deal with obstacles. The costly lesson of Dieppe had been learned. By midday UTAH Beach was clear and the 4th Division was on its way inland across the causeways to link up with the airborne forces.

By the end of the day the 4th Division had achieved almost all of its objectives. Over the beach had come 23,000 men and 1,700 vehicles. The causeways were secure and the beachhead firm.

The museum, opened in 1962 and with a major refurbishment, modernisation and expansion to two floors, re-landscaping of the memorial area around and widening of the road from Ste Marie du Mont for 1994, offers a splendid account of the events that took place here on 6 June 1944 and immediately thereafter. Funded by the local Ste Marie du Mont council, the region and veterans, it was originally built into and around German Blockhouse W5 and now offers a panoramic view over the sea. It has landing

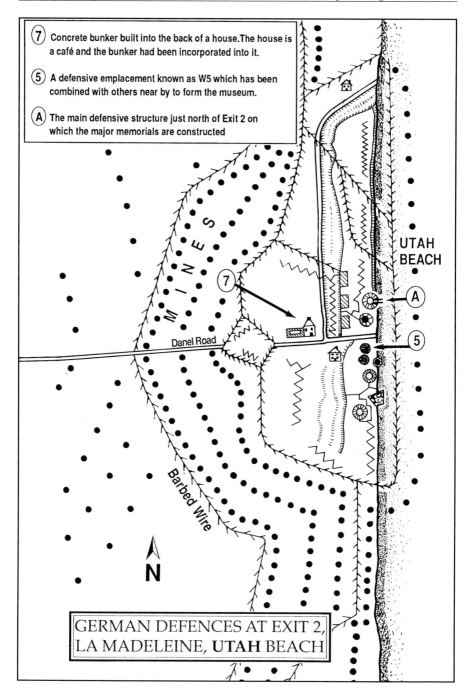

(7) Concrete bunker built into the back of a house. The house is a café and the bunker had been incorporated into it.

(5) A defensive emplacement known as W5 which has been combined with others near by to form the museum.

(A) The main defensive structure just north of Exit 2 on which the major memorials are constructed

UTAH BEACH

M I N E S

(7)

Danel Road

Barbed Wire

N

(A)

(5)

GERMAN DEFENCES AT EXIT 2, LA MADELEINE, **UTAH** BEACH

craft, films using actuality footage (English sound available), diorama, scale models, photographs, ephemera and artefacts, many donated over the years by veterans.

Veterans of the landings are asked to sign the Book of Honour (and should have complimentary entrance). Postcards and booklets are on sale.

Open:daily from 1 April-30 November. Weekends from 1 December-31 March. Entrance fee payable. Reductions for children. Tel: (0)2 33 71 53 35.

There are good parking and toilet facilities beside the museum.

The Wall of Liberty. A major project is underway for the area in front of the Museum/Memorial area which, it is said, has been privately bought (by the family who own the *Champion* Supermarket Group) and donated to the Veterans' Association. It is planned to build the US Veterans' Memorial Wall here. It had originally been intended for the Memorial Valley of the *Mémorial* Museum at Caen but, although many veterans, their families and others subscribed to the project by paying for individual names to be inscribed, the wall did not materialise and much controversy was engendered. The original idea was the brainchild of General Alvin D. Ungerlieder of the 29th Division who formed the Association. Members have now managed to trace 26,000 contributors (it was thought that 60,000 had originally subscribed). The plan is to create a 12-hectare *Parc de Souvenir*, designed by Parisian architect Jean Braltrusaitis and the landscaper Louis Coussnon. In it will be sixteen circular spaces, with a diameter of 60 metres and each touching the other, within which granite pillars bearing the names will be built. Oaks, cedars and cypresses will surround them and provide shade and harmony. The first phase will concentrate on the inscription of the 77,760 names of soldiers who landed at UTAH. It is hoped that that will be inaugurated on 6 June 2000. Next will be the names, inscribed without charge, of the 2,900 soldiers who died on 6 June. Then the subscripion will be open (at a minimum charge of $40 per name) to other names of those who took part in the D-Day landings or the Battle for Normandy - a target total of 400,000. The final cost is estimated to be approximately $3.5 million. Amongst the first major contributors are film producer Steven Spielberg and actor Tom Hanks.

Opposite is the café and bar *Le Roosevelt,* built adjoining a bunker, which serves snacks and simple meals and sells postcards and souvenirs.

Around and about the museum the following memorials and objects may be found within walking distance:

NTL Totem
Sherman Tank, Landing Craft, US Anti-aircraft Gun.
4th Division Memorial Obelisk.
Kilometer 00 - This marks the beginning of 4th Division's and Leclerc's 2nd Armoured Division's Liberty Highway which runs both into Holland and across France to the German border.
Through Normandy, markers can be seen every kilometer showing the distance from '0' at Ste Mère Eglise or '00' at UTAH Beach.
Rowe Road Marker at exit from beach.
40th Anniversary commemorative plaque, naming King Baudouin of the Belgians, Queen Elisabeth II, King Olav V of Norway, Grand-Duke Jean of Luxembourg, Queen Beatrix of the Netherlands, President Reagan, Prime Minister Pierre Trudeau of

The Museum, UTAH Beach.

Canada and President Francois Mitterand
Bronze plaque, Voie General Eisenhower, 1890-1969
Bunker System A. (See the diagram 'German Defences at Exit 2, La Madeleine, UTAH Beach). This carries the 24ft-tall polished red Baveno granite memorial obelisk to the **American forces of VII Corps,** who landed here and liberated the Cotentin Peninsula between 6 June and 1 July 1944. It was erected in 1984 by an agreement between the governments of France and America which included it as part of the permanent arrangement for commemoration, which already covered Pointe du Hoc and the St Laurent Cemetery. It bears the words 'Erected by the United States of America in humble tribute to its sons who lost their lives in the liberation of these beaches. June 6, 1944'.

There is also a marker to **90th Infantry Division,** the first follow-up division. It commemorates their dead from 6 June 1944 to 9 May 1945, and proudly carries the division's nickname, 'The Tough Hombres', and the fact that from UTAH Beach to Czechoslovakia the 90th Combat Team fought five campaigns in 300 days. On top of

Artist's impression of 'The Exotic Garden', Wall of Liberty project, UTAH Beach.

Kilometer 00.

Memorial to US Naval Reserve, Place Angelo C. Chatac.

the steps is a memorial to the **1st Engineer Special Service Brigade** and a **light anti-aircraft gun.** On the low wall to the seaward side of the Engineer Memorial are **fifty-eight markers** pointing to ship locations, to where acts of heroism were performed (including Free French pilots), to ports and towns and even to Berlin.

Below, and part of, the bunker is a **memorial crypt** with an illuminated display including a **portrait of Major General Eugene Mead Caffey,** who was responsible for erecting the memorial.

Memorial to US 90th Infantry Division, UTAH Beach.

As Colonel Caffey he commanded the Brigade in 1944 and dedicated the memorial on 11 November that year. In and on the walls of the crypt are plaques from or about:

Souvenir Français.

Major General Eugene Mead Caffey.

The Commander of the 1st US Engineer Special Brigade.

The use of the blockhouse by the US engineers.

The names of those Engineers who gave their lives.

The actions of the airborne and seaborne forces on D-Day.

A new plaque has recently been erected to the **US Coastguards.**

Some 250 metres to the east, down a small road to the left, **is a memorial to the US Naval Reserve** (Map S20).

After leaving the UTAH Beach area on the D421 direction Quinéville/Objectif un Port, take the first left and on the left-hand corner at the T junction stop.

• *Chapelle de la Madeleine 20.3 miles/ 5 minutes/Map S1*

Inside the chapel is a superb photo of US troops leaving it in June 1944, and beautiful stained glass windows. One immediately behind the altar records that in 1944 the Free French Forces took part in the Landings with the Allied troops. The chapel was rebuilt with funds donated by Jean Schwab d'Hericout who landed nearby with the Free French.

Return to Route des Alliés and continue direction Leclerc Memorial/Quinéville along Ridgway Road.

After just over a mile at a crossroads is Blair Road, Exit 3, to the left on the D67. The inland end of this causeway was due to be secured by the 502nd PIR. Their drop was so scattered that some came down on the wrong DZ, yet, despite that, the CO of the 502nd, Colonel Cole, and a force from the 3rd Battalion, moved onto the village of St Martin de Varreville, 2 miles to your left, and cleared it by 0730. An additional task for the 502nd had been the elimination of a battery of Russian 122mm guns just west of the village, but they found that the Germans had moved them. So Colonel Cole dug in his men inland of the causeway and waited. At about 0930 a number of Germans driven back from the beaches up Blair Road ran into the paratroopers who killed seventy-five of them.

Continue to the parking area on the right.

• *Leclerc Comité du Débarquement Monument/Bunkers/22.0 miles/10 minutes/Map Q6,7*

UTAH Beach was the landing place for General Patton's 3rd Army and, as part of it, Frenchman General Leclerc's 2nd Armoured Division, on 1 August. This was where Leclerc's force came ashore and there is a *Comité du Débarquement* memorial to commemorate the fact. The memorial says that the Allies landed there on 6 June but on that day the forces were American. There is little doubt that there was embarrassment in some French quarters that Leclerc's force did not land until almost a month after D-Day and the impression is given that the French landed alongside the Americans. There is a whiff of political correctness in the air. There is also an armoured car and a half-track vehicle and four low red marble monuments to the Free French Forces. In the parking area is a **NTL Totem**. There are formidable blockhouses and bunkers hidden in the sands and the defenders here held out for some hours. This was where the 4th Division had been scheduled to come ashore and things might have been quite different for them if they had.

A stroll past the Leclerc memorial through the dunes to the beach leads to the centre of what was once a typical infantry strongpoint of the Atlantic Wall.

A large blockhouse is visible 250 yards away to the left, and other remains are obvious in the sand around. The position originally stretched for some 150 yards both to left and right and also inland. Sea approaches were covered by 50mm and 4.7cm guns, plus a 3.7cm Renault turret mounting. Flank defence was provided by a 75mm and two 4.7cm anti-tank guns, while facing inland was a 50mm weapon. The whole position was surrounded by barbed wire and minefields, with remotely-controlled flamethrowers. Individual posts were connected by trenches and the artillery weapons were supported by infantry firepower, such as 81mm mortars.

Out to sea at low tide blockship debris can be seen.

Continue north following signs to Ravenoville on the D42.

Just after leaving, a junction with Begel Road is passed. This is Exit 4. Like Exit 3, it had been allotted to the 502nd PIR. Two miles inland from here the village of St Germain de Varreville sits just above the inland end of the causeway. In the village on 6 June was a German artillery battery which put up a stubborn fight and delayed Colonel Strayer and the men of the 506th who were on their way to clear Exit 2. They by-passed the enemy position, though part of Colonel Strayer's force joined up with a group of tanks from the 70th Tank Battalion, which they brought up from the beach, and destroyed the guns. Lieutenant-Colonel Patrick Cassidy, CO of the 1st Battalion of the 502nd, gathered as many of his own men as he could find, plus a few of the 506th, and established roadblocks to cover Exit 4 and Exit 3. By mid-morning he reported that Exit 4 was open.

Continue past the large bunkers on each side of the road. Continue following signs to Quinéville on the D15 through Ravenoville Plage and back onto the D421 towards Quinéville. Continue through Les Gougins and turn left by a German bunker onto the D69.

At this point out to sea the Isles de Saint Marcouf can be seen. It had been suspected that the Germans had established a minefield control post on the islands and elements of the 4th and 24th Cavalry Squadrons under Lieutenant-Colonel E. C. Dunn landed there around 0530 on D-Day. Although no Germans were present, and no major minefield was discovered, a number of casualties was suffered from mines on the islands themselves.

Continue to and stop at

• St Marcouf Batterie, Crisbecq/29.4 miles/ 10 minutes/Map Q3,4

Beside the complex is a **NTL Totem**. There are formidable concrete remains here of control bunkers and gun emplacements. The central bunker has been converted into a small open museum and information centre with signs in English, French and German, and it is possible to climb on top of it to get a good view towards UTAH Beach. The works were begun in 1941 by the Todt Organisation and on 6 June the main armament in position was two 155mm guns. In addition there were three 21mm Skodas, six 75mm anti-aircraft weapons and three 20mm guns. An all-round defensive position was established with minefields, barbed wire and seventeen machine-gun posts. As part of the coastal defence organisation the battery came under the German Navy and the position was commanded by 1st Class Ensign Walter Ohmsen with a force of some 300 men. In the early morning of 6 June, following a raid in which some 600 tons of bombs were dropped around the battery without damaging it, a number of paratroopers of the 501st and 502nd PIRs, miles off course, landed nearby and twenty were taken prisoner. As daylight came the 155mm guns opened up on the invasion fleet off UTAH Beach, hitting a cruiser and sinking a destroyer as well as damaging others. In the return fire many guns were destroyed, though the casements remained intact, and, despite continued counter-battery work from the sea and local attacks by troops from UTAH Beach, the position held out until 12 June when men of the 39th Infantry Regiment entered the silent battery.

All the officers and NCOs had been killed or wounded. Ensign Ohmsen and seventy-eight men had withdrawn during the night. The damage that can now be seen is the work of US engineers who attempted to destroy the battery after its capture.

Continue to the junction with the D14 and go straight over on the D69 signed Batterie d'Azeville. At the first junction turn left on the D269 and turn next right on the D269. Continue to the parking area on the left. The entrance to the Batterie is over the road.

• *Batterie d'Azeville/31.1 miles/20 minutes/Map Q8*

The refurbished battery was one of the first parts of the Atlantic Wall to be constructed. It consists of four powerful casemates, 30 metres apart, linked by a 300 metre long network of concrete trenches, 150 metres of which were covered and used as ammunition bunkers, shelters and electric generators. Two of the enormous structures are uncharacteristically slab-sided.

The approaches to the position from the sea had been made almost impenetrable by the use of minefields and barbed wire thickened by one-man concrete shelters. The positions at both Azeville and Crisbecq were still holding out on 8 June despite assaults by 1st Battalion 22nd Infantry preceded by artillery and naval gunfire. On 9 June Colonel Tribolet, commanding 22nd Infantry, decided to blank off Crisbecq with naval gun fire and to concentrate his efforts on Azeville. He discovered that the approach to the position from the west had apparently been overlooked by the defenders who had not cleared the undergrowth for fields of fire and sent two companies in that way. They were able to pick their way through the wire and around the mines without being seen and opened fire on the nearest blockhouse with bazookas. Demolition teams laid three charges to blow up the blockhouse and a tank joined in, but none of the assaults caused serious damage to the concrete. The attackers were about to run out of explosives and be forced to withdraw when Private Ralph Riley, on the orders of his company commander, took the remaining flamethrower and set off to give the blockhouse 'one more squirt'. Having run through enemy fire, he reached the blockhouse only to find that the flamethrower would not ignite. Taking his life into his own hands, he turned

Leclerc Monument and armoured car, Varreville.

Azeville Battery.

on the oil jet and lit it with a match, aiming the burning stream at the door. By chance the flames reached some ammunition inside and explosions followed. Within minutes a white flag was displayed and the German commander surrendered with the entire garrison of 169 men. Riley was awarded the Silver Star. The capture of Azeville allowed the Americans to ignore Crisbecq and to push on to Quinéville .

Open:daily 1 June-31 August 1400-1900. Sundays only May and September 1400-1700. Entrance fee payable. Guided tours on request. Tel: (0)2 33 05 98 83.

Return to the junction with the D14 and turn left towards Fontenay-sur-Mer. Some 600 yards after the turning is a farmhouse on the left called 'de Perrette' and just beyond it a memorial marker.

The story of Lieutenant Vourch and his 5 companions of No 10 Inter-Allied Commando, Quinéville.

• *The Perrette 365th Fighter Group Memorial 33.2 miles/5 minutes/Map Q2*

The US 9th Air Force Association in concert with friends in France has erected over a dozen memorials to commemorate its actions during the battle of Normandy. This one, marking the landing strip used by the 365th Fighter Group, who were here from 28 June to 15 August, was dedicated on 21 September 1987 by a group of veterans who came over from America for the occasion.

Continue through Fontenay-sur-Mer and turn right direction Quinéville at the junction with the D42. Continue to the Museum parking on the right, Avénue de la Plage.

• *Musée de la Liberté, Quinéville /37.2 miles/15 minutes/Map Q1*

The museum, which contains no weapons, shows life in Normandy under the occupation, using photographs, propaganda posters, dioramas, video presentations and a recreated street. A blockhouse which forms part of the building may also be visited. In front of the museum is a Liberty Highway marker and a signboard telling the story of Lieutenant Francis Vourch and 5 other Frenchmen of No 10 Inter-Allied Commando who made a reconnaissance, named HARDTACK 21, of the area on the night 26/27 December 1943, and discovered and described one of the anti-tank obstacles, 'Element C', made of steel girders and weighing 2.5 tons, that was to form one of the main beach defences. They also took back with them samples of soil in waterproof bags, the information about Element C in particular, contributing to the success of the D-Day Landings. Vourch had also taken part in the Dieppe Raid with No 10 Commando in 1942. There is a **NTL Totem.**

The village was not taken until 14 June. As the Holts' map shows, Quinéville sits at the end of a ridge that runs west to east from Montebourg, and this high ground was seen by the Germans as essential for the protection of the route to Cherbourg and they established strong positions upon it. Equally, General Collins knew that the capture of the Montebourg-Quinéville ridge was an essential prelude to an attack upon Valognes and thence Cherbourg. Establishing a firm position on the western end of the ridge, to the east of Montebourg which had yet to fall, he sent the 22nd and 39th Infantry along the crest of the ridge, west to east, and they fought their way in column of companies down to the nose and into the village with the support of an air strike by thirty six A-20s.

Open:daily March-May/Oct-Nov 1000-1800. June-Sept 0930-1930. Entrance fee payable. Reductions for veterans, OAPs and students. Tel: (0)2 33 21 40 44.

• *End of Itinerary One*

• *OR continue with the Extra Visit below.*

Extra Visit to Montebourg/German Cemetery, Orglandes/Patton's HQ, Néhou/Valognes (Map P1,2). Round trip approximately 32 miles. Approximate time: 1 hour, 30 minutes

Take the D42 to Montebourg.

Montebourg was bitterly fought over from 6 June until the Germans were finally forced out on 19 June. On the night of 6 June, General Dollmann, commanding the German 7th Army, moved the 243rd Division to Montebourg to counter the American advance. For the civilians of the little town, all hell already seemed to have broken loose. See the civilian eyewitness account below.

Rommel became increasingly aware of the threat to Cherbourg and feared that the Cotentin Peninsula was about to be cut off. On 7 June he rushed more troops to the area, including the 77th Division which was eventually sent to Montebourg. From 8 June to 1 July, General von Schlieben set up a defensive line from le Ham

Extra visit continued

to the west of the N13, through Montebourg to Quinéville on the coast to the east. On 10 June the 505th Parachute Infantry attacked le Ham, with the objective of taking Montebourg station. The attack bogged down after a successful start, and Montebourg was still in enemy hands by 12 June. The Germans were prepared to fight hard for what they felt was the vital key town to the defence of Cherbourg. They repelled attacks over the following days until finally, on 18 June, Quinéville having been taken, (see above), Generals Collins and Bradley, knowing that Schlieben was withdrawing to Cherbourg, headed once again for Montebourg. The attacking American divisions encountered little resistance. When the 3rd Battalion of the 22nd Infantry entered Montebourg at 1800 hours on 19 June they found it deserted, but 90% destroyed. Today there is a monument to the US 4th Infantry Division and a street named for them.

A D-DAY MEMORY

From a 12-year-old French girl living in Montebourg.

"My father was the local doctor.... But at Easter time he was taken ill and was sent to a sanatorium in the Alps. On 5 June my mother had a phone call to say he was dying. We were a large family (twelve in all, ten living still at home) and she called us together to brief us as to how we were to look after each other in her absence. Each older child was given direct responsibility for a younger, and should we have to evacuate, for looking after the practical necessities for the little one.

I was responsible for my 7-month-old brother, who had an ear infection. So I had to keep a bottle of hydrogen peroxide, as many nappies (a rare commodity at the time) as I could find and most precious of all, a tiny burnous [a hooded woollen cape] which we kept in a pillowcase.

After five o'clock in the morning on 6 June, the doctor who was my father's replacement was called out to tend wounded soldiers - Allied soldiers - the Invasion had started.

At first we stayed on in our home, but it was terrifying. Phosphorous bombs were falling and there were fires everywhere. The Germans had recently commandeered all the town pumps and the townspeople tried to put out the fires with buckets of water. It was hopeless. Eventually a vehicle full of ammunition was hit by a bomb and exploded near our house. There was artillery fire too. We were very frightened - especially as we were without our parents. We bundled as much as we could into the baby's pram, including cans of milk - there was a large compartment under the mattress - and took refuge in a nearby abbey, then in use as a boys' school. Then the battle came to the very courtyard and there was fierce fighting. We managed to get out to a nearby farm, but it was already full of refugees. We had lost all our possessions - except the little *burnous*, still in its pillowcase.

The entrance, German Cemetery, Orglandes.

Headstones in the German Cemetery.

Memorial to General Patton's HQ, Néhou.

EN HOMMAGE
A NOS LIBERATEURS
DES 9ÈME ET 90ÈME DIVISION
POUR LE 50ÈME ANNIVERSAIRE
DU 17 JUIN 1944
LE 7 JUIN 1994

Plaque to the US 9th and 90th Divisions, church wall, Orglandes.

Sherman tank, General Patton's HQ.

A D-Day Memory continued

People were very kind and generous to each other in those dangerous days. The brothers gave us linen to use as nappies and when we were in the cowshed, a family whose farm was burnt out passed us. One of the girls was doing the washing when the house was hit. She still had the soap in her hand. It was all she had. She gave it to us for the baby.

The first Allied soldier I saw was an American. This surprised me. I had always expected to be liberated by the English. It was by the German battery in the wood on the farm and he had been taken prisoner. The Germans seemed sorry for our plight and offered us sweets. We all refused. It was our little form of 'Resistance'. The American soldier appreciated this and gave us the 'V' sign."

Extra visit continued

From the main street (the old N13), take the D42, direction Ecausseville/Eroudeville.

A 9th USAAF Museum is being constructed by the Franco-American 9th USAAF Normandy Airfields Association in an old hangar in Ecausseville. Planned opening - 2002.

Continue through Ham to the junction with the D24. Turn left signed to Deutscher Soldaten Friedhof, Orglandes. On entering the village the cemetery parking is on the right.

German Cemetery. This contains 10,152 burials from the battles around Valognes during the American push towards Cherbourg. Originally the dead of both sides were buried here, but the Americans were moved to Saint Laurent in 1945. To the original 7,358 German dead were added a further 2,794, exhumed by the French *Service des Sepultères* from many isolated small cemeteries and graves in the surrounding area. Landscaping work by the German Volksbund began in 1958. 28 lines of graves, marked by dark stone crosses bearing two or three names in white on each side, stand on the vast lawn. The cemetery was inaugurated on 20 September 1961. It has an impressive entrance complex with a large square tower. To the left beneath it is a room with the cemetery registers and a large mosaic of Christ. Outside is a **NTL Totem.**

Continue into the village and turn right following signs to Cobra La Percée on the D126.

Just beyond the turning is Orglandes Church, on the wall of which is a black marble plaque with, in gold lettering, the message *'A Nos Libérateurs'*, **the US 9th and 90th Divisions'** (Map P3), erected on the 50th Anniversary.

Continue to the junction with the D142. Turn right signed Néhou. Continue to the junction with the D2. Go straight over. On entering Néhou there is a sign by the church to Camp Patton on the D42. At the junction with the D900 turn

Extra visit continued

right signed Bricquebec. Continue to a small turn to the right (just before the sign Bricquebec 6 kilometers) signed Camp Patton/La Belle Manière. Continue to the parking area on the right.

General Patton's Headquarters.

The inspiration for the creation of this impressive memorial site was M Jean Baptiste Tyson, founder of the Association *'Souvenir du Général Patton'*, whose headquarters are in the *Mairie* of Néhou. He was aided by the State of Connecticut and, once the project was underway, the *Département* of La Manche bought the area up to the hedge and barrier and now maintains it. The site contains a Sherman tank ('Lucky Forward') in immaculate condition, acquired from the Saumur Armoured Vehicles Museum.

There is a descriptive board about the M4 Tank behind it. Beyond on the right hand side is a memorial stating that General Patton had his command post on this site from 6 July-2 August, during which time he planned the Avranches Breakthrough. To the right of the memorial is a plaque to M Tyson and to the left a 2ème Division Blindé plaque. Beyond are **NTL Totems.** One, bearing a photo of Patton, describes the 'Legendary Commander in Chief of the Glorious 3rd Army'. The other describes the configuration of the 3rd Army bivouac - the trailer-caravans of Patton and his Chief of Staff General Gaffey, the mess tent, and the generators which were in a field in La Belle Manière Farm (over the road).

Beyond the barrier is the orchard where many bivouacs were sited. One original apple tree remains, the others were replanted in 1993. This land belongs to the Benedictine Nuns, whose Abbess was a novice in France during the war and who founded a convent in Bethlehem, Connecticut. Coincidentally, General Patton's grand-daughter Georgina, belongs to the order, which has bought a house in Néhou. The Abbess, Georgina and other members of the Patton family were present at the unveiling of the memorials, at which two nuns of the Order sang George Patton's favourite song 'The Fox' (Rommel's nickname). In this area is a large boulder memorial bearing plaques with quotations beloved by Patton: *'De l'audace, encore de l'audace, toujours de l'audace'* [Danton] and Patton's own saying, 'Do not take counsel of your fears'.

Return to the D900 and continue through Bricquebec. Continue on the D902 to the N13 at Valognes.

Valognes. This was Schlieben's headquarters (though on 6 June he was attending the War Games at Rennes) until the retreat to Cherbourg on 20 June. On that day, the 315th Infantry cleared stragglers in the area as they advanced towards Cherbourg.

If **Cherbourg** has not been visited on Approach One, it can be visited now.

Follow signs to Cherbourg along the N13 (Map Ch).

En route is the town of Tourlaville, in the cemetery of which are the graves of American Civil War casualties from the USS *Kersage* and the USS *Alabama*.

For information on the Port, see the end of Approach One.

ITINERARY TWO

- **Itinerary Two** starts at St Côme du Mont, looks at the southern edge of the 101st US Airborne Division landing area and works eastwards over the area of the US Rangers operation to the 116th and 16th Infantry Regiments landings at OMAHA BEACH. See Map 5 below.
- **The Route:** St Côme du Mont; 502nd PIR Memorial; Carentan - Town Hall and Memorials, Stained Glass Window in Church; Brévands Church Stained Glass Window; Isigny - 29th US Division Stained Glass Window, Church, Comité du Débarquement Monument; German Cemetery, Peace Garden and Exhibition, La Cambe; Grandcamp-Maisy - Heavy Group Bomber Command RAF Memorial, Rangers' Museum; Pointe du Hoc - Rangers' Memorial; 147th Engineer Combat Memorial, Englesqueville; Vierville - HQ 11th Port US Army Plaque, US Memorials; OMAHA Beach Memorials, Operation AQUATINT Memorial; St Laurent - Comité du Débarquement Monument; 2nd Infantry Division, Provisional Engineers Memorial, Le Ruquet; AQUATINT Graves, St Laurent Churchyard, American National Cemetery and Memorials.
- **Extra Visits** are suggested to Cricqueville-en-Bessin Church Rangers' Memorial, A2 9th USAAF Airstrip ; Memorial Church to Massacre at Graignes.

Planned duration, without stops for refreshment or Extra Visits: **5 hours, 45 minutes**

Total distance: 41.5 miles.

BACKGROUND TO OMAHA AND POINTE DU HOC

'Bloody OMAHA' is how most Americans who know refer to the more easterly of the American landing beaches. OMAHA was the critical beach and on the 4 miles of sands below its 100ft high frowning cliffs the Allied invasion came perilously close to failure. Once again, as with the paratroopers, it was the spirit and determination of small groups of GIs that won through.

During World War I groups of men from British villages, football teams and local clubs had volunteered together to fight. They had joined up together and, in the mass casualties on the Western Front, died together. Villages lost almost all their men at one stroke. Battalions that had been formed from such groups of friends were known as 'Pals Battalions'. On OMAHA the Americans were to have their own Pals Battalions and it is a story that had been overlooked in the popular history of the landings - until the making of Spielberg's film, *Saving Private Ryan*.

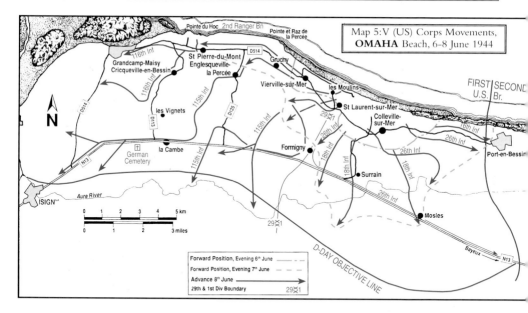

OMAHA BEACH

Assault Time:	0630 hours
Leading Formations:	116th Infantry Regiment (attached from 29th Division) and 16th Infantry Regiment of the 1st Infantry Division
US 1st Division Commander:	Major General Clarence R. Huebner
Bombarding Force C:	Battleships: USS *Texas* (flagship)
	USS *Arkansas*
	Cruisers: HMS *Glasgow*
	FFS *Montcalm* (French)
	FFS *Georges Leygues* (French)
	Eleven destroyers
German Defenders:	352nd Infantry Division and elements of 716th Coastal Defence Division
352nd Division Commander:	Lieutenant General Dietrich Kraiss

The Plan - Omaha Beach (See Map 5)

General Huebner's plan was to attack on a two-regiment front with the 16th Regiment on the left and the 116th Regiment on the right. In turn each regiment was to land two battalion teams on its own section of front with the task of clearing the beach obstacles and moving some two miles inland to secure the beachhead for follow-on landings. Almost 300 special assault engineers were to follow the leading waves of infantry in order to blow up the obstacles.

The set-piece plan had been prepared in great detail and perhaps reminded General Huebner of the way plans had been prepared for the highly successful American offensive at St Mihiel in 1918 in which he had taken part. The beach had been divided into eight sectors of different lengths beginning with DOG in the west and ending with FOX in the east. The infantry landings were to follow the air and naval bombardment at 0631 hours. The beach approaches were to be cleared by 0700 hours when for the next two hours another wave of infantry was scheduled to come ashore every thirty minutes. The plan continued in its detail - enemy strongholds to be neutralised by 0830 hours - artillery to begin landing at 0830. It was a plan that in its detailed precision had similarities to the one in September 1944 for Operation Market Garden which prompted the Pole, General Sosabowski, to complain, 'But what about the Germans?' Here, as in Holland, the enemy was not prepared to co-operate.

What Happened on D-Day

The effect of the weather on Force O for OMAHA was far worse than on Force U for UTAH because the 1st Division did not have the benefit of shelter at sea from the Cotentin Peninsula. The troops were loaded into their assault craft some eleven miles offshore, about twice the distance out that the British would use and against

'Flying Fortress' over OMAHA Beach.

the latter's advice. Being so far out, the operation had to be done well before 0630 hours and it was, therefore, dark. Many craft got out of position, including those carrying the engineers, whose task it was to clear the beach obstacles.

Six thousand yards offshore twenty-nine DD (duplex drive) floating tanks were launched. Only two of these reached the beach. Many did not float at all, but went straight to the bottom taking their crews with them.

There were losses too among the LCVPs carrying the infantry. Ten were swamped by the heavy seas and sank. The men, loaded with almost 70lb of equipment each, had little chance of survival. Much of the intrinsic artillery to provide close-support for the infantry combat teams had been loaded on to amphibious DUKWs, but they proved to be top heavy and as a result they capsized, losing more than twenty guns.

As the leading waves of landing craft approached the beach they were off target, without their beach-clearing engineers, without supporting armour and short on artillery. The men, crouched down in the bellies of the LCVPs, had been there for three hours. They were cramped, cold and sea-sick and then, before they reached the shore, the enemy opened fire on them.

What happened on the beach is told in the battlefield tour. Despite all difficulties, despite a situation that looked so desperate to General Bradley that he considered evacuating OMAHA, by the end of D-Day the Americans were on the cliffs above the beach and around the villages of Vierville and Colleville. They owed a great deal to the on-the-spot leadership of Brigadier General Cota, the Assistant Divisional Commander of the 29th Division. That evening the first follow-up force, the 26th Infantry Regiment, came ashore to defend the bridgehead. However, the landing was behind schedule and only two of the five exits from the beach were secure. If the Germans were to counter-attack with armour within 48 hours, the beach might yet be lost.

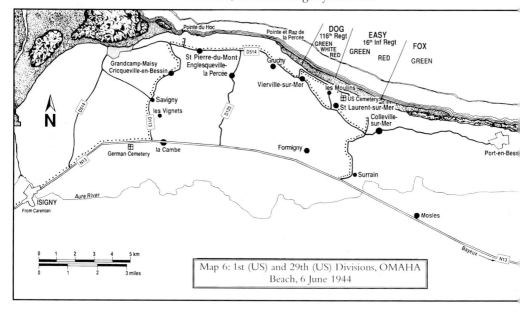

Map 6: 1st (US) and 29th (US) Divisions, OMAHA Beach, 6 June 1944

THE TOUR

• *St Côme du Mont/ 0 miles/Map R*

The itinerary starts here as the natural progression from Itinerary One and so as to get an impression of the waterway obstacles en route to Carentan.

Exit the N13 on the D913 direction St Côme du Mont. Turn left following signs to Carentan.

At the end of D-Day the 101st Airborne Division had achieved most of its objectives, but around the locks on the outskirts of Carentan, which controlled the flood waters of the Douve River, the paratroopers were struggling against fierce resistance.

The High Command of the German 7th Army, responsible for the defence of the area, was still not certain that the main invasion had arrived. Reports coming in were confusing. The use of WINDOW had upset German radar and the Rupert dummy parachutists had fooled the Germans into believing that air drops had been made very far afield from the true DZs. The scattered drop also made life difficult for the defenders. Although some German forces, such as elements of von der Heydte's 6th Parachute Regiment, were fighting well, there was little co-ordinated resistance. It was small unit against small unit, often in contest over the possession of a village strongpoint or a road or railway bridge.

The N13 leading south from St Côme du Mont had been turned into a causeway by opening the locks on the Douve and flooding the fields. It was the obvious route to Carentan from the 101st Airborne landing areas and German resistance in St Côme was stubborn.

At 0430 hours on 7 June the 506th PIR with half-a-dozen Sherman tanks of 746th Tank Battalion advanced on the village from the direction of Vierville in the north-east. Attack and counter-attack followed, but by nightfall the Germans had not been moved. Over at the locks, after a day's fighting and following the initiative of Colonel Johnson, CO of the 501st PIR, who walked towards the enemy carrying a flag and suggested that they might capitulate, remnants of the 1st Battalion of the 6th Parachute Regiment surrendered - though not before some had been shot by their own officers for wanting to give up. However, enemy fire from Carentan prevented any exploitation south.

At 0445 hours on 8 June, behind a rolling barrage, a mixed force of the 101st Airborne Division under Colonel Sink attacked St Côme from the north-east. Some eight fierce actions followed, but when the Americans established a defensive line south of the village across the N13 at about 1600 hours the Germans withdrew to the west. Equipment abandoned in St Côme suggested that the defenders had been the young paratroopers of the 6th Parachute Regiment.

In concert with the attack from the east there had been an assault from the north in the area of Houesville by the 502nd PIR and it was there that General McAuliffe (the same General that would say 'Nuts' to the Germans in Bastogne) found Colonel George

Van Horn, the Commanding Officer of the 502nd, sitting in a wheelbarrow with his ankle in plaster directing the assault. It is a story depicted in the film *The Longest Day*. John Wayne played the part of Colonel Horn.

Steadily over the next two days, the Americans linked up along the Douve and reorganised for a drive upon Carentan.

Between St Côme and Carentan were four bridges over the four main waterways (see the Holts' map) - the Jourdan, the Douve, the Groult and the Madeleine. Before Carentan could be taken the bridges had to be crossed.

On 7 June, Lieutenant General Omar N. Bradley, Commanding the American First Army, had decided to alter the priority task given to Major General J. Lawton Collins' VII Corps which had landed on UTAH (4th Infantry Division was part of VII Corps) The corps' objective was changed from the capture of Cherbourg to the linking up with V Corps on OMAHA, i.e. that the corps' direction should shift to the south. The heavy resistance encountered, particularly on OMAHA, made it advisable to concentrate and co-ordinate the two American forces before the Germans could exploit the gap between them. This gap is evident from the Holts' map when comparing the advances made from each beach on D-Day.

The key to the joining of the forces was Carentan, set squarely on the N13 and at the base of the Douve, and its canal system running to the sea. The Germans were aware of the town's importance and 7th Army Headquarters ordered 6th Parachute Regiment to 'defend Carentan to the last man.'

On 10 June glider and paratroop forces of the 101st Division began their move astride the N13 towards Carentan, scrambling over and under the bridges and paddling in rubber dinghies. The Germans countered with 88mm and machine-gun fire, supported by a brief air attack by two German planes, but the Americans pressed steadily on towards Bridge Number 4, the last one before the town.

Continue on the N13 towards Carentan, crossing the rivers, Jourdan, Douve, (and passing Kilometer Marker 10) Groult and Madeleine. The bridge over La Madeleine was Bridge Number 4. *300 yards after crossing it and going straight over the roundabout, stop on the right by a memorial and flagpoles in front of a warehouse building (Agralco).*

• 502nd PIR Memorial, the Cabbage Patch, Carentan/1.9 miles/10 minutes/Map R24

The American attack petered out in the early hours after the leading company lost fifty-seven men out of the eighty that had begun the assault, and both sides, exhausted by their efforts, rested during the remainder of the night. So many casualties were suffered on the Causeway that it became known as 'Purple Heart Alley.' Taking advantage of the lull, Lieutenant-Colonel Robert G. Cole, commanding the 3rd Battalion 502nd PIR, led his men over Bridge Number 4 and then came under fire from a house in a field behind the warehouse (which was not built at the time). Calling down a smoke screen from the artillery, the Colonel told his men to fix bayonets and at 0615 hours on 11 June he and Major John Stopka led a charge upon the house from across the road and past where the memorial now

Memorial to the 502nd PIR at the 'Cabbage Patch'.

Comité du Débarquement monument, Carentan Mairie.

stands which was then a cabbage patch. It was probably the first bayonet charge in France since the one led by Major Pat Porteous at Dieppe in 1942. Major Porteous won the VC for his leadership. Colonel Cole won the Medal of Honour, the first man in the 101st to do so, and Major Stopka won the DSC - sadly the colonel was killed in Holland (without knowing about his award) and the major at Bastogne. Major Porteous, who landed on SWORD beach with No 4 Commando, survived the war. The memorial reads:

"11 June 1944. Here, in a cabbage patch, the decisive attack of the 502nd Parachute Infantry Regiment of the 101st Airborne drove out the Germans and liberated Carentan."

At the bottom is an additional plaque, headed 'Hancock Field', to Captain Fred A. Hancock of the 502nd PIR, a Silver Star winner.

Continue into Carentan and turn left immediately after at the town hall (which is opposite the railway station). Park in the square and walk back to

• Carentan: Town Hall/Comité du Débarquement Monument/101st Airborne Memorials/ Stained Glass Window, Eglise Notre-Dame/2.9 miles/30minutes/RWC/Map R 20,21,22,23

The first contact between troops from UTAH and OMAHA, that is between the Vth and VIIth Corps, had been made near Brévands, east of Carentan, when men of 327th Glider Infantry Regiment met soldiers from the 29th (Blue and Gray) Division on the afternoon of 10 June. That contact was sealed when Carentan was cleared by an attack from the east by the 327th on 12 June. The German 7th Army's appreciation of the importance of Carentan led to a counter-attack on the town on 13 June along the railway from Baupte, by the 17th SS Panzer Grenadier Division supported by thirty-seven assault guns and what was left of the 6th Parachute Regiment. The 101st Airborne Division was badly mauled, but, with support from the 2nd Infantry Division from OMAHA and a P47 strike by the American 9th Air Force, the town was held. General Maxwell Taylor recalled, 'The battle for Carentan lasted for three days during which I was constantly scuttling in my Jeep from one flank of the division to the other.'

The paratroopers then pushed out defensive lines to the south and south-west of Carentan and stayed there until they were relieved by the 83rd Infantry Division on 29 June. It was the last serious battle for the division which was ordered back to the UK after the fall of Cherbourg. It was not quiet in Carentan all the time though. On 20 June the representatives of units within the 101st Division had assembled in the *Place de la République* behind the town hall for a ceremony in which the Silver Star was to be presented to officers and men when German artillery fire hit the square - however, not before Colonels Sink, Johnson and Michaelis received their awards. The ceremony ended quickly. There was another one though on 7 July in Cherbourg. Then General Maxwell Taylor, the division's commander, was awarded the DSO by General Montgomery in recognition of the division's achievements. On 13 July the division arrived back in England.

In front of the town hall are a *Comité du Débarquement* Memorial, a plaque commemorating the Screaming Eagles, presented by the 101st Airborne Association on their 'Heritage Tour' in 1973 and a **NTL Totem**. Inside the town hall are flags, plaques and souvenirs of US veterans' visits.

Behind the town hall is the

TOURIST OFFICE. Boulevard de Verdun. Tel: (0)2 33 42 74 01

Here a town plan and details of the town's hotels and restaurants are available. Note that Monday is Market Day.

Return to the square past

Hotel du Commerce et de la Gare/Restaurant Escapade on the left. It has a good variety of menus. Tel: (0)2 33 42 02 00.

Walk to the Post Office at the far end of the Square and turn along rue des Prêtres to the Church.

In the Church of Notre-Dame there is a fine **101st Airborne Division memorial stained-glass window** on the right as you enter the main door.

Return to your car and continue towards Isigny. Cross the River Taute and turn left on the D443, signed to 'Mairie'. Continue, passing the local cemetery on the left.

200 yards from the turning the road to the left (signed to the *Ecole Maternelle*) is named after John Tucker, *Commandant de l'Armée Americaine*, in 1944.

Continue, crossing the N13, to the crossroad with the D89 at Catz.

Extra Visit to the Memorial Church to the Massacre at Graignes(Map V1)

Round trip: 12.2 miles. Approximate time: 35 minutes

Turn right on the D89, direction St Lô, N174. Continue, passing Kilometer 44 marker and the railway line. Turn right on the D89 signed Graignes. At the junction with the D444 fork right, signed Graignes and continue over a causeway across the marshes. Enter Graignes and turn right on rue du 11 juin, signed Mémorial. Stop in the car park on the right in Place de la Libération 12 juillet 1944.
In the parking area is a **NTL Totem** and there are WCs.
Walk through the local cemetery to the preserved ruined church.
In the early hours of 6 June, the sleepy village of Graignes was astounded to see in the bright moonlight a cloud of young American parachutists dropping into the marshes that ringed Graignes on three sides. Many of them, weighted down with their 100lbs of combat gear, drowned. The survivors made their way towards the church, silhouetted against the dark sky, until, 48 hours later, 14 officers and 168 men had struggled into the village. They were men of the 507th Parachute Infantry of the 82nd Airborne, dropped from 8 to 15 miles south of their intended drop zone, plus a glider pilot, a C47 pilot and 2 soldiers of the 29th Division who had landed at OMAHA. On the morning of 7 June the Mayor of Graignes, Alphonse Voydie, held an emotional town meeting in the church attended by practically every man, woman and child in the village. They unanimously agreed to help the young Americans, even though they knew the risks - summary execution if caught - and, led by the Mayor and their priest, l'Abbé Leblastier, they searched the swamps for the equipment dropped in them. Soon the soldiers were equipped with machine guns, mortars and ammunition. Major Charles D. Johnson of the 3rd Battalion took command of the group and set up a command post and strong points around the village.

On 8 June they ran out of rations and the village greengrocer and café owner, 50-year-old Madame Boursier, organised a ration collection from the villagers. They prepared two meals a day and transported them to the men in the outlying observation positions and occasionally made the hazardous trip over mined roads by horse-drawn cart to nearby Saint Jean de Daye, held by the Germans, to fetch bread. Several of the youngsters of Graignes scoured the surrounding countryside to bring back valuable intelligence reports and guide the American patrols.

On 8 June came the first encounter between an Americans patrol and a truck filled with German grenadiers. Several Germans were killed, but, out-gunned, the Americans withdrew to Graignes. Later that day another patrol collided with a German field artillery unit, with the same result. Then Johnson sent a group under Lieutenant Francis E. Norton to blow a bridge on the road to Carentan. As the men set charges, a 12-year-old girl warned them of the approaching Boches. Waiting until several Germans were on the bridge, the Americans blew the charge, killing several of the enemy.

Extra visit continued

On 10 June another patrol encountered a German motorcycle patrol, killing all but one man, who returned to his base with the news of the American presence in Graignes. A medic, Captain Abraham Sophian, set up an aid station in the church to treat the wounded, with the women and girls of the village acting as nurses. On 11 June the citizens were attending 1000 Mass when the news of approaching Germans burst. After a short but bitter exchange of fire, the Germans pulled out, leaving behind many of their dead. It was a mere reconnaissance in force, and at 1900 hours the real gun and mortar attack began. Soon Major Johnson and Lieutenant Elmer Farnham and his assistant were killed during the two-hour bombardment. It soon became obvious that the American force was surrounded and just before dusk they were charged from all directions. Running out of ammunition, they attempted to pull out, in many cases only to run into the hands of the Germans. The small band that remained in the church were pinned down by their attackers. Most of the villagers managed to flee into the swamps, but Madame Boursier, the Abbé and a young Franciscan priest, Father Lebarbarchon, and two of the self-appointed nurses refused to leave the wounded. Infuriated by their own losses, the Germans dragged 12 captured American paratroopers into the village square, then transported them by truck to nearby Mesnil-Angot where they were shot or bayoneted. The Abbé and the Franciscan were also murdered. The next day another 12 Americans were killed in Graignes - as were the two 'nurses' - and thrown into the pond. Among them was the surgeon, Captain Sophian. 44 of

Ruined Memorial Church, Graignes.

Plaque unveiled by US Ambassador,12 June 1949.

Extra visit continued

the remaining citizens of Graignes were arrested, 66 homes destroyed and 139 badly damaged in the German reprisals, leaving only two houses untouched. The eight-centuries-old church was blown up.

About 100 of the fleeing Americans eventually managed to reach their own lines, exhausted from their hair-rising near encounters with the enemy. After sleeping for 18 hours, they were fed, showered and issued with new uniforms and were back with their units and in the fighting again within 24 hours.

The ruined church has been left as a dramatic and moving reminder of the terrible events that took place here in June 1944. Under the vaulted roof is the tomb of Curé Albert Leblastier and on the wall to the left is a plaque commemorating the inauguration of the memorial by US Ambassador David Bruce on 12 June 1949. Beneath it is a blue 507th PIR plaque. On the rear wall is an imposing marble plaque bearing in gold letters the names of the citizens of Graignes and the American soldiers killed 6-12 June 1944.

From the memorial are incredible 360° views over the flat marshland and the Marais de la Taute which during wet winters flood spectacularly, giving the land the appearance it had in 1944. Below the church wall is a viewing platform of the *Parc Naturel Régional des Marais du Cotentin et du Bessin*.

Return to crossing with the N13 and rejoin the main itinerary.

Continue on the D89 and turn left signed Brévands. Enter Brévands and turn left signed to the Church and Le Port. Drive to the entrance of the church.

• Brévands Church Stained Glass Window and RAF Grave/8.1 miles/10 minutes/Map S 18

In the churchyard, to the left of the church, is the grave of Sergeant R.F.C. Dean, Pilot, 17 November 1941. In the church, on the right-hand side, is a stained glass window with the caption, *La Paroisse de Brévands Reconnaissante. Juin 1944.*

Forces from OMAHA and UTAH first made contact in the Commune of Brévands.
Return to Catz and continue on the D89 to the first junction. Turn left signed Isigny.
On the left is passed the **Hotel/Restaurant Aire de la Baie. Tel: (0)2 33 42 00 99. The River Vire, marking the junction between La Manche and Calvados, is then crossed.
Continue into Isigny and stop near the church on the left.

• US 29th Division Stained Glass Window, Isigny Church/12.9 miles/10 minutes/Map S19

This striking, modern window was unveiled on the 50th Anniversary.
Next to the church is the **TOURIST OFFICE**. 1 rue Victor Hugo. Tel: (0)2 31 21 46 00.
Continue to the centre of the town and stop beside the Comité du Débarquement monument on the left.

• Isigny Comité du Débarquement Monument/13 miles/5 minutes/RWC/Map S16

Beside the monument is a **NTL Totem**.

The towns of Isigny, Bayeux and Caen, all off the N13 road behind the landing beaches, were D-Day objectives. None was taken on D-Day. Isigny was scheduled to be taken by 29th Division who were due to land in strength once a foothold had been established at OMAHA by the 1st Division. Major General Gehrhardt, commanding the 29th Division, was to take back under command the units attached to 1st Division for the landings and head for Isigny, while the 1st Division under Major General Huebner was to drive east to link up with the British at Port-en-Bessin.

When the Americans landed at OMAHA they had expected formidable fortifications, but less than formidable defenders of the 'ear-nose-and-throat' 716th Static Division. What they found were good quality troops of the 352nd First Attack Division. Instead of there being just four battalions of indifferent troops to overcome between Bayeux and Isigny, there were those, plus four from the 352nd Infantry Division.

Because of the difficulties on OMAHA, Major General Gehrhardt did not assume formal command of the 29th Division until 1700 hours on 7 June and that evening the task of taking Isigny was given to the 175th Infantry Regiment supported by the 747th Tank Battalion. In a remarkable night-time offensive the 29th Division cleared la Cambe before dawn on 8 June, though a mistaken attack by allied aircraft caused 20 'friendly' casualties, and that night, following a naval bombardment that destroyed 60 per cent of the town, moved unopposed into Isigny. Omar Bradley was so overwhelmed by the devasting effects of the naval fire, for which he had frequently pestered Admiral Ernest King, (C-in-C of the US Fleet), that he gathered the Admiral, General George Marshall (Chief of Staff of the US Army), General Henry Arnold (Commanding General of the US Army Air Forces) and General Eisenhower all together in the square to show them the damage. As they were sitting in open cars, it was, he said, an opportunity from which 'an enemy sniper could have won immortality as a hero of the Reich'.

Known by the Americans as 'Easy Knee', Isigny claims to be the birthplace of Walt Disney's forebears who were 'd'Isigny', i.e. 'from Isigny'

To the right is the **Hotel de France. Tel: (0)2 31 20 00 33 and there are a couple of convenient restaurants nearby, notably the good value Le Globe, Tel: (0)2 31 51 96 70.

Turn right on the Avénue de Versailles and rejoin the N13 signed D-Day Le Choc/Toutes Directions/Bayeux/Grandcamp Maisy. Continue to the La Cambe exit on the D113 and follow signs to Cimetière Militaire.

• The German Cemetery/Exhibition/Peace Garden, La Cambe/20.8 miles/30 minutes/MapT18

The Cemetery. This was originally an American cemetery, with burials of both American and German dead. In 1947 the Americans were repatriated or re-buried at St Laurent. The following year the British and French War Graves organisations began bringing in German dead and in 1956 work began on concentrating all German burials in the area into six cemeteries. The German People's Organisation for the care of War Graves (*Deutsche Kriegsgräberfürsorge*) established, and continues to care for, this and similar cemeteries. (See War Graves Organisations below). The work here was completed on 21 September, 1961, most of the reinterments and landscaping having been done by students of many nations at an International Youth Camp in 1958. Groups of German school children and students regularly come and camp nearby and spend time in tidying the area. The Allied nations would do well to follow this example in order to bring home to their citizens the terrible cost of war to their young.

To the left and right of the arched entrance are rooms which house the visitors' book, the cemetery registers and war graves literature. On the walls are the names of the missing and there are frequently wreaths of dried ferns and flowers on the floor left by visiting relatives. The cemetery receives around 112,000 visitors per year.

A D-DAY MEMORY

A memory of 1944 by an American soldier of VII Corps

"I was present when this cemetery was inaugurated. Three people were picked from each company of the 175th Regimental Combat Team. We were trucked down to la Cambe and dedicated this cemetery, which was for the dead of 29th Division. I happened to be one of the people chosen. It was a very touching ceremony with the dead not yet buried piled up on either side of the honour guard. We were dressed in the cleanest battle uniforms we could find and three people from each Regiment carried guidons."

Inside the cemetery are small groups of black stone crosses. These are symbolic and do not mark graves. The graves are marked by flat stones engraved with the names of those below - often four or more together. The Germans call this 'comradeship in death', though a more practical reason is that the French were unwilling to give up land for the invader to use and the Germans have had to bury all their Normandy dead in six cemeteries. Here there are 21,160 dead, including 296 in a mass grave under the grassed mound in the centre of the cemetery.

The mound, or ossuary, is ringed at the bottom by stones carrying the names of the dead and surmounted by a huge black cross and two figures representing mourning parents. There are steps to the top of the mound from the rear and it is quite proper to climb up and to look over the graves. In winter the steps can be extremely slippery, as can be the stone path leading from the entrance to the mound.

The impression here is one of solemnity and of sadness, a typical reaction in German cemeteries. Whether this is due to the Teutonic inheritance showing through in the cemetery architecture, or to the wide use of dark oak trees (symbols of strength) or to a deliberate intent to express remorse is impossible to say. It is, however, worthwhile making an effort to contrast the style of the three national cemeteries that are visited on the recommended tours - German, American and British - and asking the rhetorical question, 'What is their purpose?'

In Block 47, Grave 3 121F lies the body of SS Obersturmführer Michael Wittmann,

Information Centre
outside the German
Cemetery, la Cambe.

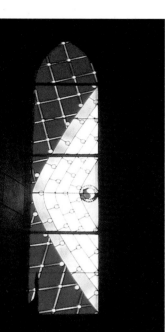

Stained glass window
to US 29th Division,
Isigny church.

Stained glass window, Brévands
Church.

Graves of Michael Wittman and his crew.

Landscaping the cemetery, International Youth Camp 1958.

Mass grave, sculptures and symbolic crosses in the cemetery.

found near Cramesnil on the N158 (on the other side of the road to the Canadian Cemetery at Cintheaux) with the remains of his tank and other members of his crew, then reinterred here in May 1983. A veteran of the Russian campaign, Wittmann is most famous for his exploits at Villers-Bocage on 13 July 1944. He was leading his force of 4 Tigers and 1 PzKpfw towards the village when he spotted a British column (of 22nd Armoured Brigade of 7th Armoured Division) leaving it in the direction of Point 213 on the N175. Soon they halted and the crews got out to take a break. Wittmann cut round behind the unwary British and entered the village to carry out a recce. There he spotted 4 Cromwells lined up one behind the other in the main street and quickly knocked out three of them. The first one was the tank of the commanding officer of the 4th County of London Yeomanry (the Sharpshooters) - Lieutenant-Colonel Arthur, the Viscount Cranleigh - although he himself had gone forward in a scout car to Point 213. The second was that of the second-in-command, Major Carr, and the third that of the RSM. The fourth, that of Major Pat Dyas, managed to reverse and take cover in a garden. Wittmann continued to the Caumont road where he came up against the tanks of 'B' Squadron parked on the road. Shots were exchanged and, as he was outnumbered, Wittmann turned round and proceeded back into the town. Meanwhile Major Dyas had loaded his gun and followed the Tiger. When it turned round Wittman returned Dyas's fire, knocking out the tank and killing two of the crew. The wounded Dyas got away on foot and joined 'B' Squadron. Wittmann then rejoined the other Tigers to replenish his ammunition, after which he moved against 'A' Squadron parked on the N175. First he knocked out the Fireflys, whose 17-pounder guns were the only weapons that could damage a Tiger, then one by one shot up the rest of the squadron. All the crews were either killed or captured. In total, 25 tanks, 14 armoured trucks and 14 Bren carriers were lost in the engagement. Wittman's personal total of tanks destroyed was almost 140, more than 100 of which had been on the Russian front. In this engagement his tank was eventually disabled in the centre of Villers Bocage but he and his crew escaped back to the German lines. He was awarded the Oak Leaves and Swords to embellish his Knight's Cross, the highest order of the Iron Cross. He was eventually killed on 8 August.

The Exhibition and Peace Garden. In September 1996 the modern building of the exhibition, just outside the cemetery entrance, was inaugurated. Its aim is to show how war affected the individual and there are many moving displays of photographs of soldiers (German and Allied) who died in Normandy, with extracts from letters and other personal documents. There are also uplifting quotations from Martin Luther King, ('If we accept that life is worth living and that man has a right to live, we must find an alternative to war'), Professor Theodor Heuss ('Those who rest in the graves are waiting for us ... But when we stand in silence at the crosses, we hear their now-tranquil voices: Make sure, you who are still alive, that peace endures') and Albert Schweitzer ('Wargraves are the great communicators of peace'). Panels describe the cemeteries in Normandy and there is a computer where visitors can freely use the keyboard to look up the burial place/memorial of all the soldiers on both sides who are commemorated in Normandy. This is a remarkable facility that, hopefully, will be copied by the other war graves organisations. The Commonwealth War Graves Commission has a limited search facility on the Internet but for Normandy the la

Cambe offering is more comprehensive. A book, produced by the German-American Memorial Foundation, describing the exhibition is on sale. On the day of the inuaguration a Peace Garden was started, which now stretches along the side of the road towards Bayeux. Each of its more than 1,000 trees is sponsored by an individual, an organisation or a municipal community. There is a **NTL Totem** beside the garden.

Return to the roundabout and follow signs to la Cambe and Grandcamp-Maisy on the D113. Continue to les Vignets.

By turning right here and continuing to Savigny the memorial to **367th Fighter Group of 9th US Airforce Memorial (Map T17)** could be seen.

Continue on the D113 into Grandcamp-Maisy and follow signs to the Port.

There are some fine sea food restaurants around the harbour, which become very popular on Sundays in the season, notably La Marie on the right. Tel: (0)2 31 21 41 00. **TOURIST OFFICE.** 118 rue Aristide Briand. Tel: (0)2 31 22 18 47
Boat trips to the Landing Beaches leave the harbour during May-November on the mini-cruiser *Colonel Rudder*. Contact Mme Vicquelin. Tel: (02) 31 21 42 93

Stop on the quay as near to the sea as possible. On the corner is

• *Monument to Heavy Group Bomber Command RAF/26.9 miles/10 minutes/ RWC/Map S13*

During 1944 two French bomber squadrons, Groupe Guyenne and Groupe Tunisie formed part of No 4 Group Bomber Command (Yorkshire Group), and were given the RAF numbers 346 and 347 respectively. The squadrons became operational on the night of 5 June 1944 and the first target for their Halifaxes were German gun emplacements just outside Grandcamp Maisy. The memorial was unveiled on 8 June 1988 to music provided by a French Air Force band accompanied by a fly past by French Mirage jets and an RAF Nimrod. Many of the French crews had been stationed in the village of Elvington and members of the Parish Council plus a party from the Yorkshire Air Museum and Allied Air Forces Memorial were present.

Walk along the seafront on the Quai Crampon, which has a No Entry sign. Stop at the Museum on the right. [Alternatively you can drive to the museum on the way out of Grandcamp by following the signs in the centre of the town.]

An important new memorial to the Rangers is planned outside the Town Hall for the 55th Anniversary (Map S15).

• *Rangers Museum/15 minutes/Map S14.*

The exhibitions show the history of the Rangers, plus an 18-minute film.
Open: June, July, August 1000-1900 (closed Monday mornings). April, May, September, October 1000-1300 and 1500-1800 (closed Mondays). Tel: (0)2 31 92 33 51

By the museum is a **NTL Totem.** It describes the 47mm gun that was the port's only defence and the powerful 100mm and 155mm guns sited to the east of the town that could range over UTAH and as far as Saint-Marcouf which were silenced on D-Day by a bombardment by the US Navy. Grandcamp (the port area) and the separate town of

Memorial to US 367th Fighter Group, les Vignets.

Memorial to French Units, Bomber Command, Grandcamp-Maisy.

Memorial to Sergeant Peregory MoH.

Maisy (to the east) were liberated on 8 June by the 116th Infantry Regiment. From then on the port played an important role in the landing and bringing up of reinforcements and equipment.

Return to your car and turn left signed Centre Ville. At 27.1 miles there is a sign to the left to the Rangers Museum, a route which you could drive. Continue on rue Commandant Keiffer to the junction with the D514.

• *National Guard/Sergeant Peregory Memorial/Memorial Gardens/27.2 miles/5 minutes/Map T20*

The monument and the memorial garden behind it were inaugurated on the 50th Anniversary. Medal of Honour winner Sergeant Frank Peregory, 29th Division, is buried in the US Cemetery. On 8 June advance elements of the 3rd Battalion, the 116th Regiment were halted by the deadly fire of a German machine gun. Sergeant Peregory attacked the enemy with daring using grenades and his bayonet. He captured 35 enemy soldiers and opened the way for the leading elements of the battalion to advance and secure its objectives.

Continue on the D514, direction Vierville sur Mer/Pointe du Hoc to the turning to the right on the D19 signed to Criqueville-en-Bessin (28.1 miles).

Up this road in Criqueville-en-Bessin Church there is a memorial to Colonel Rudder and the **American Rangers (Map T1)** and near the village **a marker to 9th USAAF Airstrip A2.**

Continue and then follow signs to the left to Pointe du Hoc and stop in the large parking area.

• *Pointe du Hoc/Ranger Memorial/Bunkers/29.9 miles/30 minutes/ WC/Map T2,3*

The small road down which you have driven from the D514 is Rangers Road. In June 1944 it was much narrower and the entrance to the coastal area was controlled halfway down by a manned guard post. The area between the guard post and the sea, which is today the memorial area, was completely sealed off by barbed wire and sentries. The only way in was past the guard post.

Allied intelligence had taken great pains to locate all coastal gun batteries that could menace the invasion, and a total of seventy-three in fixed emplacements had been identified. The most formidable along the American beaches was the six-gun battery at Pointe du Hoc, which was capable of engaging targets at sea and of firing directly onto UTAH and OMAHA Beaches.

The guns were thought to be 155mm, with a range of 25,000 yards and, in preparing their bombardment plans, the Americans placed Pointe du Hoc on top priority. It was decided that the gun positions would be steadily bombed during May, with a heavier than average attack by both day and night three days before D-Day, and then again during the night of 5 June. The potential threat of the Pointe du Hoc battery was seen to be so great that the 2nd Ranger Battalion was given the task of capturing the position directly after H-Hour.

The battery position is set upon cliffs that drop vertically some 100ft to a very small rocky beach. In addition to the main concrete emplacements, many of which were connected by tunnels or protected walkways, there were trenches and machine-gun posts constructed around the perimeter fences and the cliff's edge. The German garrison numbered about two hundred - men of the static 716th Coastal Defence Division, mostly non-Germans.

The responsibility for the assault on Pointe du Hoc lay with General Gerow's V Corps and hence with the 1st Infantry Division and thence with the right-hand assault formation, the 116th Infantry Regiment attached from 29th Division. They were given two Ranger battalions under command to do the job.

The man commanding the Rangers was Lieutenant-Colonel James E. Rudder from Texas who at the last minute, when his Executive Officer who was supposed to be heading the assault was not fit to do so, determined that he would lead the assault himself. General Huebner protested at the idea, but Rudder said, 'I'm going to have to disobey you. If I don't take it, it may not go'. Rudder trained his men on the cliffs on the Isle of Wight, helped by British Commandos.

The position was out on a limb, separated from DOG Green, the nearest edge of the main OMAHA beach at Vierville, by four miles of close country. Between them was another prominent feature, Pointe de la Percée, which like Pointe du Hoc, jutted out into the sea.

The plan called for three companies of 2nd Ranger Battalion to land below the cliffs, climb them and then make a direct assault on the battery. Meanwhile, a fourth company was scheduled to land on DOG Green with the 116th Infantry and to move west to tackle fortifications at Pointe de la Percée in order to cover the flank of the main Ranger force here.

On D-Day the Rangers were late. The strong easterly tide had pulled them too far east, and in the morning light and confusion of the air and sea bombardment Lieutenant-Colonel James E. Rudder, commanding the 2nd Battalion, mistook Pointe de la Percée for Pointe du Hoc.

Walk along the James E. Rudder footpath to the Ranger Memorial at the edge of the cliff.

Over to the right the prominent feature jutting into the sea is Pointe de la Percée. Realising his mistake, the Colonel turned his small flotilla of seven British-crewed LCAs (three had already sunk in the heavy seas and the men were bailing out with their steel helmets in the ones which remained afloat), and moved in this direction, parallel to the shore and some 100 yards out. They came under the direct fire of those manning the trenches, and the Rangers turned inshore and landed some 500 yards away to your right, Rudder's boat being the first to hit the beach. There Colonel Rudder established his HQ, featured in a well known photograph showing the spread-out American flag. The Rangers headed for the cliffs. In a novel approach they had fitted DUKWs with firemen's ladders, but the small beach had been so cratered by the earlier fire support by the battleship *Texas* and others, that the vehicles could not reach the cliff. Rocket-fired grapples were tried, but the ropes, heavy with sea water, held many down, and so with ladders and daggers the Americans began to climb.

The responsibility for the defence of the area had been taken over by the 352nd Division, a full attack formation, following its move forward to the coast by Rommel in February 1944, but fortunately the troops here were those of the Coastal Defence Force. In anticipation of commando landings, the Germans had placed 240mm shells attached to trip wires at 100 yards intervals along the cliff, and the forward troops were amply supplied with hand grenades which they rolled down as the Americans climbed up. The area was in a state of great confusion. Minutes before the Rangers arrived eighteen medium bombers raided the German positions, driving the defenders underground and, as the attacking troops struggled to gain the top of the cliffs, they had direct and very effective fire support from the US destroyer *Satterlee* and the British destroyer *Talybont*. Only very stubborn or foolhardy defenders remained at the cliff's edge to take a personal part in the proceedings and, once on top, the Rangers, scattering small arms fire around them, worked quickly across the torn and smoking ground to the gun emplacements. When they got there they found that the guns had been removed.

Colonel Rudder then split his small command into two. One stayed where it was and prepared a defensive position while the other set off up the road, now called Rangers Road, to find the guns, which fortunately they did. Five of the six (one had been damaged by bombing and the Germans had removed it for repair) were hidden in an orchard at the back of the field where Rangers Road meets the D514. They were well camouflaged but unguarded and, using thermite grenades, the Rangers destroyed them.

To this point, despite the difficulty of assault and because of the air and naval fire support, the Americans' casualties had been relatively light, probably thirty to forty, but later that day the 1st Battalion of the 914th Regiment began a series of counter-attacks that nearly wiped out the small bridgehead and caused most casualties. Aware of the isolation of the men at Pointe du Hoc, the 116th Infantry Regiment, with the 5th Ranger Battalion which had landed with them at OMAHA four miles to your right (east), attempted to link up with the 2nd Ranger Battalion but were stopped 1,000 yards short. That night the 914th Regiment drove the Americans into a small enclave along the cliff, barely 200 yards wide, but the Rangers held on, helped by fire from destroyers. The concrete OP bunker upon which the symbolic dagger stands was attacked by grenade and with a bazooka, but despite this a radio could be heard working inside. Having silenced the machine gun which had been firing from the bunker, the Rangers by-passed it and it was not cleared until 24 hours later when, following the use of a satchel charge, eight Germans surrendered, leaving one man dead inside.

On the night of 7 June General Kraiss ordered the 352nd Division to withdraw during the following day to a defensive position along the River Aure, just south of the N13, but it was not until just before noon on 8 June that the Rangers were relieved by a tank and infantry force of 116th Infantry Regiment, supported by the 5th Ranger Battalion. Before that, however, they had been bombed by Allied planes and fired on by their own side. Such is the fog of war. Their final casualties were 135 killed, wounded and missing out of a total of 225 that landed at Pointe du Hoc. This is a casualty rate of 60 per cent.

Perhaps the most difficult question to answer about the struggle at Pointe du Hoc is, 'Why was the assault made from the sea when the cliffs alone were so formidable?' It

Rangers' Memorial, Pointe du Hoc.

One of the bunkers, Pointe du Hoc.

seems in retrospect, and appears reasonable to assume, that the same conclusion could have been drawn at the time, i.e. that an airborne assault would have been the best way of carrying out the task, and with less likelihood of such a high casualty rate. It may be that the Rangers existed and therefore had to be used; perhaps all available airborne forces, including aircraft, were committed elsewhere; or maybe the position was too near the cliff's edge to plan operations like Merville (qv) or Pegasus Bridge (qv). In the light of what happened to the drops of the 82nd and 101st Airborne Divisions, it was fortunate that the planners had opted for an assault from the sea.

It is interesting to note that most accounts refer to 'Pointe du Hoc' as 'Pointe du Hoe'. The latter is incorrect, and probably has been carried onward from a spelling mistake in early secret planning documents or perhaps an unwitting angliscised literal version of the correct French pronunciation. The puzzle over the name leads on to the puzzle about the guns. Why did Allied intelligence not know that they had been moved? The answer probably rests with the strict security that the Germans maintained in the area. The only access was via the guard post and no Frenchmen were allowed in under any circumstances, so that the French Resistance, who sent back details about most other gun positions before D-Day, were unable to help. The largest question of all in regard to Allied intelligence, however, lies with their total failure to notice Rommel's movement of the 352nd Division onto the beach called OMAHA. That slip might have cost the Allies the war. As it was, it was a close run thing.

In 1954 James Rudder returned to Pointe du Hoc with his 14-year-old son Bud. His visit was covered by a feature in the 11 June 1954 issue of *Collier's* magazine, with a picture of father and son on the cover.

The memorial area is $30^1/2$ acres and the site was preserved by the *French Comité de la Pointe du Hoc*. In 1960 a dramatic granite 'dagger' memorial was raised on top of the German concrete OP bunker, with inscriptions in English and French that commemorate the Rangers' action. On 6 June 1979, in a ceremony attended by General Omar Bradley, the American Battle Monuments Commission took over responsibility for maintenance of the area and just prior to, and since, the visit of President Reagan in 1984, a great deal of tidying-up has taken place. There is a widened Rangers Road, a substantial car park, modern toilets, telephones, gravel paths and easy access to many of the bunkers and gun positions and an explanatory **NTL Totem.**

The ground is still scarred with huge craters from the bombing or from the 14in guns of the *Texas* (which is now a floating museum in Houston). On 6 June 1944 Pointe du Hoc must have been the nearest earthly equivalent to Hades.

Return to the D514 and follow the signs to Vierville/OMAHA Beach.

It is invidious to single out particular actions for special mention since every soldier who took part in the events of 6 June 1944 did the best he could measured by his own standards. Some did a great deal more. However, there are perhaps three events of the day that attract the greatest comment - the Rangers assault on Pointe du Hoc, the 6th Airborne *coup-de-main* on Pegasus Bridge and the landings on OMAHA Beach. It was on OMAHA that the Americans suffered grievous losses - almost one-third as many again as the combined totals of the 82nd Airborne Division, the 101st Airborne Division and UTAH Beach, and more than the entire total of all British casualties for D-Day. As a result, OMAHA Beach has become a

particular place of pilgrimage and there are a number of memorials and features to be seen.
Continue along the D514 to the large château/farm on the right, signed Château de l'Englesqueville/Cidre bouché.

• 147th Engineer Combat Battalion Memorial, Château d'Englesqueville/32.3 miles/10 minutes/Map T21

Drive in through the narrow main gates of the château and ask permission to see the memorial from the helpful owner, Monsieur Lebrec (who speaks excellent English).

The memorial, which was rededicated on 6 June 1994 by the 147th Veterans' Association commemorates the 600 men who were stationed here in June 1944, when the grounds of the château were filled with the Battalion's tents. On its base is the castle emblem of the combat engineers which was made from a ship's propellor.

Continue to Vierville Château on the right.

• HQ 11th Port US Army, Vierville Château/34.6 miles/5 minutes/ Map T10

There is a plaque on the right hand gatepost to commemorate the HQ and nearby a **NTL Totem**.

Turn left down the D517 to a plaque on the wall to the left and a complex of memorials to the right.

• 5th Ranger Battalion Plaque/6th Engineer Special Brigade Memorial/29th Infantry Division Memorial/35.0 miles/10 minutes/Map T9,8,12

The Rangers' plaque is on the wall to the left. Colonel Rudder's force had consisted of the 2nd and 5th Ranger Battalions. The 2nd had been given the task of taking Pointe du Hoc, while the 5th was charged with taking the cliff Pointe de la Percée immediately to the east of Pointe du Hoc, and between it and OMAHA beach. The Rangers had to scale the cliffs using bayonets to secure handholds and the fighting went on all day.

To the right is the 6th Engineers Special Brigade Memorial, moved in 1998 from its situation above the other end of OMAHA Beach. On D-Day the failure of the preliminary air and naval attacks to neutralise the beach defences and the appalling casualties on the beach, which caused the German commander watching from Pointe de la Percée to believe that the invasion had failed, meant that the 6th Engineer Special Brigade coming in with the second wave, was unable to get on with its job of blowing gaps in the obstacles. Half of the engineers and their accompanying naval demolition parties were delayed and only one third landed where they were supposed to, the others being carried east by the strong current. Enemy fire was devastating. Of sixteen bulldozers only three were able to operate on the beach and by the end of the day casualties had reached 40%. Such was the heroism of the troops in tackling the obstacles that fifteen officers and men were awarded the Distinguished Service Cross.

Below it is the 29th (Blue and Grey) Division Memorial, unveiled in 1988 in the presence of a party of veterans of the Division and an Honour Guard. On the heights to the right is a German gun position.

Continue down the road to the sea. Stop in the car park beside the memorial
To the left is the Hotel du Casino. Tel: (0)2 31 22 41 02.

• *National Guard Memorial/58th Armoured Field Artillery Memorial/Bunkers/35.1 miles/10 minutes/RWC/Map T4,5,6,7,*

OMAHA Beach and the 'Pals Battalion' (see Map 6)

The general aspect of the memorial is that of a three-sided concrete box and a plaque in English and in French thanks the people of Vierville for helping to build the memorial and is dated June 1989. On opposite arms on the outside of the box are quotations from Winston Churchill and Charles de Gaulle.

> 'I am all for volunteers who come from some uplifting of the human soul some spirit arising in the human breast.' Winston Churchill 6 May 1947 *'Les armes ont torturé mais aussi façonné le monde honteuse et magnifique. Leur histoire est celle des hommes.'* Charles de Gaulle. [Weapons have tortured, but also shaped the shameful yet magnificent world. Their history is that of mankind.]

Inside the arms of the memorial the story of the National Guard in 1917-1918 and 1940-1945 is told in English and in French and the whole structure has been built upon blockhouse WN72. The Germans had built two *Widerstandsnest* (WN) 'resistance points' to cover each of the five exits from the beach.

On D-Day this position's two casemates, one with a 50mm weapon and the other with a 75mm gun, enfiladed the beach left and right. The position was overcome by a Sherman DD of 743 Tank Battalion with assistance from the USS *Texas* shortly after midday.

In the cliffs to the left of the memorial other bunkers can be seen. To the left (west) along the beach can be seen Pointe de la Percée. Where you are, however, is effectively the western end of OMAHA Beach and it stretches away to the right in a concave arc for almost four miles. Nowhere less than 100ft high, cliffs stand guard over the seashore and there are only the five exit gullies (the Americans called them 'draws') through to the heights above. You are standing at the entrance to the Vierville draw, D1. (DOG 1) On the right hand side of the path down to the beach from the memorial is another memorial - to the **US 58th Armoured Field Artillery.**

Below the cliffs is a mixture of dunes, scrub and waterpools leading down to the beach road on the sea-side of which is a wall marking the edge of the beach some six feet below. The beach is broad and flat and at low tide a good 100 yards separate the beach wall from the water's edge. Those 100 yards are clearly visible to anyone on the cliffs.

On 6 June 1944 there were many people on the cliffs and they were not, as had been thought, just the conscript mixture of the 716th Static Division, but a force hardened by the addition of trained combat soldiers of the 352nd Division. To compound the

Memorial to US 147th Engineers in the grounds of the Château d'Englesqueville, with the owner, M Lebrec.

Memorial to US 6th Engineer Special Brigade.

situation further, one of the battalions of the 352nd Division was just completing an anti-invasion exercise in the area and was therefore deployed correctly to counter a landing - a situation oddly akin to that at Salerno when, following a similar exercise, Kesselring's Panzers seemed to be waiting for Mark Clark's 5th Army to come ashore. The defensive positions were formidable too, though they tended to be bunched around the five draws. Estimates indicate that along the beach were eight big guns in concrete bunkers, thirty-five anti-tank guns in pillboxes and more than eighty machine-gun posts. Then there were the beach obstacles.

The thickening of the Atlantic Wall that Rommel had inspired was very evident at OMAHA. On the sand were log obstacles in three jumbled lines each about 20ft apart, carrying mines and shells, whose function was to prevent landing craft reaching the shore. Among and inland of them were metal hedgehogs producing a combined obstacle belt of some 50 yards thick which was totally submerged at high tide. From the beach wall to the bottom of the cliffs were mines and wire, particularly concentrated in the five draws and, sprinkled along the slopes as if from some ghastly pepper-pot, were anti-personnel mines.

The 1st Division's landing plan was simple. The beach was divided into two main sectors, DOG where you are now, and EASY to the east (to the right). On DOG would land the 116th Infantry Regiment under command from the 29th Division. Once a foothold had been established the 116th would revert to its division and clear the area to the River Aure beyond the N13 as far west as, and inclusive of, Isigny. On EASY the 16th Infantry Regiment were to land and then head east to link up with the British at Port-en-Bessin. Each regiment had attached to it supporting forces to help it in its task - two battalions of floating DD tanks to provide direct fire support against enemy fortified positions and two special brigades of engineers to clear beach obstacles ahead of the bulk of the landing craft carrying the infantry. The combined forces were known as RCTs (Regimental Combat Teams), i.e. the 116th RCT and 16th RCT. It was planned that by the end of D-Day the 1st Division force would have a bridgehead 16 miles wide and 5 miles deep. In reality by nightfall on the day the bridgehead was barely the length of the beach and averaged less than 1 mile deep with most units still below the cliffs. This situation is clearly indicated on the Holts' map.

At first, despite the swamping of the DD tanks almost as soon as they were launched, the loss of supporting artillery in the top-heavy DUKWs and the absence of the main force of the special engineers who had got out of position in the heavy seas, things seemed to be going well. The landing craft were not being fired upon. It was when the ramps were dropped for the men to go ashore that the enemy made his presence felt. The leading company of the 116th Regiment was Company 'A'. It came ashore below where the National Guard Memorial stands and a regimental

Memorial to US 58th Armoured Field Artillery.

National Guard Memorial, OMAHA Beach.

account of what happened was prepared by survivors and approved by the Commanding General. This is an extract:-

The first ramps were dropped at 0636 in water that was waist deep. As if this had been the signal for which the enemy waited, the ramps were instantly enveloped in a crossing of automatic fire which was accurate and in great volume. It came at the boats from both ends of the beach. Company 'A' had planned to move in three files from each boat, center file going first, then flank files peeling off to the right and left. The first men tried it. They crumpled as they sprang from the ship, forward into the water. Then order was lost. It seemed to the men that the only way to get ashore with a chance for safety was to dive head-first into the water. (Pvt Howard L. Gresser)

A few had jumped off, trying to follow the SOP, and had gone down into water over their heads. They were around the boat now, struggling with their equipment and trying to keep afloat. In one of the boats, a third of the men had become engaged in this struggle to save themselves from a quick drowning. (Pfc Gilbert G. Murdock)

That many were lost before they had a chance to face the enemy. Some of them were hit in the water and wounded. Some drowned then. Others, wounded, dragged themselves ashore and upon finding the sand, lay quiet and gave themselves shots, only to be caught and drowned within a few minutes by the on-racing tide. (Murdock)

But some men moved safely through the bullet fire to the sands, then found that they could not hold there; they went back into the water and used it as cover, only their heads sticking out above it. Others sought the cover of the underwater obstacles. Many were shot while doing so. Those who survived kept moving shoreward with the tide and in this way finally made their landing. (Murdock and Pfc Leo J. Nash)

They were in this tide-borne movement when Company 'B' came in behind them. (Pvt Crosser)

Others who had gotten into the sands and had burrowed in, remained in their holes until the tide caught up to them, then they, too, joined the men in the water.

Within 7 to 10 minutes after the ramps had dropped, Company A had become inert, leaderless and almost incapable of action. The Company was almost entirely bereft of Officers. Lieutenant Edward N. Gearing was back where the first boat had foundered. All the officers were dead except Lieutenant Elijah Nance who had been hit in the head as he left the boat, and then again in the body as he reached the sands. Lieutenant Edward Tidrick was hit in the throat as he jumped from the ramp into the water. He went on to the sands and flopped down 15ft from Pvt Leo J. Nash. He raised up to give Nash an order. Him bleeding from the throat and heard his words: 'ADVANCE WITH THE WIRE CUTTERS!' It was futile, Nash had no wire cutters. In giving the order, Tidrick himself a target for just an instant, Nash saw machine-gun bullet cleave him from head to pelvis.

German machine-gunners along the cliff directly ahead were now firing straight down into the party. Captain Taylor N. Fellers and Lieutenant Benjamin R. Kearfoot had come in with 30 men of Company 'A' aboard L.C.A. No. 1015, but what happened to that boat team in detail will never be known. Every man was killed; most of them being found along the beach.

In those first 5 to 10 minutes when the men were fighting in the water, they dropped their weapons and even their helmets to save themselves from drowning, and learning by what they saw that their landing had deteriorated into a struggle for personal survival, every sergeant was either killed or wounded. It seemed to the others that enemy snipers had spotted their leaders and had directed their fire so as to exterminate them. A medical boat came in on the right of Tidrick's boat. The Germans machine-gunned every man in the section. (Nash)

Their bodies floated with the tide. By this time the leaderless infantrymen had foregone any attempt to get forward against the enemy and where men moved at all, their efforts were directed toward trying to save any of their comrades they could reach. The men in the water pushed wounded men ahead of them so as to get them ashore. (Grosser and Murdock) Those who reached the sands crawled back and further into the water, pulling men to land to save them from drowning, in many cases, only to have them shot out of their hands or to be hit themselves while in these exertions. The weight of the infantry equipment handicapped all of this rescue work. It left many unhelped and the wounded drowned because of it. The able-bodied who pulled them in stripped themselves of their equipment so as to move more freely in the water, then cut away the assault jackets and the equipment of the wounded and dropped them in the water. (Grosser, Murdock and Cpl. M. Gurry)

Within 20 minutes of striking of the beach, Company 'A' ceased to be an assault company and had become a forlorn little rescue party bent on survival and the saving of the lives of the other men.

The 29th Division was a National Guard Division. The nearest British equivalent would be a Territorial Division, but the British geographical recruitment net was much wider than the American one. The Americans were pals and many had been since childhood. The leading companies of the 1st Battalion were A, B and D, recruited and based respectively around the Virginian towns of Bedford, Lynchburg and Roanoke. Sergeant John R. Slaughter who landed with D Company and who returned to OMAHA in 1988 to share in the unveiling of the 29th Division Memorial, took time to tell the authors his story: -

We landed in column of companies. 'A' Company about 0630, B Company some ten to fifteen minutes later and D Company about 0710, though we probably all were late. We hit the eye of the storm. The battalion was decimated. Hell, after that we didn't have enough to whip a cat with.'

The tactical story of OMAHA beach, the casualties and the bravery are usually associated with the 1st Division, because their General commanded the landing. In a sense they get the glory, yet the heaviest casualties on this bloody beach, indeed anywhere along the whole invasion coastline, were taken here on DOG Green, just below where you stand, by A Company of the 1st Battalion of the 116th Infantry Regiment of 29th Division, a Pals Battalion from Bedford Virginia. It is this part of the OMAHA landing that opens the film *Saving Private Ryan* John Slaughter tells the story as it happened:-

The small town of Bedford lost twenty-three men on D-Day. It's a town of 3,000 people. Twenty-two of those men were from A Company of the 116th Regiment. There were three sets of brothers in A Company. Raymond and Bedford Hoback were killed. Raymond was wounded and lay on the beach. Then when the tide came in he was washed out to sea and drowned. They never found his body. He was carrying a Bible and it washed up upon the sand. The day after D-Day a GI found it. It had Raymond's name and address in Bedford inside and the soldier mailed it to the family. On the Saturday (D-Day was a Tuesday) the family got a telegram that Bedford was killed and then on Sunday they got another one saying that Raymond was too. There were two Parkers killed. Then Roy and Ray Stevens who were twins, Roy was wounded and Ray was killed.

It was because of family tragedies like this, in particular the loss of 5 Sullivan brothers who were serving on the same ship, that the policy was adopted to remove from the active front remaining close family members when two members of that family had been killed in action. This fact was the inspiration for the Steven Spielberg film. His story was based on an actual family - the Nilands from Buffalo New York, six of whom, four brothers and two cousins, were on active service. Three of the brothers were in Normandy and one of the cousins also jumped at Ste Mère Eglise. When Fritz Niland was asked to identify the body of his brother he was shocked to find it was not the brother he had been told was killed and that he had therefore lost two brothers. They were Sergeant Robert J. Niland of the 505th PIR, 82nd Airborne, killed on 6 June, and 2nd Lieutenant Preston T. Niland of the 22nd Infantry, 4th Division, killed on 7 June. They are buried in the American Cemetery at St Laurent (qv). A third brother was declared missing in the Pacific (but happily was found as a POW after the war). Fritz Niland was then withdrawn from active service. He survived the war, but after returning home was never again able to go upstairs as he could not bear his brothers' empty bedrooms. He became a a dental surgeon. Coincidentally the Niland cousins - who both attended the premier of *Saving Private Ryan* - went to school with Charles Deglopper, the only 82nd Airborne Medal of Honour winner (won at the bridge at la Fière, qv.)

A D-Day Memory

Pte Lee Ratel. 18 years old. 16th Infantry Regiment, 2nd wave, Never in action before. A replacement. Landed on OMAHA beach.

"It was waist deep when we went in and we lost, I'd say, probably one third between getting off the boats and to the edge of the water and then probably another third between there to the base where you get any protection at all, because it was straight down and they were zeroed in there. They're very, very good defensive soldiers, but they're not trained the same ... they're trained to think how they're told to think and Americans are more independent, they can think on their own resources and this makes a lot of difference in a battle. Most, except myself, were seasoned men, they knew what to do ... there were landing craft blown up in the water, lying in the water, they never got in ... direct hits ... bodies of men who didn't even get into the sand and there were a lot of them lying on the sand ... there was crossfire from pillboxes ... the beach here cost an awful price in men, good men ... it was a job that had to be done and we were allotted to it. That's it. You do what you have to do."

Further east, at the next draw, designated D3 (there was no D2) and known as *les Moulins* where DOG sector became EASY, the two other battalions of the 116th landed on either side of the exit. There was less opposition on the beach, and smoke, from grass and buildings set on fire by the naval bombardment, produced a screen that saved many lives. On EASY Red though, the 2nd Battalion of the 16th Infantry Regiment of the 1st Division were suffering the same fate as the 1st

Battalion of the 116th on DOG Green, having landed opposite the Colleville draw, E3. The minefields claimed many victims and the Americans, without the specialised armoured vehicles developed by the British for clearing beach obstacles, were confined to single-file movement through the mined areas. This led to slowness in getting off the beaches and a log-jam of men and material, excellent targets for enemy fire from strong points, unaffected by the pre-assault bombing which had been dropped too far inland.

The Americans come in for much criticism over the planning for the OMAHA assault. In particular the following are singled out:

1. The decision not to use the British-developed specialised armour was foolhardy in view of the lessons of Dieppe.

2. The assault plan was too 'clockwork' and in particular ignored British advice about when and where to launch assault craft.

3. The frontal assault went against British advice, with rumours that a bloody victory in a Presidential election year would not only re-elect the President but also reaffirm the nation's pledge to deal with Germany before Japan.

Later the British, in particular Montgomery, were to have their share of criticism for being too slow in breaking out from the Normandy beachheads - Monty had already been accused of being slow, first when following up Rommel after El Alamein and second when fighting across Sicily. Much of the criticism would come from the Deputy Supreme Commander, the same officer that had said that it would be too dangerous to use the 82nd and 101st Airborne Divisions on the Cotentin Peninsula. We have the benefit of hindsight to aid our assessments of both viewpoints.

Immediately opposite the National Guard Memorial is a small bronze plaque mounted on the wall. It reads (in French) - 'An anti-tank wall blocked this exit from the beach at Vierville. It was destroyed 6.6.44 about 1700 by assault engineers of **29th Div USNG, 121 Battalion,** Company C, 3rd Peloton, 9th Escouade'.

Landing on EASY Red with the 16th was veteran war photographer Robert Capa who had covered the Spanish Civil War and the Italian and North African campaigns. Capa kept his camera shooting as he made for the shore between dead bodies and German obstacles, eventually dropping down on the sand to escape the constant small arms fire, only to be strafed by a mortar bombardment. Capa stood up and ran to a landing craft. He had shot 106 pictures and he wanted to get them back. The three rolls were rushed to the office of *Life* for whom Capa was working, and the darkroom technician in his eagerness to develop the films quickly, dried them too fast and melted the emulsion, ruining all but twelve frames. Those twelve frames are today the most evocative and familiar of the whole invasion operation. What Capa said when he learned what had happened is not recorded.

Perhaps the most telling comment made on D-Day was by Colonel George Taylor of the 'Big Red One' who, on seeing what was happening on the shore, shouted, "Only two kinds of people are staying on this beach - the dead and those who are going to die. Now let's get the blazes out of here." [It is doubtful that he actually said 'blazes'.]

Continue along the beach. To the right is the

• First American Cemetery in Europe Marker/36 miles/5 minutes/ Map T13

The memorial marks the site of the first US burials on Continental Europe.
Continue to the small plaque in the wall to the left.

• Operation AQUATINT Plaque/36.2 miles/5 minutes/Map T14

The plaque commemorates an unsuccesful British Commando raid of 1942 by eleven men of the Small Scale Raiding Force commanded by Major Gus March-Phillips. The idea was to land in the dark and to take a prisoner. The team was transported by MTB. Once ashore a firefight began and shouts were heard from the shore, presumably hailing the boat. However one of the MTB's motors was damaged by a bullet and it lay offshore for a while. When she attempted to go in-shore again she was fired on by German patrol vessels, and with the beach illuminated and under machine gun fire, efforts to pick up the landing party had to be abandoned. By monitoring German radio broadcasts it was learnt that Major March-Phillips had drowned while trying to swim out to the MTB and Sergeant A. Williams and Private R. Leonard were shot by the Germans on 13 September. All three are buried in the churchyard of St Laurent-sur-Mer. The other members of the force were taken prisoner and some later escaped.
Continue to the Comité du Débarquement Monument.

• Comité du Débarquement Signal Monument/36.2 miles/5 minutes/Map T15

On the sides of the monument are panels to 1st Infantry Division and 116th Infantry Regimental Combat Team of the 29th Infantry Division. The monument marks the junction between DOG and EASY sectors and is at the bottom of Exit D3, les Moulins. A **NTL Totem** also tells the story here.
Continue along the Beach, signed to le Ruquet, to the memorials on the right.

• 2nd Infantry Division/Provisional Engineers Special Brigade Memorials/Bunker, le Ruquet/37.2 miles/ 10 minutes/Map U1,2,3

The beach here is EASY Red and the exit which runs uphill past the obvious bunker is E1. The American official history records this as the St Laurent exit and mistakenly calls the river Ruquet, the 'Ruguet'.

The bunker was designated WN 65 - *Widerstandsnest* 65. The WN defences were generally the smallest structures, usually manned by one or two squads though not always with heavy weapons. When several WNs were combined for defence of a greater area the arrangement was called a *Stutzpunkt* (strong point) and had a 'garrison' of about platoon strength, plus a local reserve, though none of this form were found along the beaches (the defences in the area of the Leclerc Monument were probably the nearest to a Stutzpunkt. Larger combinations, such as that around Cherbourg, were known as *Verteidigungsbereiche* (defensive areas).

Thanks to the determined efforts of the 37th and 149th Engineer Combat Battalions the 16th Infantry were able to move off the beach here relatively quickly and it became the main exit for OMAHA on D-Day. E Company of the 16th, with the help of the 37th, three of whose men won the DSC that day, took the bunker in a fight that left 40 Germans dead. Serving in the 149th were twin brothers Jay B. Moreland and William W. Moreland, both of whom were killed on D-Day. They are commemorated on the wall in the Garden of the Missing in the American Cemetery. Following its capture, the bunker was used by the Provisional Engineer Special Brigade Group as its HQ on D-Day and there is a plaque on the bunker recording that fact and giving a list of the units in the Brigade.

Over the gun port is another plaque to the **'467th AAA AW Bn (SP)** [who] landed here am 6 June. Dedicated by the survivors of the Bn June 6 1994.'

In front of the bunker is a black monolith memorial to the 2nd Infantry Division which was part of the follow-up force on 7 June and on the heights behind and to the left of the bunker can be seen the fir trees that form the boundary to the American National Cemetery.

Below the memorial is a **NTL Totem** describing how on 7 June the Engineers built an airfield on the flat ground between Le Ruquet and Les Moulins, the first airfield on liberated territory. By 1900 hours that night it was in use to evacuate the wounded.

Return to the Comité Monument and turn left uphill. Continue to the museum on the right.

• OMAHA MUSEE, 6 JUIN 1944/38.4 miles/15 minutes/Map T16

This private museum has a chronological presentation of the events from the occupation to the landings. There is an impressive display of guns, uniforms and military vehicles from the campaign. The rusting Sherman tank which stands outside 'arrived' at the museum on 15 May 1988 according to a plaque beside it and '49,230 examples' were made. There is also a 155mm 'Long Tom' gun in the car park. **Open:** 15 Feb-15 March 1000-1230 and 1430-1800. 16 March-15 May 0930-1900 (1930 in July and August). 1 October-20 November 0930-1830. Entrance fee payable. Tel: (0)2 31 21 97 44.

Continue to the D514. On the wall of the church ahead is a plaque to 81st Chemical Mortar Battalion. Turn left. Continue to the church on the left.

• AQUATINT Graves, St Laurent Churchyard/38.6 miles/10 minutes

To the right on entering the churchyard are the CWGC graves of: R. Lehnigen, who served as Private R. Leonard, Pioneer Corps Commando, age 42, personal inscription *"Die Internationale wird die Menschheit sein"*; Major G.H. March-Phillips, DSO, MBE, Royal Artillery Commando, age 34, personal inscription, "A gallant, beloved husband, 'He that loveth, flyeth, runneth and rejoiceth: He is free'", and 609816 Sergeant A.M. Williams, The Queen's Royal Regiment Commando, age 22, personal inscripton, "R.I.P." All took part in the AQUATINT Raid (see above) of 12 September 1942.

Continue following signs to the American Cemetery and stop in the large parking area.

Plaque to the AQUATINT Commando Raid, OMAHA Beach.

Plaque to the 467th AAA A W Battalion (SP) and gun, Bunker WN 65 at Exit E1.

View of Bunker WN65, the St Laurent draw, (Exit E1) le Ruquet, OMAHA Beach.

OMAHA Museum, St Laurent.

• The Normandy American National Cemetery and Memorial, St Laurent/41.5 miles/45 minutes/WC/Map U4,10

This cemetery was built and is maintained by the American Battle Monuments Commission. The architects for the memorial features were Harbeson, Hugh, Livingston and Larson of Philadelphia, Pennsylvania, and the cemetery was dedicated on 18 July 1956. The site was chosen for its historical importance - overlooking the OMAHA beaches - and includes the area of one of the original battle cemeteries used during the landings. It covers 172 acres, all beautifully landscaped and tended, which were donated by the French people 'without charge or taxation'.

It contains 9,286 burials, 307 of whom are unknown and whose white marble crosses or Stars of David bear the inscription, 'Here rests in honoured glory a comrade in arms known but to God'. On the known graves is inscribed the rank, unit, name, date of death and home state of the serviceman or woman commemorated. The headstones are set out in straight lines, perpendicular, horizontal and diagonal, which form a dramatic geometric pattern on the immaculate emerald green grass, whichever way the eye looks.

Medal of Honour winners' headstones are lettered in gold. This is America's highest award for gallantry, the equivalent of the British Victoria Cross. The most famous is that of **Brigadier General Theodore Roosevelt** (Plot D, Row 28, Grave 45), who died of a heart attack on 12 July 1944. His award was won on 6 June at UTAH for 'his valor, courage and presence in the very front of the attack and his complete unconcern at being under heavy fire inspired the troops to heights of enthusiasm and self-sacrifice... He thus contributed substantially to the successful establishment of the beachhead in France.' Beside him lies his youngest brother, Lieutenant Quentin Roosevelt, a World War I aviator who died in France on 14 July 1918, and who was reinterred here when the cemetery was made.

There are thirty other pairs of brothers who lie side by side, including the Nilands (qv) in Plot F, Row 15, graves 11 and 12. Eight other pairs of brothers are buried here, but in different rows, and a father and son, Colonel Ollie Reed (Plot E, Row 20, Grave 19) and Ollie Reed Junior (Grave 20).

Two other Medals of Honour winners of the Normandy campaign buried in the cemetery are: **Tech Sergeant Frank Peregory** (qv) of the 116th Infantry Division whose story is told where it happened at Grandcamp Maisy on 8 June, and **1st Lieutenant Jimmie W. Monteith,** Jr. of the 16th Infantry, 1st Division whose act of conspicuous gallantry took place on 6 June on OMAHA. Monteith landed with the initial assault waves under heavy fire. Without regard for his personal safety he continually moved up and down the beach reorganizing men for further assaults, which he then led. He then went back to lead two tanks on foot through a minefield and then rejoined his company. He continued to attempt to strengthen links in his defensive chain under heavy fire until he and his unit were completely surrounded and he was killed by enemy fire.

There are also some women Red Cross nurses and WACs (Mary Bankston Pfc, D-20-19; Mary Barlow Pfc, A-19-30; Dolores Brown, Sgt, F-13-10; Elizabeth Richardson, Red Cross, A-21-5). The servicemen and women resting here were re-interred from temporary cemeteries (e.g. at Ste Mère Eglise, la Cambe and OMAHA Beach - now marked by memorials). 14,000 others of their comrades were repatriated at government expense. This impressive cemetery receives more than 1.25 million visitors each year -

not only veterans or their families, but local French people. It was the setting for the beginning and end of the film *Saving Private Ryan*. It contains the following areas of interest:

Approach Avenue/Car Parks. A tree-bordered avenue, leads from the N514 to the main entrance. To the right are ample, well-signed car parks.

In the car park is a **NTL Totem** which bears the lines,

Visitor
Look how many of them there were
Look how young they were
They died for your freedom
Hold back your tears and be silent.

On entering the cemetery from the car park there are WCs on the right. The park is a horticulturist's joy, with many species of trees, bushes and shrubs which are rare and unusual to the area, such as Canadian maple trees and red-flower potentilla. The beds and lawns are immaculately tended, with the avenue of trees leading to the memorial shaped and trimmed.

Visitor's Building. To the left of the main entrance, this well-appointed room houses the superintendent's office, the cemetery registers, and the visitor's book, as well as literature about this and other American Battle Monuments cemeteries. The staff are splendidly helpful and the culture is of ordered peace and quiet. The long-time resident American superintendent Phil Rivers has moved on to be replaced by the equally dedicated Gene Dillinger, assisted by Michael Green. Visitors can always go to them for help – a facility that, sadly, has no counterpart in the British sector.

Time Capsule. Embedded in the ground on the right-hand side just inside the entrance, the time capsule, dedicated to General Eisenhower, contains sealed reports of the 6 June 1944 landings. It is to be opened 6 June 2044.

Memorial. This area, to the right as one progresses into the cemetery, consists of a semi-circular colonnade, with stone loggias at each side which are engraved with vivid battle maps, picked out in coloured enamel and designed by Robert Foster of New York. Ornamental urns at each side flank a 22ft-high bronze statue of *The Spirit of American Youth Rising from the Waves,* sculpted by Donald de Lue of New York.

In 1987 the American Veterans' Association donated a memorial bell which tolls every hour and at noon and at 1700 hours plays a tuneful sequence. It is reminiscent of the memorial bell in the church of Belloy on the Somme, donated as a memorial by the parents of the American poet Alan Seeger, who fell in July 1916. They both toll for Americans who gave their lives in France.

Garden of the Missing. Behind the memorial, the garden's semi-circular wall bears the names of 1,557 missing with no known graves, who came from 49 of the 50 States that make up the Union. An asterisk against a name means that the person has since been identified, two of whom, Jay and William Moreland (qv), were twin brothers. The garden is planted with ornamental shrubs and roses.

Reflective Pool/Stars and Stripes. To the left of the memorial is the rectangular reflective pool with water lilies and, beyond it, two enormous flagstaffs. The American flag flies proudly from each of them, raised each morning, lowered each evening. As the last flag is lowered, twenty minutes before closing time, one of the

The Reflective Pool, US Cemetery, St Laurent.

Graves of Preston and Robert Niland, who inspired the 'Sergeant Ryan' story.

The Spirit of America statue.

Detail, Orientation Table.

*Grave of Brigadier General
Theodore Roosevelt, MoH.*

gardeners plays 'Taps', the American equivalent of the Last Post. It is a haunting sound in this sad but beautiful setting.

Orientation Tables. Continuing past the memorial, one reaches the first orientation table, overlooking OMAHA Beach, with a map pointing to features on the nearby landing beaches. From here one can descend a deceptively gentle-looking path down to the beach itself. (It seems very long and steep on the way up.) It is well worth the effort as from the bottom one can look up at the formidable cliffs and the sites of the heavily defended German positions which faced the Americans as they landed.

On the way down, a second orientation table shows the Mulberry Harbour designed for OMAHA, washed away in the storm of 19 June.

Graves Area. This is laid out in ten lettered plots (A-J), with numbered rows and graves to help visitors to find the graves of friends and relatives. Plans and registers are kept in the visitors' building.

Chapel. Along the central pathway is the non-denominational chapel with a fine ceiling mosaic designed by Leon Kroll of New York depicting 'America' blessing her sons as they leave to fight for freedom in France and 'France' bestowing a laurel wreath upon American dead who gave their lives to liberate Europe.

Statues of United States and France. At the end of the main axis beyond the chapel are two granite figures sculpted by Donald de Lue representing the two countries.

Open: Summer, weekdays 0900-1800, weekends, holidays 1000-1800; winter, weekdays 0900-1700, weekends and holidays 1000-1700. Tel: (0)2 31 22 40 62.

Extra Visits to 2nd Armoured Division and 149th Tank Battalion 'Hell on Wheels' Plaques, VVF (Map U7); 1st Infantry Division Memorial (Map U8); 5th Engineer Special Brigade Memorial/20th & 299th Engineer Plaques/146th Engineer Combat Battalion Plaque/Bunker WN62/OP/(Map U6). Round trip: 2.6 miles. Approximate time: 35 minutes

Return to the main entrance to the cemetery and turn left. Continue past the church into the village and turn left onto the small road signed to 'VVF' (Village de Vacances Familles). You will probably notice the turning just after you have passed it. Continue down the road past the boat club to the 'Village' and stop in the car park.

Village de Vacances Familles. This basic hostel-type accommodation has a superb setting on OMAHA Beach. Open: April-September. Tel: (0)2 31 22 41 81 *Walk up through the buildings.*

The memorial is on the left, halfway up the slope.

2nd Armoured Division and 149th Tank Battalion 'Hell on Wheels' Plaques, VVF (Map U7)

The plaques are mounted on what is known locally as a 'tank wall' because the wall has been built across what was once a tank exit from the beach. This was Exit E3. The 2nd Armoured Division had begun landing on 9 June and went

Extra visits continued

into action two days later, being greatly involved in the fighting for Carentan. It earned the nickname 'Hell on Wheels' for its exploits and was the first American Division to enter Berlin.

Return to your car, go back up the small road and follow the one-way circuit uphill to the car park and stop.

You are now behind the American Cemetery and by following the signed footpath you will come to:

1st Infantry Division Memorial

This tall column commemorates the men of the 'Big Red One' who fell on D-Day and their names are listed on it. It stands on WN62, as does the other memorial further down the slope.

Walk down the slope to the next memorial.

5th Engineer Special Brigade Memorial/20th & 299th Engineer Plaques/146th Engineer Combat Battalion Plaque/Bunker WN62/ OP.

A story related by Winston Ramsay in his formidable and unique work, *D-Day Then and Now*, concerns an infantry landing craft that beached just below here. Its commander, 2nd Lieutenant Phill C. Wood Jr, was apparently under the impression that H-Hour was 0620 and not 0630 and brought his craft in at 0625, thus according to the engineers he was leading the rest of the invasion by 5 minutes. Sadly, as he ran ashore, an artillery shell hit the LCI and killed most of the men in it.

Around the middle of the morning on D-Day two destroyers moved within 1,000 yards of the beach and began to shell the German positions along the length of OMAHA and two landing craft drove straight onto the beach below you and added their fire to that of the navy. Under cover of this fire the 37th and 146th Engineer Combat Battalions bulldozed two gaps in the dunes on either side of E1, filled in the anti-tank ditch and cleared the minefields. The 146th memorial plaque says '35 men died here'.

The Engineers were awarded the *Croix de Guerre* for their achievements and the emblem of the award is on the back of the memorial.

This is a remarkable observation point on a clear day. Immediately to the right can be seen Exit 3, the Vierville draw. Further along the coast, jutting out into the sea, is the harbour wall of Port-en-Bessin, the boundary between the British and American beaches, and further still the shapes of the Mulberries at Arromanches will be visible. To the left are the firs of the American Cemetery, the whole sweep of OMAHA Beach and at its end the jutting cliffs of Pointe de la Percée that Colonel Rudder mistook for Pointe du Hoc.

Return to your car and follow the circuit around to the entrance to the American Cemetery.

• End of Itinerary Two

Memorial to US 149th
Tank Battalion ('Hell on
Wheels'), VVF.

Memorial to 5th Engineer
Special brigade, overlooking
OMAHA Beach,

Croix de Guerre,
reverse of the
Engineers' memorial.

Memorial to the 'Big Red One', overlooking OMAHA Beach.

ITINERARY THREE

* **Itinerary Three** starts at Bayeux, covers the GOLD Sector landing beaches, General Montgomery's first HQ, and finishes at Tierceville.
* **The Route:** Bayeux - General Eisenhower Statue, Battle of Normandy Museum, CWGC Cemetery and Memorial, Liberation Memorial/Général de Gaulle Bas Relief, Cathedral, Place Général de Gaulle Column, Général de Gaulle Museum; Port-en-Bessin – D-Day Wrecks Museum, General Montgomery Roundabout, *Comité du Débarquement* Monument, No 47 (RM) Commando Memorial, Bunker; Batterie de Longues (Chaos); Arromanches - Groupe Lorraine Memorial, D-Day Landings Museum, Brigadier General Stanier Memorial, Mulberry Harbour; St Côme de Fresne - Orientation Table, Bunker, RE Memorial, 360° Museum/Film; Le Hamel/Asnelles - Bunker, Place Brigadier Stanier (sic)/De Gaulle Message Monument; 231st Brigade, 50th Division Memorial, Bunker; Ver-sur-Mer - General Leclerc Memorial, RA HQ Memorial, 2nd Battalion Herts Memorial, Admiral Ramsay's HQ Plaque; Bunker; America/GOLD Beach Museum, Ver-sur-Mer; Green Howards Memorial, Crépon; General Montgomery's HQ, Creullet Chbteau; Creully - 4th/7th Royal Dragoon Guards Memorial, Château and BBC Studio; Tierceville Eros.
* **Extra Visits** are suggested to: 846th Air Engineers Battalion Memorial, Vaucelles; 'Big Red One' Memorial, Tour-en-Bessin; General Montgomery's HQ and American Liberators Memorial at Blay, General Eisenhower's HQ, Tourneville; 2nd *'Indian Head'* Division Memorial and Stained Glass Windows, Trevières; 'Big Red One' Memorial, Etreham.

Planned Duration, without stops for refreshments or Extra Visits: **8 hours**
Total distance: 31.4 miles

BACKGROUND TO GOLD SECTOR

The background information given first covers the whole 2nd (British) Army plan. The actions on GOLD, the beach adjacent to Arromanches, are then described, in conjunction with a battlefield tour.

The 2nd Army (See Map 2)

The Supreme Commander had three subordinate Commanders in Chief - for the sea, the air and the land. Although General Montgomery was never formally appointed C-in-C Land Forces, that was in effect his position. Under his command were four armies, known collectively as 21st Army Group. They were divided as follows:

Assault armies	First (US Army	General Bradley
	Second (British) Army	General Dempsey
Follow-up armies	Third (US) Army	General Patton
	First (Canadian) Army	General Crerar

General Montgomery stated that:

> In the initial stages of this campaign [OVERLORD] the object [is] to secure a lodgement on the Continent from which further offensive operations [can] be developed.

This basic aim was later expanded and in the expansion developed a point of controversy which was to lead to some senior Allied officers petitioning the Supreme Commander to have General Montgomery removed as C-in-C Land Forces. In a speech to the Royal United Services Institution in October 1945 the then Field Marshal said:

> Once ashore and firmly established, my plan was to threaten to break out on the eastern front, that is in the Caen sector, by this threat to draw the main enemy reserves into that sector, to fight them there and keep them there using the British and Canadian armies for the purpose. Having got the main enemy reserves committed on the eastern flank my plan was to make the break-out on the western flank, using for this task the American armies under General Bradley and pivoting on Caen.

To many observers this explanation sounded like being wise after the event. True, the British had stuck at Caen and there *had* been bloody battles there attracting the main force of German armoured reserves, and the Americans on the western flank *had* benefited and broken out, but not everyone believed that it had been planned that way in advance. The Americans and the Deputy Supreme Commander believed that in the days following D-Day General Montgomery was too cautious, too bound by the lessons he had learned as a junior officer in the trenches of the Western Front during World War I. They petitioned for his removal. He was slow to follow up Rommel after El Alamein, the argument persisted, and everyone knew what had happened at Anzio when General John P. Lucas was too cautious and sat on the beach after landing instead of immediately heading inland for the Alban Hills.

The Supreme Commander was not moved by the arguments. He kept his team intact, manipulating the senior prima-donnas to give of their best, using their rivalries to spur each to greater effort. If one man can be said to have ensured the success of the D-Day Landings it has to be General Eisenhower. Yet Monty was to claim that the Americans, including Eisenhower, did not ever really understand his plan, even though he had spelled it out well in advance of the invasion. In his October 1945 speech he had continued:

> This general plan was given out by me to the General Officers of the field armies in London in March 1944, that is to say, three months before D-Day. The operations developed in June, July and August exactly as planned.

The British Second Army's part in the plan was 'to make straight for Caen to establish the pivot while 6th Airborne Division was given the task of seizing the crossings over the Caen canal and of operating on our extreme left.'

The Second Army's seaborne element was made up from two Corps: XXX Corps under General G.C. Bucknall, landing on GOLD Beach, and 1st Corps under General Dempsey landing on JUNO and SWORD Beaches.

The preparatory fire-plan of bomber strikes, naval bombardment and tactical fighter support was common along all beaches, though timings varied slightly to allow for the different H-Hours occasioned by the variation in tide from west to east. However, there was one major difference in assault tactics between the American and British beaches, and that was in the use of specialised armour to provide close support to the assaulting infantry. The British had it, and the Americans did not, which has since resulted in a lot of criticism of the Americans.

The specialised armour used on GOLD, JUNO and SWORD Beaches had been developed by Major General Sir Percy Hobart's 79th Armoured Division. General Hobart, a brother-in-law of General Montgomery, had commanded the first tank brigade created in 1934, but his innovative ideas were strongly resisted by an Army high command which was still wedded to the horse. Hobart had served in the First World War and joined the Tank Corps in 1923 rising to become its head. In 1938, while in Egypt, he built up the 7th Armoured Division, later to be known as 'The Desert Rats', but, still frustrated by a blinkered military hierarchy, he retired in 1940 to become a corporal in the Home Guard. In 1942 the débacle of the Dieppe raid made it clear that assaulting infantry needed close armoured support if they were to get ashore against determined opposition - that is, if they were to get ashore without suffering horrendous casualties.

The Chief of Staff to the Supreme Allied Commander (COSSAC), prompted by Winston Churchill, recalled General Hobart to command 79th Armoured Division which from 1943 was given the task of developing armour to accompany a seaborne assault. The range of equipment produced was extraordinary and with a colourful vocabulary to match:

DD Tanks: floating ('Donald Duck') Duplex Drive M4 Sherman tanks. Engine power could be transferred from the tracks to twin propellers and, by erecting high canvas screens all around, it could float. Once on shore, power was returned to the tracks and the screen jettisoned.

Crocodiles: mainly Churchill tanks modified to be flamethrowers.

Crabs: generally a standard M4 Sherman tank fitted with an extended pair of arms carrying a flail. Its purpose was to clear minefields by beating the mines into explosion - a sort of military Hoover, beating, sweeping and cleaning at $1^1/_2$ mph.

BARV: Beach Armoured Recovery Vehicle, usually, but not invariably, a Sherman. The gun turret was replaced by a superstructure allowing the tank to drive into deep water and through fitted winches or small dozer blades it was able to clear beaches of stranded vehicles.

Petard: an AVRE (Armoured Vehicle Royal Engineers, see below) based on a Churchill chassis with its normal main armament replaced by a 290mm short-barrelled mortar which fired a 40lb 'flying dustbin' explosive charge. Its function was to destroy enemy pillboxes and fixed obstructions.

Bobbin: a normal Churchill tank adapted to carry a 110-yard long spool of flexible coir coconut matting that could be laid in front of the vehicle to form a road over soft or slippery ground for itself and following vehicles.

ARK: 'Armoured Ramp Carrier', a turretless Churchill tank carrying two runways across its flat top. It could be used to provide a ramped road up and over a beach wall or could be dropped into ditches or streams to form a bridge.

AVRE: 'Armoured Vehicle Royal Engineers'. This is a generic title for a whole range of specialised armoured vehicles. They include those above, plus others carrying huge 2-ton bundles of wood called fascines used to fill holes in roadways, bridge-layers, craned recovery vehicles, etc.

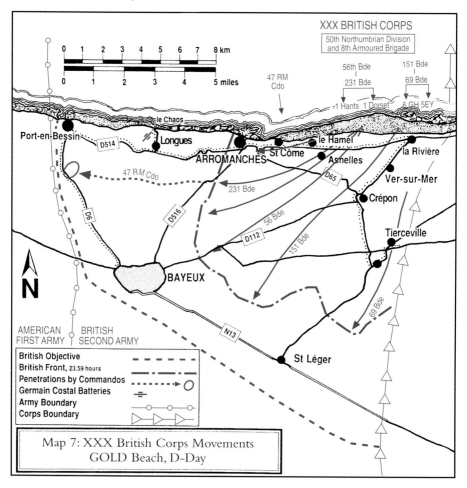

Map 7: XXX British Corps Movements
GOLD Beach, D–Day

The specialised armoured vehicles were known to most soldiers as 'Hobart's Funnies'. Despite the complexity of types, the Funnies divide into just two main varieties defined by their purpose. One is the DD tank, designed to float ashore with the infantry in order to provide immediate fire support, the other is the rest. The second collective type came from General Hobart's recognition that the destruction of the few Churchill tanks that were landed at Dieppe was due to the failure of the assault

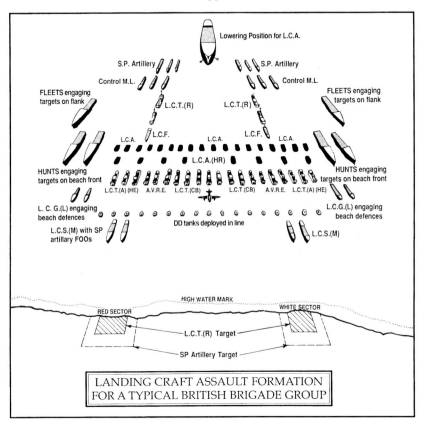

LANDING CRAFT ASSAULT FORMATION
FOR A TYPICAL BRITISH BRIGADE GROUP

Key:

LCA	Landing craft, Assault	AVRE	Assault Vehicle, Royal Engineers
ML	Motor Launch	LCT(CB)	Landing Craft, Tank (Concrete Buster)
LCT(R)	Landing Craft, Tank (Rocket)	DD Tanks	Duplex Drive Tanks, fitted with flotation device
LCF	Landing Craft, Flak		
LCA(HR)	Landing Craft, Assault (Hedgerow). Used to explode enemy minefields	LCS(M)	Landing Craft, Support (Medium)
		LCGL	Landing Craft, Gun (Large)
LCT(A)(HE)	Landing Craft, Tank (Armoured) (High Explosive)	FOO	Forward Observation Officer to direct artillery fire

engineers to clear the mines and obstacles, or to prepare exits from the beach. The Americans, offered the opportunity to have their pick of the Funnies, opted for a few DD tanks, but decided against having any specialised armour to help them to get off the beaches. There is no doubt that the men of the 1st and 29th Divisions could have done with some Funnies on D-Day. British casualties were comparatively low, thanks in part to the specialised armoured support. Casualties on OMAHA Beach might have been dramatically fewer if armoured obstacle clearance had been possible. However, it must be remembered that the landings on UTAH Beach went almost perfectly without the specialised armoured support and that OMAHA Beach was backed by very high cliffs where armoured manoeuvrability was limited. Therefore while any additional obstacle clearance capability would have been effective on OMAHA Beach on D-Day, the presence of the 79th Division equipment might not have made a major difference. The question remains, however, 'Why didn't the Americans take the Funnies?'

General Montgomery had no doubts about the value of the 79th Armoured Division and divided the division's force between the British beaches, putting its components (and those of the RM Armd Spt Gp) under command of the assaulting division. Thus, in the planned approach of the sea armada to the French shore along GOLD, JUNO and SWORD Beaches, the DD tanks and AVREs were prominent. See diagram above.

GOLD BEACH

Assault Time:	0725 hours
Leading Formations:	8th Armoured Brigade DD tanks
	6th Battalion, The Green Howards.
	5th Battalion, East Yorkshire Regiment
	1st Battalion, Dorset Regiment
	1st Battalion, Royal Hampshire Regiment
50th Division Commander:	Major General D.A.H. Graham
Bombarding Force K:	Cruisers : HMS *Orion*
	HMS *Ajax*
	HMS *Argonaut*
	HMS *Emerald*
	Gunboat : HNMS *Flores* (Dutch)
	13 destroyers including ORP *Krakowiak* (Polish)
German Defenders:	716th Division
	352nd Division
352nd Div Commander:	Lieutenant General Dietrich Kraiss
716th Div Commander:	Lieutenant General Wilhelm Richter

The Plan (See Map 7)

The D-Day mission of the 50th Northumbrian Division was complicated. It was to capture Bayeux, to establish a bridgehead across the N13 Bayeux to Caen road, to take the German gun battery at Longues and to establish contact with flanking formations. This latter involved the capture of Port-en-Bessin to link up with Americans from OMAHA Beach.

The beach was subdivided into JIG and KING sectors, west and east respectively, and each sector given to a brigade formation to attack. Thus there were two leading brigades, 231st Brigade on JIG and 69th Brigade on KING. The non-military reader can be easily misled by statements such as 'the attack was made on a brigade front'. A simplistic and apparently correct interpretation would be that a whole brigade's complement of men attacked simultaneously. Nothing could be further from the truth. The art of delegation from higher to lower formation steadily reduces the size of force. Thus a brigade of four battalions might only use two in an attack and keep two in reserve. Then each of the two battalions might only use two of their four companies, keeping the others in reserve. Hence, in effect, the 'brigade' attack might only have an assault strength of one battalion. On KING, for example, the formation which attacked at H-Hour was not of brigade size but the size of two battalions - the Green Howards and the East Yorkshires, although this ignores the complications of forces being attached for special purposes such as Royal Engineers and DD tanks. It does, however, help to keep the relative sizes of formations in perspective.

The divisional plan was that the 231st Brigade would land east of le Hamel (Asnelles), clear the village and then drive along the coast towards the Americans at Port-en-Bessin, the latter having been taken by commandos from the rear. The 69th Brigade was to land west of la Rivière (Ver-sur-Mer) and to head inland towards the N13 Bayeux to Caen road. The leading brigades were thus moving apart. Into the gap between them at 1000 hours were to come two follow-up brigades, the 56th and the 151st. Their task was to take Bayeux.

What Happened on D-Day

The weather was bad, probably at its worst, opposite GOLD Beach. When the troops clambered down into their LCAs some 10,000 yards offshore, the Force 5 wind was whipping up waves of over 4ft. Those who had survived sea-sickness in the relative calm of their transport ship now fell prey to the pitching and rolling of their small craft. Despite their hyoscine hydrobromide anti-sea sickness tablets few men failed to fill their 'Bags, Vomit'. So rough was the sea that it was decided that the DD tanks, scheduled to land ahead of the infantry and to be launched some 7,000 yards out, would not be launched until within 700 yards of the beach. The Sherwood Rangers supporting the assault lost three tanks in 'B' Squadron and five tanks in 'C' Squadron. 'A' Squadron, with Keith Douglas (see below) landed dry at 1400 hours.

The air and naval bombardment followed the pattern established on the American beaches, although the British opted for a longer naval bombardment. Anticipating that the German armoured threat would come against the British beaches, General Montgomery had over 130 warships in the British Task Force begin firing twenty minutes before the Americans at 0530 hours and continue until H-Hour. His idea was to give the assaulting troops the maximum opportunity to break through the crust of defenders and to move inland at speed in anticipation of a German armoured counter-attack.

The leading formations touched down within a minute or two of their allotted time and at the right place. At le Hamel a German strongpoint held out until noon, causing considerable casualties by raking the beach with machine-gun fire. At la Rivière the preliminary bombardment had been very effective and there was relatively little opposition, although German resistance was stiffer than had been anticipated because of the presence of troops of the 352nd Division. The reserve and follow-up formations were landed successfully and, while not all of the D-Day objectives had been achieved, by the end of the day (see the Holts' map) the 50th Division beachhead measured six miles by six, the N13 was in sight, reconnaissance patrols had entered the outskirts of Bayeux and No 47 Royal Marine Commando were on the heights above Port-en-Bessin. Although there had not been any contact with the Americans from OMAHA Beach in the west, contact had been established with the Canadians from JUNO Beach in the east.

THE TOUR

Bayeux

This historical city was one of the D-Day objectives of 50th Northumbrian Division landing on GOLD Beach, and reconnaissance patrols of the 151st Brigade entered its outskirts at about 2030 hours on the evening of 6 June. They spent the night in the Saint Sulpice suburb.

There is no disputing Bayeux's claim to be the first major town to be liberated. German resistance was weak. German General Kraiss had vacillated, moving troops of his 915th Regiment towards the Cotentin Peninsula when he had heard of the American drops, then pulling back towards Bayeux as the British approached, and finally withdrawing.

By midday on 7 June members of 56th Brigade and tanks were entering the city. Miraculously its historic treasures - the cathedral, the ancient and picturesque buildings - were all spared the fearful damage that many Norman towns endured. The precious Bayeux Tapestry had long since been removed and was hidden in the Château de Sourches near Le Mans. The citizens celebrated their liberation by flying their *Tricolores*, but their greatest joy was to be shown a week later.

At 1530 hours on 14 June a car with a loudspeaker raced through the narrow streets blazoning the marvellous news that General de Gaulle was in France and would address the citizens at the Place du Château (now renamed Place Gen de Gaulle) in half an hour. De Gaulle was the focus of Free French determination, the symbol of resistance, the hope for a return to freedom. His single-minded crusade often made him unpopular with Allied leaders, but his broadcasts on the forbidden BBC rallied the spirit of France, the morale of the resistance workers: 'My aim, my only aim, is to act in such a way that ... the French forces shall not cease to fight, that the French forces shall be present at the Victory....'

De Gaulle's aim was fulfilled. French forces landed with the Commandos at Ouistreham, with Leclerc at UTAH Beach. French pilots flew with the RAF, and they made a meaningful contribution to the Invasion.

In Bayeux de Gaulle was greeted with rapture. His long, lonely struggle had been fully rewarded. The citizens, at first almost too overwhelmed with emotion to react, eventually broke into joyous cheers. De Gaulle marched through the main street. The people fell in behind him in a spontaneous victory procession, singing the *Marseillaise*. The moment is crystallised for posterity as a striking bas relief in Bayeux, on the Liberation Memorial, Rond Point de Vaucelles - see below - and by an oft-published photograph which shows him towering above the surrounding townsfolk.

As there was no French government recognised by the Allies, they were urged to accept General de Gaulle's *Comité Français de la Libération Nationale* as the provisional government of France. His reception in Normandy on this historic visit - unanimously acclaimed by all political shades - convinced them that they should recognise it.

De Gaulle then created Monsieur Raymond Triboulet (qv) Sous-Prefet of the newly liberated *arrondissement* - the first political appointment to be made in Free France.

The intervening week had been very active for the British. Their engineers constructed a wide road round the city, its ancient streets being too narrow for modern military transport. That road was the prototype of today's ring road. Hospitals were set up, as were supply dumps, and Bayeux was to remain as a major supply base for the Allies on the route of the American 'Red Ball Express' all the way to Brussels.

Note that by the year 2002 the new Bayeux bypass - part of the A13, 'the motorway without tolls', as it is advertised - should be completed. By 1999 many of the bridges crossing it were well underway. The dual carriageway will start from the existing N13 at Vieux Pont on the Caen side and sweep round to the north through Monceaux en Bessin to skirt the old N13 again at Vaucelles, rejoining the dual carriageway just beyond Mosles, on the Cherbourg side.

Approach Bayeux on the N13 from the Caen direction (or if coming from the Cherbourg direction, drive around the ring road to the Eisenhower roundabout.

• General Eisenhower Statue/Memorial Roundabout/0 miles/Map A15

This impressive, nine foot tall statue, cast in bronze, the work of sculptor Robert Dean, was dedicated on 5 June 1994 for the 50th Anniversary. It is cast from the same mould as the statue of the General which stands in front of the American Embassy in Grosvenor Square, London. The $100,000 finance was provided by the Battle of Normandy Foundation and the City of Bayeux undertook the

Statue of General Eisenhower, Bayeux.

erection and perpetual maintenance of the statue. John Eisenhower, son of the General, unveiled the statue. In retirement the Eisenhowers bought a farm in Gettysburg, Pennsylvania, the town where the American Civil War reached its climax, and, outside his office in the town, is a bronze statue of a smiling Eisenhower in civilian clothes sitting on a bench. Both representations capture the substance of the Supreme commander's personality - humanity.

Take the ring road, direction St Lô on the D572 and continue, passing the **Hotel Campanile, Tel:(0)2 31 21 40 40, on the left, over the traffic light and along Boulevard Fabian Ware (named after the founder of the Commonwealth War Graves Commission) *to the Museum parking area on the right.*

• Musée de la Bataille de Normandie/Notts Yeomanry Memorial/ 1.1 miles/45 minutes*/RWC/Map A12, 13

In the parking area is a blue **NTL Totem** signboard.

This superb museum is, as its name explains, about the battle for Normandy, not the landings, which are covered in the museums such as Arromanches, Ste Mère Eglise and UTAH Beach.

It is the story of the 'battle of the hedgerows', of 'the break out', of operations EPSOM, GOODWOOD, TOTALISE and TRIDENT, and the 'Falaise Pocket'. The battles are vividly portrayed in this modern, custom-built museum, with a cinema (35-minute film with French or English sound showing the battle for Normandy), diorama of the Falaise Pocket battle and separate galleries for the Americans, British, Canadians and Germans and some impressive set-piece, life-sized scenes, with models and original 1944 vehicles. Thankfully this museum has not become high-tech with endless video screens showing things that could equally as well have been seen at home, nor has it demeaning 'games' supposedly giving 'interactive education' to visitors.

*Allow more time (at least $1^1/_2$ hours) if you wish not only to see the film, but to peruse thoroughly the fascinating documents, photographs, posters and newspapers. There are also uniforms and weapons, rations and maps. The book stall is temptingly well equipped (even with books in English) about World War II and Normandy; there is a snack/drinks dispensing machine, clean WCs and ample free parking.

The basis for the original museum, now extended, was the personal collection of local dentist, collector, historian, researcher and author of many books on the Normandy Campaigns, Dr Jean Pierre Benamou. Local buffs quibble about the over-emphasis on German exhibits to the detriment of the recognition of Resistance and Free French participation, and an embarrassment of riches where documents are concerned. It is, however, an indisputably magnificent museum and not to be missed.

Open: 1 May -15 Sept 0930-1830. 16 Sept - 30 April 1000-1130 and 1400-1800. Entrance fee payable. Tel: (0)2 31 92 93 41

Outside are a number of well-restored vehicles, guns, and tanks (including a Hetzer SP anti-tank gun, a Sherman tank, a Churchill AVRE, and a 40mm Bofors gun). In September 1993 a memorial was unveiled in the grounds to the Notts (Sherwood Rangers) Yeomanry.

For the assault on Bayeux, the Sherwood Rangers changed from support of the 231st

Infantry Brigade to 55th Infantry Brigade. Troop leader Lieutenant Mike Howden of 'A' Squadron was the first person to enter the outskirts of Bayeux on the evening of 6 June in his tank. He was held up by a string of mines across the road and asked for Sapper support. As none was available at this stage, he was instructed to return to his squadron. It was decided by the Rangers' Infantry, the Essex Regiment, to remain on the outskirts of the town and the Sherwoods laagered their tanks on the site of what is now the Amazon Hotel on the ring road - disappointed not to be fulfilling Monty's plan to take Bayeux that night. After a short night they entered the town the next morning, 'A' Squadron in support of the Essex Regiment and 'B' Squadron coming in from the north of the town supporting the South Wales Borderers. 'C' Squadron remained in reserve at St. Sulpice. A machine-gun post to the south of the town set a house alight with its fire and the Bayeux fire-engine came clanging its bell, with a full crew in their shiny helmets, and put the fire out. This brought out a German machine-gun section - the only opposition encountered by the Sherwoods other than the odd sniper fire. It was because they were the liberators of the first city in Normandy, Bayeux, that the honour of erecting their memorial in the museum grounds was granted to them.

The Sherwood Rangers went on to Tilly-sur-Seulles where they have another memorial. There, on 9 June their most famous son, the war poet Keith Douglas, 2 i/c of 'A' Squadron, was killed. He is buried in Tilly CWGC Cemetery (Holts' Map F5). Douglas, from an early age both a rebel and a poet, enlisted at the outbreak of war, but, like other undergraduates, his call up was delayed until July 1940. After four months of cavalry training, Douglas did three months at Sandhurst and five months' training with armoured cars in Gloucestershire with the 2nd Derbyshire Yeomanry, into which he had been commissioned - and whose collar dogs he insisted on wearing thereafter. Posted to the Middle East in June 1941 and, prevented by illness from joining his own regiment, he joined the Sherwood Rangers Yeomanry. His experiences in North Africa are vividly described in his book, *Alamein to Zem Zem*, and it was during this period that some of his most brilliant and enduring poems were written, establishing his reputation as probably the finest poet of the Second World War. In December 1943, after acquitting himself with credit in the North African campaign and becoming thoroughly attached to his adopted Regiment, Douglas returned with them to the UK. Preparing for the Normandy invasion, he continued to write poetry, as well as revising the manuscript of his book. In March he wrote an unfinished poem called *Actors waiting in the wings of Europe.* It includes the lines,

> Everyone, I suppose will use these minutes
> To look back, to hear music and recall
> What we were doing and saying that year
> During our last few months as people, near
> The sucking mouth of the day that swallowed us all
> Into the stomach of a war. Now we are in it.....

On a foot recce during the morning of 9 June a mortar fragmentation bomb exploded in a tree above him and Douglas was killed by a splinter so fine that there was no mark on his body. His loss to literature has been compared with that of Wilfred Owen during the First World War.

Leave your car in the museum car park and walk up the road to

Battle of Normandy Museum, Bayeux.

Interior of the Museum.

• *Bayeux Commonwealth War Graves Commission Memorial and Cemetery/30 minutes/Map A10,11*

On the same side of the road as the museum is the Bayeux Memorial to the Missing with No Known Graves, designed by Philip Hepworth. It bears the names of 1,805 Commonwealth service men and women (1,534 from Britain, 270 from Canada and 1 from South Africa) who fell in the Battle of Normandy.

The Latin inscription above reads *'NOS A GULIELMO VICTI VICTORIS PATRIAM LIBERAVIMUS'*. Over the road is the beautifully maintained cemetery - the largest British World War II cemetery in France. It contains 4,648 graves - 3,935 from the United Kingdom, 181 from Canada, 17 from Australia, 8 from New Zealand, 1 from South Africa, 25 from Poland, 3 from France, 2 from Czechoslovakia, 2 from Italy, 7 from Russia, 466 from Germany and 1 unidentified. The internationality of the invasion, and the support given by the Commonwealth and other Allies, is well illustrated here. All lie under standard CWGC headstones, but the visitor will note that each nationality has a differently shaped top to its stones. In the shelter to the left of the stone of remembrance, the visitors' book and cemetery register are housed in a bronze box.

One of the burials of note is that of Corporal Sidney Bates, 1st Battalion the Norfolk Regiment, who won the VC for an action on 6 August involving 10th SS Panzer Division on the Periers Ridge. Although wounded, he picked up a light machine gun and charged the enemy. He was wounded for a third time but kept on firing until the enemy had withdrawn. He died two days later.

Return to your car and continue round the ring road, direction Cherbourg to the roundabout. Park in the Novotel car park. The memorial is in the centre of the roundabout opposite the hotel.

***Hotel Novotel, Rond Point de Vaucelles. Heated outdoor pool. Highly recommended. Tel: (0)2 31 92 1611).

•*Bayeux Liberation Memorial/2.1 miles/10 minutes/Map A9*

This striking bas relief, sculpted by M. Lamourdedieu, commemorates the D-Day Landings and General de Gaulle's historic visit to Bayeux on 14 June. In a conversation with a French citizen who was present on the day that de Gaulle came to Bayeux, the authors were given an account somewhat at variance with the accepted version. The memory recounted to us was that the 'crowd' numbered no more than 500 and it was made up more by those who were curious as to what was happening than by those who were excited by the visitor. 'No-one knew who he was,' we were told. 'As for a welcome by the Resistance, that was not so. They were mostly Communists and hated what de Gaulle stood for.'

In the grassed centre is the holder for the Flame of Liberty.

The Ceremony of the Flame

In September each year young people came from Eindhoven in Holland to Bayeux, as the two towns are twinned, to rekindle the Flame of Liberty and Friendship, at the Bayeux Liberation Memorial. This event started in 1945 as, although smaller villages and towns in Holland were liberated before Eindhoven, it, like Bayeux, was the first important city to be liberated.

Sporting and social events take place between young Dutch boys and girls and local Bayeux youngsters. Then, at 2100 hours on 16 September the local band accompanies the procession from the town centre to the memorial. There local World War II veterans, resistance workers and others bring their standards as the children, the Mayor of Bayeux and members of the Bayeux Council, members of the twinning committee and representatives from Eindhoven Council congregate. Messages of remembrance, friendship and peace are exchanged, the flame is rekindled and the young light their torches from the flame, around which stand young people bearing the national flags of France, Holland, Great Britain, America and Canada. During this moving ceremony the national anthems of the countries are also played.

The following morning the flame starts its journey to Holland (630 kilometers) transported by young Dutch cyclists. At 2100 hours on 18 September the young people with their torches arrive in Eindhoven and the flame is rekindled there at a similar ceremony, which is always extremely well attended by veterans' organisations and local people. A ceremony is also held here on the morning of 6 June.

Drive out of the car park and turn right off the ring road towards Centre Ville and continue through the main street of the town, rue Saint Malo, to the traffic lights at the bottom of the hill. Turn left on rue Maréchal Foch and park in the car park on the right.

By the car park are: Le Printanier - charming restaurant with good daily menu as well as à la carte. Tel: (0)2 31 92 03 01. Pizzeria Roma - Italian specialities. Tel: (0)2 31 51 94 14.

Walk back to the traffic lights and the Tourist Office is to your left.

TOURIST OFFICE. Helpful English-speaking staff. Books and maps on sale, local information. Pont St Jean. Tel: (0)2 31 51 28 28. Pick up a town plan here to locate the following - all within walking distance. Allow one hour:

Bayeux Cathedral

Inside, to the left of the nave, is a plaque to commemorate the 56th Brigade, who liberated the city on the afternoon of 7 June. There is also a standard Lutyens WW1 plaque and a stained glass window similar to the one in Portsmouth. Both windows were established by the 'D-Day and Normandy Fellowship', an organisation whose members come from those who served in Normandy in any of the three arms. It was unveiled by the Queen Mother on 6 June 1989. The 56th Brigade was part of 50th Division and on the wall to the left of the entrance gate to the Hotel du Doyen (situated in rue Leforestier opposite the western side of the cathedral) is a plaque to the division. 50th Division was in turn part of XXX Corps which was later to play a prominent role in Operation Market Garden. There is also an unusual plaque to Major Peter Dewey who was killed in Saigon in 1945 and who in 1944 ran the OSS operations in the south of France. His father was a rich banker who married a French lady from Port-en-Bessin. Distraught at his son's asassination, the father raised this plaque. He was also the first person to get aid parcels into Port-en-Bessin after the war.

Place Général de Gaulle

Column to commemorate de Gaulle's speech on 14 June 1944. Plaque on wall of Sous-Préfecture, erected on 14 December 1946.

Musée Mémorial du Général de Gaulle
In rue de Bourbesneur, off Place Général de Gaulle. A museum recalling the 14 June 1944 speech, plus personal memorabilia. There is a **NTL Totem** here describing the General's speech, the setting up of the provisional government of the French Republic and the publication of *La Renaissance du Bessin,* the first newspaper of liberated France to be published. Tel: (0)2 31 92 45 55.

And, of course,
The famous ***Tapisserie de la Reine Mathilde.*** Cinema with English commentary. Book and souvenir shop. Entrance fee. Tel: (0)2 31 51 25 50, and Musée Baron Gérard. Paintings, lace, porcelain etc. Tapestry ticket gives you entry here too. Tel: (0)2 31 92 14 21.

Market day in Bayeux is Saturday, with a fine array of flowers, plants, fruit, vegetables, cheeses etc. There is a variety of restaurants, souvenir shops, enticing *patisseries* and hotels within walking distance, e.g:
***Lion d'Or. Rue Saint Jean. The traditional hotel in the heart of the town, favoured by war correspondents for its crab omelettes in 1944. Highly recommended.   Tel: (0)2 31 92 06 90
**Hotel de Luxembourg/Hotel de Brunville. Family owned, well run. Good value.Tel: (0)2 31 92 00 04.
**Hotel d'Argouges. Pleasant Relais de Silence. No restaurant. Tel: (0)2 31 92 88 86.
* Hotel Notre-Dame. Good restaurant. Opposite cathedral. Tel: (0)2 31 92 87 24.
   Drive out of the car park. Return to the traffic lights, go straight over.
On the right is the Post office and the *Mairie* in Place des Déportés, in front of which is a dramatic statue to the civilians who were deported.
   Continue to the roundabout and turn right onto the ring road (past the museum and the British cemetery) to the Liberation monument roundabout.

Extra Visits to US 846th US Air Engineers Memorial, Vaucelles (Map A8)/ 'Big Red One' Memorial, Tour-en-Bessin (Map U16)/General Montgomery's Headquarters/US Liberators at Blay (Map X1)/US 1st Division Plaque, Etreham (Map U12). Round trip: 13.5 miles. Approximate time: 30 minutes. Additional Visit to General Eisenhower's HQ, Tournières (Map W1)/US 2nd 'Indian Head' Division, Trevières (Map T19). Extra miles: 20.2 miles. Approximate extra time: 45 minutes.

When taking this visit, the main itinerary can be re-joined just before the D-Day Wrecks Museum at Port-en-Bessin - see below. It is a long 'Extra Visit', taking in some extremely interesting but little-visited sites, that could well be treated as a separate itinerary.
   From the Liberation Memorial, Vaucelles Roundabout, take the N13 direction Cherbourg. Continue through Vaucelles to the memorial on the right to
The 846th US Air Engineers Battalion Memorial.

British War Memorial, Bayeux.

CWGC Cemetery, Bayeux.

*Lighting the flame, Liberation
Memorial, annually, 16 September.*

*Général de Gaulle bas relief,
Liberation Memorial.*

*Memorial to Blay's American
Liberators.*

General Montgomery's Tac HQ, Blay.

Extra Visits continued

Continue to Tour-en-Bessin.

Englishman Eddy Spink and his wife helped inspire the memorials at Etreham, and on the wall here, in the parking area to the right, in the centre of the village, to **The US 1st Division, 'The Big Red One'.** The village was liberated by the 3rd Battalion of the 26th Infantry Regiment of 1st Division on 8 June. They advanced down the N13 from Isigny.

Continue to the large Coopérative de Creully complex on the right. Turn left on the D206 signed to Blay. Continue to the junction with the D96 and turn right. Continue to the memorial in the bank on the left.

Orientation Table showing the site of General Montgomery's T.A.C. HQ when he moved here from Creullet on 23 June1944, staying until 3 August. The table shows a plan indicating the position of the General's caravan, the cookhouse, captured German tanks and the airstrip (which was in the field behind). It was erected on the instigation of local farmer Ernest Debourdon de Gramont, on whose land the HQ was. M Debourdon formed a committee (of which one of the authors was Honorary President) which managed to locate Monty's pilot, Trevor Martin, and his interpreter, Norman Kirby, who gave many invaluable details about the General's period here. The memorial was unveiled on the 50th Anniversary but unfortunately the present Viscount Montgomery (son of the General) was not able to be present as he was committed to the inauguration of the Montgomery Roundabout at Port-en-Bessin (see below). However, he and Lady Montgomery attended an impressive wreath-laying ceremony in June 1996, attended by Monsieur Triboulet (qv), Trevor Martin and Norman Kirby, local members of the Resistance - and the authors.

Continue down the hill to the junction. In the bank on the left is the

Monument to Blay's American Liberators. When the Montgomery HQ memorial was being planned, another village committee was formed to erect this memorial to Blay's American Liberators, 9 June 1944. It also pays tribute to Maréchal Montgomery's headquarters here at Blay.

Either return to the Coopérative de Creully and pick up the directions from there at the end of the Additional Extra Visit which follows, OR Turn left on the D97E signed Blay/Breuil en Bessin. Continue to the church and the Mairie (which has the signatures of Lord and Lady Montgomery in the Livre d'Or) of Blay, go straight over the crossroads to Breuil (when in doubt continue straight on!) over the railway signed to le Molay Littry.Turn right on the D5 and continue through the central square of le Molay Littry signed Tournières. Drive through the village following signs to American Monument. As the road bends to the right turn left following American monument signs and continue to the memorial staight ahead.

General Eisenhower's HQ. When the Franco-American 9th US Airforce Normandy Airfields Association (qv) located the site, the Eisenhower Foundation erected this monument near the actual HQ. The original had been

Extra Visits continued

in a field which was part of a farm between Le Percas and Bailleul. The field was commandeered from the farmer who was totally excluded from the high security area, patrolled by MPs. The inscription reads, 'The United States of America recognizes the selfless service and manifold contributions of General Dwight David Eisenhower, Supreme Allied Commander 1944-1945. Near this site General Eisenhower established the Supreme Headquarters' first command post on the European Continent. This plaque was dedicated by a United States Department of Defense delegation and the Eisenhower family on 6 June 1990 during the centennial year of his birth and the 46th Anniversary of Operation OVERLORD.'

Turn round and return towards le Molay Littry. In Tournières turn left on the D191 signed to Trevières. Continue to the junction with the D5 and turn right signed Trevières and next left on the D191 and at the junction with the D96 turn left. On entering Trevières the road to the right just before the Trésor Publique is called Allée de la 2ème Division Americaine. Continue to the T junction, turn right direction Mosles and immediately park by the Church.

Treviéres War Memorial. The face of this striking bronze female figure wearing a Poilu's helmet was damaged by a shell during the Battle of Trevières in June 1944. It was, of course, the village First World War Memorial. The citizens decided to keep the damaged figure as a reminder of the dreadful suffering that Normandy had to undergo for her liberty. A small plaque to the right shows the statue in her pre-war glory and explains the story in French and in English. In the church are two **stained glass windows to the 2nd US (Indian Head) Division** and on the wall to the right of the entrance to the *Mairie* opposite is a **plaque to the 9th and 38th Regiments of the Second Infantry Division** who took part in the battle of Trevières 8-10 June 1944. It was erected by the 2nd Infantry Division Association Monument Foundation on 6 June 1989. There are strong links between the Association and the citizens of Trevières and there have been several pilgrimages here by veterans and their families. Inside the *Mairie* is the Divisional History of the 2nd 'Indian Head' Infantry Division, whose motto is 'Second to None'.

In the words of a survivor, the Battle of 'Trevières was a tough nut to crack'. The attack by 9th and 38th Regiments began at 1200 hours on 9 June on this important German HQ, with its carefully prepared positions. By the end of the day the 38th had entered the town, but it was not until the end of 10 June that they cleared Trevières after a house-to-house battle. 2nd Medical Battalion Clearing Station at St Laurent quickly established a collecting station near the town to evacuate the casualties of the fighting.

Continue on the D29 to Mosles and turn right on the N13 direction Bayeux.

On the right you pass the simple, excellent value 'Routier' café, Restaurant de la Poste. It is extremely popular with lorry drivers and also has a small dining room.

Detail, Trevières WW1 Memorial.

Extra Visits continued

Continue to the Coopérative de Creully and turn left. Continue on the D206 direction Etreham to the bridge over the Aure.

The plaque on the bridge dates from 1846 and thanks the local landowner for erecting the bridge which facilitated the passage of vehicles.

Continue to the fork and go left towards the church on the D20A. On the wall of the Presbytery opposite is

Plaque to the Ist US Infantry Division, 'the Big Red One', 7 June 1944, erected in 1994. The 2nd Battalion 26th Infantry Regiment moved through here on the night of 7 June followed by the 1st Battalion on the morning of the 8th.

Continue round the church and join the D123. Continue to the junction with the D6 and turn left. Rejoin the main itinerary en route from Bayeux at the museum of Underwater Wrecks.

Turn right, direction Arromanches, on the ring road. There are several useful supermarkets on the ring road. *Take the first left signed to Port-en-Bessin on the D6. Continue.*

On the right you will pass two excellent 18th Century château/manor house hotel-restaurants in beautiful grounds: the *** Château de Sully (which would seem worthy of an extra star for the opulence of its setting and public rooms) Tel: (0)2 31 22 29 48, and the **** Chenevière, Tel: (0)2 31 51 25 25, popular with exclusive British and American groups.

Continue to the museum on the right.

• Museum of Under-Water Wrecks/9.4 miles/25 minutes/Map A7

After the war a great many wrecks lay under the coastal waters of Normandy, posing a threat to local shipping. They became the property of the French Government, provided they were salvaged. Several million tons of scrap iron were recovered by specialised firms during the 20 years that followed. In 1970, however, more wrecks emerged which were impeding the access to local ports and Jaques Lemonchois was asked to clear them. For many days he and his team worked on this absorbing but dangerous task. The results are here preserved for future generations as a reminder of Operation NEPTUNE. As well as items salvaged from D-Day warships, there are tanks, parts of aeroplanes, contemporary documents, films and photos.
Open: June-September 1000-1300 and 1400-1900 (1 July-31 August open all day). Tel: (0)2 31 21 17 06.

Continue to the roundabout.

• General Montgomery Roundabout/9.7 miles/Map A6.

Inaugurated by Viscount Montgomery, the Field-Marshal's son, for the 50th Anniversary, the sculpture is called 'ESSOR'. The revolving sphere represents the world of the sea and the pillars the Pipeline under the Ocean - PLUTO. The architect is Henri Lebihan.

Go straight over, following signs to 'le Port' to the traffic lights.

Up the hill to the left, signed Grandcamp/Golf Omaha Beach, is the ***Hotel Mercure Omaha Beach, a smart modern hotel with swimming pool, adjacent to the magnificent 27-hole golf club whose club house shares the restaurant with the hotel. Tel: (0)2 31 21 72 94. Highly recommended. The tees on the golf course are named after D-Day personalities, e.g. Piper Bill Millin and the Commanding Generals.

Continue towards the sea to the Mairie on the right.

On the corner opposite is a *plaque to the Croiseur Georges Leygues,* 6 juin 1944. The French cruiser was one of the ships which, following a sea/land duel, silenced the German guns at Longues (see below).

Continue to the harbour and drive over the lock road to the hard standing below the cliffs. Park and walk to the memorials described below.

• Port-en-Bessin/RM Commando and Comité du Débarquement Memorials/Bunker/10.5 miles/20 minutes/RWC/Map A3,4,5

In order to supply the estimated one million gallons of petrol that the Liberation Army would need, pipe lines were laid under the sea from England. The PLUTO (Pipe Line Under The Ocean) system in its various forms supplied most of the needs of the Allies from August 1944 onwards. At Escures, a village on the D6 en route to Port-en-Bessin, there was a junction in the PLUTO line that started in Port-en-Bessin. The main line ran some 200 yards to the east of the D6 to Bayeux and around behind the British War Cemetery. The other leg ran to the N13 to the west and thence to Cherbourg. The idea for PLUTO was said to have come from Lord Louis Mountbatten and development began in 1942. There were two different types of pipe. The main one, laid at sea, was flexible and called HAMEL. The name derived from the first letters of the names of the men who invented it: Mr H.A. Hammick of the Iraq Petroleum Company and Mr B.J. Ellis of the Burmah Oil Company. The pipe was towed across the Channel from Southampton in 70-mile lengths on enormous 'cotton reels' called CONUNDRUMS, each with a wound weight of 1,600 tons, which is roughly the weight of a destroyer. The whole operation, known as 'Force PLUTO', was run by about a thousand men from a main base at Southampton and pipe laying began as soon as the routes across the Channel had been cleared of mines.

The town boasts a tower built by Vauban in 1694 as defence against English and Dutch pirates. Later it became a magazine to supply the batteries at nearby Huppain and du Castel. Although damaged, the tower survived the invasion. Below it on the beaches, beside the hard, is a **Todt bunker,** facing out to sea, with a **memorial plaque to the No 47 (RM) Commando.** On the jetty of the outer harbour is a *Comité du Débarquement* **Monument,** commemorating the landings, a **NTL Totem** and a dramatic statue to fishermen who have lost their lives at sea. On the cliffs overlooking the port there are gun emplacements and bunkers. These formidable positions were attacked by No 47 RM Commando on the afternoon of D+1, having worked their way, some ten miles, along the coast from Le Hamel carrying almost 90lb per man of weapons and supplies. Two of the strongpoints were taken with the help of a naval bombardment from HMS *Emerald's* 6in guns, rocket-firing Typhoons and artillery smoke. A German counter-attack, supported by flak-ships in the harbour, retook one of the hills, but at dusk the German commander and 100 men surrendered, though sadly the commandos' troop leader, Captain T.F. Cousins, was killed by a sniper. The commandos had captured a port which was to play an important role in maintaining the flow of vital supplies, and they had secured the junction between the British 50th Division on GOLD Beach and the US 1st Division on OMAHA Beach. By 14 June the port was handling more than 1,000 tons of supplies a day, much more than it had ever done in peacetime.

Along the coast to the east the remains of the Mulberry harbour at Arromanches can be seen.

Today Port-en-Bessin is one of the premier fishing ports of France with between 10,500 and 12,000 tonnes of fish passing through its market and distribution system annually, one of the most modern in Europe. Its natural harbour, protected on each side by high cliffs made it a safe haven for the Romans, Saxons, and Normans - some of William the Conqueror's fleet was made here. In the 15th Century the two jetties were made. Damaged in the 17th Century by heavy storms, they were reconstructed in the 19th Century and the latest modernisation was in 1970. Christened by Françoise Sagan 'le petit Saint-Tropez normand', the port has been popular with literary, artistic and political personalities - from Seurat to Flaubert to Simenon to Presidents Félix Faure, Vincent Auriol and François Mittérand. It was in Port-en-Bessin that the scene in the film,*The Longest Day*, which purported to show the taking of the Casino at Ouistreham by Commandant Kieffer and his men, was actually shot.

There is a wonderful fish market here on Sunday mornings along the quay with its variety of interesting shops, patisseries and restaurants. Sunday lunch is very popular and it is advisable to book. Highly recommended is La Marie du Port. Tel: (0)2 31 21 72 45.

Return towards Bayeux along the one-way system following 'Toutes Directions'. On the right is the *King Hotel. Tel: (0)2 31 21 44 44. At the junction with the D514 coast road turn left following signs to Longues or Arromanches on the rue du Croiseur Montcalm.*

Immediately on the right is a **plaque to the Cruiser Montcalm** next to the Cultural Centre and the **Office de Tourisme**, Tel: (0)2 31 21 92 33. The Free French vessel *Montcalm* was part of Bombarding Force C which supported the Americans on OMAHA Beach.

Continue to the College Hemingway on the left. Just beyond it is

• *No 47 Royal Marine Commando Memorial/11.5 miles/5 minutes/Map A22.*

Links between Port-en-Bessin and No 47 RM Commando Association have remained strong, with frequent pilgrimages being made over the years since 1944. In 1996 the students of the Hemingway Institute started an oral history project to which the Commandos contributed many memories. This memorial was inaugurated during their visit on 7 June 1997.

Continue to Longues and at the crossroads after the church turn left towards the sea following signs to 'Batteries de Longues' and stop in the car park.

* Longues (le Chaos) Battery/14.8 miles/20 minutes/Map A2

Construction began in September 1943. There were four gun positions, a two-storey observation bunker, anti-aircraft guns, defence works and searchlights.

The battery has been well preserved and progressively restored in recent years, although rock falls at the cliff's edge have put the observation bunker out of bounds. Each of the four casemates contained a 155mm rapid-firing naval gun and, although 1,500 tons of bombs had been dropped around the weapons, they were totally protected by the thick concrete. When the Allied naval bombardment began, just before sunrise, the Longues battery replied. Its first salvo straddled HMS *Bulolo* carrying the HQ of the British XXX Corps. HMS *Ajax* immediately brought her own 6in guns into action and, at a range of some 7¹/₂ miles, despatched 114 rounds at Longues. Within 20 minutes the battery was silenced. Three guns were destroyed, and it was claimed that shells from *Ajax* entered the slits of two of the casemates. The fourth gun recommenced firing in the afternoon and, following a duel with the French cruiser *Georges Leygues*, fell silent shortly after 1800 hours. The total number of shells fired by the battery was estimated to exceed 115. The garrison surrendered to the 231st Brigade advancing from Arromanches on D+1 yielding 120 prisoners.

By the car park is a 'boutique' offering guided tours in the season and a **NTL Totem**.

Return to the D514 and continue east following signs to Arromanches, passing through Tracy.

In the church at Tracy is a **stained glass window commemorating 6 June 1944**.

On entering Arromanches, pass the newly refurbished *Hotel Chanteclair, Tel: (0)2 31 21 38 97 on the left.

Arromanches

Arromanches was made ready to resist an invasion, houses were blown up to improve fields of fire and machine-gun positions prepared, but the invaders did not come from the sea. The town was liberated on the afternoon of D-Day by the 1st Battalion Royal Hampshire Regiment who had landed on GOLD Beach and descended upon the German defenders from the heights of St Côme to the east, where they had spent the whole morning dislodging elements of the 352nd Division. There was very little damage to buildings in the town and only six civilian deaths, despite the naval fire support that preceded the Hampshires' arrival.

Arromanches is remembered for the harbour that was towed across the English Channel - the Mulberry. The name has no special meaning. When a code word was needed for the project the list of available words was consulted and the next one was 'Mulberry'. The idea of the floating harbour is said to have originated in a memo from Sir Winston Churchill to Vice-Admiral Mountbatten Chief of Combined Operations on 30 May 1942. It ran:

Museum of Underwater Wrecks, Port-en-Bessin.

The Longues Battery.

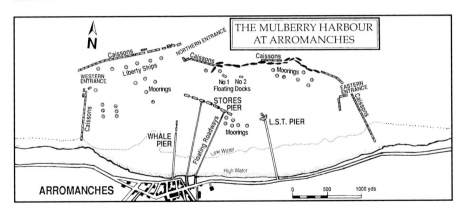

THE MULBERRY HARBOUR
AT ARROMANCHES

PIERS FOR USE ON BEACHES
CCO or deputy
They must float up and down with the tide. The anchor problem must be
mastered. Let me have the best solution worked out. Don't argue the matter. The
difficulties will argue for themselves.

It may well be that Churchill had thought back to 1915 and to his ill-fated idea that
became the Gallipoli campaign. At that time he had proposed that one method of
landing men on a shore was to use pathways that would 'float up and down'.

In August 1942 the frontal attack on the harbour at Dieppe proved that such a thing
should not be done again, and that since an army invading France would need
harbours for re-supply, they would either have to be captured from behind or built in
England and taken across the Channel. In June 1943 the Normandy coastline was
chosen as the site for the invasion and in August, at the Quebec Conference, the
Combined Chiefs of Staff approved the construction of artificial harbours code named
Mulberry. The Directorate of Ports and Inland War Transport under Sir Bruce White,
and a special staff known as 'X Staff' in Norfolk House, St James's Square, London
under Commodore Hughes-Hallett set to work. They had less than ten months to
design and construct two harbours each roughly the size of that at Dover. One was to
be for the Americans at OMAHA Beach, the other for the British at Arromanches.

The basic concept was simple. First a line of sixty old ships would be sunk off all five
beaches. It would provide an elemental breakwater on the landward side of which the
seas would be calmed. These ships were called 'Gooseberries'. Inside the Gooseberries,
off OMAHA Beach and Arromanches, a huge semi-circle of hollow concrete boxes,
called caissons and codenamed Phoenixes, would be sunk to form a harbour wall. In
all 146 Phoenixes would be needed, the sixty largest displacing over 6,000 tons of water
each. Work on the caissons went on around the country, but the greatest number in a
single location were built in pits dug along the banks of the River Thames. The
movement of men and material from the Mulberry caissons to the shore was to be along
flexible roadways, named Whales or Beetles, running over floating pontoons. Seven
miles of floating roadway was constructed for the two harbours. Even so it was felt that
in order for the ships within the Mulberry Harbour to be unloaded quickly enough a

The Mulberry Harbour at Arromanches in 1944.

ferry service of small craft would be needed and over 2,000 vessels with some 15,000 staff were earmarked for the purpose. The whole complex Mulberry structure involved over four hundred towed components weighing $1^1/_2$ million tons.

The Mulberry force began to sail to France on the afternoon of D-Day. The aim was to have both harbours in place within fourteen days. The British naval officer in charge of the Arromanches harbour had as his HQ ship the old light cruiser *Despatch,* bristling with anti-aircraft weapons and manned by soldiers with a major as the gunnery officer. It was the first time in over 280 years that the main armament of one of the ships of the king's navy had been manned by soldiers. Then it had been the Queen's Regiment and in 1944 it was again the Queen's.

The first Phoenix arrived at Arromanches at dawn on 9 June and by 18 June 115 had been sunk in a huge 5-mile-long arc around the town, from Tracy in the west to Asnelles in the east. The area was festooned with barrage balloons and anti-aircraft weapons, but the Luftwaffe was very little in evidence. It was the weather that was to prove the enemy. Thirteen days after D-Day a north-east storm broke that shattered the OMAHA Mulberry and even settled the Gooseberry ships there in the mud so that they became ineffective. After the storm, which lasted three days, there was no harbour left at OMAHA and a special camp had to be established on the beach to accommodate some 1,100 crew from the small vessels destroyed or blown on to the beach. The Arromanches harbour fared better and survived, battered but serviceable, a thankful matter since there were over 150 craft in the harbour at the time. Nevertheless over 800 vessels were stranded and almost 50 per cent of the 650 LCTs (Landing Craft Tank) available for the build-up were incapacitated. The gale caused more damage in three days than the Germans did in two weeks, yet by the end of the year 39,000 vehicles and 220,000 soldiers had made dry landings at Arromanches.

The town calls itself 'Arromanches Port Winston' and has adopted a coat of arms showing the British Lion, and the American Eagle breaking the chains of occupation. *Continue into Arromanches.*

• Memorial 'Groupe Lorraine Forces Aériennes Françaises Libres'/19.1 miles/ 5 minutes/Map B21

The area around the coach park as one enters Arromanches has been renamed 'Place du Groupe d'Alsace'. The memorial is on the left-hand corner.

Follow signs to the Museum/Caen/Courseulles and park in the car park on the sea front by the museum. There is a 'buy your own ticket' parking meter and a uniformed attendant to make sure that you use it.

•D-Day Landings Museum/Brigadier General Stanier Memorial/ 19.5 miles/60 minutes/RWC/Map B20, 31

The parking area, once tennis courts, faces the museum, the *Exposition Permanente du Débarquement,* designed by François Carpentier, sometime Mayor of Arromanches. Financed by the *Comité du Débarquement,* it was opened by Président René Coty in 1954. It has a working model of the Landing Beaches, a model of the Mulberry Harbour, a diorama of the landings with a commentary by Monsieur Triboulet, the first Sous-Prefet appointed by General de Gaulle in June 1944 and instigator of the museum, a variety of documentary exhibits and a 1944 British Admiralty film of the construction of Port Winston. Commentaries are given in French, English and German. This important museum is the focal point of the British Landing Beaches. Outside are a number of artillery pieces and a Sherman tank on the hill behind. There is a good book/souvenir shop in the museum. In the season it gets very busy - in 1998 there were 265,000 visitors.

Open: Feb-March 0930-1700. April 0900-1800. May-end August 0900-1900. Sept-end Oct 0900-1800. Nov-end Dec 0930-1700. Oct, Nov, Dec, Feb, March - closed 1200-1330. Jan -closed. Tel: (0)2 31 22 34 31.

On the sea wall is a **memorial to General Sir Alexander Stanier Bt.** [sic] 231st Brigade, 50th Division, 1899-1995. *'Libérateur d'Arromanches le 6 juin 1944.'* This memorial, while admirable, is incorrect. Sir Alexander's rank was Brigadier, not General, (though to be fair, the French who use the rank 'Brigadier-Général' which has long been out of use in the British Army, probably dropped the 'Brigadier' bit for brevity).

Around the museum parking area is a variety of hotels (eg **Hotel de la Marine, Tel: (0)2 31 22 3419 on the promenade, super sea view. *Hotel de Normandie, Tel: (0)2 31 21 34 32, in square) restaurants/souvenir shops, and just along the road running beyond it is the **TOURIST OFFICE,** 4 rue du Mal Joffre,Tel: (0)2 31 22 36 45.

Leave Arromanches eastward on the D514 coast road, following signs to Courseulles/Cinéma Circulaire and stop in the parking area (for which there is a fee in the season) on the left just past the Statue of the Virgin Mary on the cliffs above the town.

• St Côme de Fresne Table d'Orientation/ Bunker/RE Memorial/ Free French Airforce Memorial/360° Film/20.3 miles/30 minutes/MapB16, 17, 18,19.

By the cliff edge are the remains of German bunkers which contained field guns which menaced GOLD Beach and were silenced by HMS *Belfast*. In the sea, the remains of the Arromanches Mulberry Harbour can be seen, and to the left below is Arromanches itself. This position, and Arromanches, were taken by the Hampshires before 2100 hours on D-Day, by which time the 50th Division bridgehead measured 5 miles by 5 miles.

No 47 RM Commando landed on your right on GOLD Beach, just below these heights, and swung around behind you going to your left, heading for Port-en-Bessin, a 10-mile march away, due west.

360° Museum, St Côme.

Memorial to Brigadier General Stanier.

The 6 June 1944 Museum, Arromanches.

View over Arromanches from St Côme, showing the remains of the Mulberry Harbour.

A D-DAY MEMORY

Lieutenant L.E. Anderson. The Border Regiment. Beach Signals officer, No 1 Beach Group. Landed on GOLD beach.

"D-Day 7.30a.m. An assault craft heading for GOLD Beach with some of my signallers and myself, together with a Naval boatswain. The rule was that, as long as we were at sea, the boatswain was in charge, but that I was in command as soon as we touched shore. We ended up on an underwater obstacle sticking up through the bottom of the boat, which made it spin round like a roulette wheel in the rough sea. There then ensued what seemed to be a lengthy discussion between the boatswain and myself as to whether we were at sea or ashore. Ultimately I won and he let down the ramp. With the famous cry of 'Follow me chaps', I ran off the ramp to find myself up to my neck in water."

On the downward slope of the hill along the footpath towards Arromanches is a memorial commemorating a Napoleonic naval battle off Arromanches in 1811 which was erected on the 100th anniversary. The *table d'orientation* by the parking area gives excellent views over the remains of the Mulberry Harbour. Near it are traces of the radar station destroyed by allied airforce raids a few weeks before OVERLORD, including the truncated pyramid-shaped Würzburg radar mounting, gun emplacements and concrete shelters. There is a **NTL Totem** beside it.

Walk towards the 360° Cinema to the memorial with the badge of the Free French Airforce.

The Memorial is headed **'Esplanade du Général d'Armée Aérienne Michel Fourquet'** (known as 'Gorré), the Commander of Groupe Lorraine 'Leader of the Mission of 6 June 1944, 1914-1992'.

Continue to

The **RE Memorial** on the left with a fine display of unit badges. Operation OVERLORD was an assault upon a defended coastline - defended not just by weapons but by obstacles. Therefore well forward in the assault forces had to be engineer units equipped to clear whatever devices the Germans had erected to impede the invasion - from the beaches onward. The Americans called these forces 'Assault' or 'Special' engineer formations. The British employed the Royal Engineers, all of whom were part of 1 (British) Corps, and for the landing the engineer units were split up and put under the command of the assaulting divisions. The Corps Engineer plan identified its tasks as follows: -

On the beaches - obstacle clearance, construction of exits and subsequent beach organisation Operations inland - bridging, airfields and routes. The importance that the British attached to the engineers and to Hobart's Funnies, which were operated by them, is well illustrated by the planned landing sequence given in the orders for the landing of 8th Infantry Brigade Group at la Brêche (visited later). It was: -

A and B Squadrons 13/18 Hussars (DD tanks)

Eight gapping teams, each of two flail tanks, three AVREs, one bulldozer and two obstacle clearing teams

The assaulting infantry.

The **360° Cinema** presentation uses an original 'Circorama' process employing 9 synchronised cameras to give a unique and moving account of the events of 6 June 1944 at Arromanches and the surrounding area. It has a good book and souvenir shop. **Open:** every day June, July, August 0910-1840. May, September 1010-1740. Feb, March, April, Oct, Nov, Dec 1010-1640. Shows at 10 and 40 minutes past each hour. Entrance fee payable. Tel: (0)2 31 22 30 30.

Continue on the D514 downhill.

In the church of St Côme that is passed on the right is a **plaque commemorating the ringing of the bells on D-Day.**

Continue to the crossroads with the D205 just east of le Hamel (Asnelles). Stop and walk 100 yards down the small road to the sea.

• *D514/D205 Crossroads/21.3 miles/10 minutes/OP*

At low tide there is a good view of the remaining Phoenixes of the Arromanches Mulberry, built to last a hundred days and still around at the Millenium. There is a typical German shore bunker with deadly fields of fire across the open beaches, yet many of the German guns had limited traverse and this was to save countless British lives.

The Germans had assumed that the invaders would try to float over the beach obstacles and that therefore any landing would be made close to high tide. Thus they had arranged their arcs of fire to cover an area of the beach between the high water level and the sea wall. The landings, however, were made before half tide and thus not into the teeth of small arms opposition at the moment of landing.

The 1st Battalion Royal Hampshires landed on the beach here and to the east, accompanied by DD tanks and Hobart's Funnies. With the armour ahead of them as they jumped from their landing craft, the soldiers of the Hampshires had the firepower to cover their movement across the sands. The German fire from le Hamel was heavy and the first three CRABS which flailed their way up the beach were bogged down or stopped by an anti-tank gun. A fourth CRAB beat its way into le Hamel giving cover for two companies of the Hampshires to bypass the village and to take Asnelles behind it. Even so it was not until after midday that the area was cleared. The enemy was able to hold out longer here because both the CO and the 2nd in Command of the Hampshires became casualties early on and, therefore, due to lack of central control, no requests were made for naval fire support against the strongpoints.

Continue on the D514.

After some 200 yards there is a small road to the left leading down to the beach and to a large bunker on which are **memorial plaques to the Essex Yeomanry and the 147th (Essex Yeomanry) Field Regiment, RA (Map B33).** The Essex and the Sherwoods came ashore at 0730 with Sherman DD tanks and Sextons, supporting the Hampshires and the Dorsets of 231st Brigade, and were given much trouble by this blockhouse which was eventually knocked out by Sergeant R. E. Palmer, using a 25-pounder self-propelled gun at 300 yards, in an action that won him the Military Medal. Oddly the Official History makes little of the participation of the

Yeomanry regiments in the landings - the Essex are not mentioned at all - and in the various commemorative ceremonies held over the major anniversaries the Yeomans are frequently forgotten. The Sherwood Rangers lost eight DD tanks in the swim to the beach and another four during the day.

It was about one mile to the east along this stretch of beach that No 47 RM Commando landed at 0825 hours, having boarded their LCAs some seven miles offshore. The fourteen LCAs headed in towards Arromanches and had to turn east towards their correct beach at le Hamel, losing four craft in the process. There was considerable confusion at the water's edge with burning vehicles, mined beach obstacles and a strong running tide, not to mention the intense German machine-gun and mortar fire, and the Commandos got mixed up with the Hampshires and the Dorsets who had landed further east at Asnelles and were working their way west. All of this delayed their departure for Port-en-Bessin until the late afternoon, otherwise it might have been taken on D-Day.

Continue to the crossroads in the centre of Asnelles where the D514 meets the Rue de Southampton. Stop by the memorials on the left.

• *Asnelles/Place Alexander Stanier/50th Division, SW Borderers Memorials/Gen de Gaulle Message/21.8 miles/10 minutes/Map B10,11,12,13*

The crossroads area is known as 'Place Alexander Stanier', in honour of the commander of the 231st Infantry Brigade of the 50th Northumbrian Division, Sir Alexander Stanier Bart (sic), DSO MC. At the small road 'Rue The Devonshire Regiment', there is a memorial to the division, the leading brigade of the 231st, and three battalions - the 2nd Battalion Devonshire Regiment, the 1st Battalion Hampshire Regiment and the 1st Battalion the Dorset Regiment. The two assault battalions, the Hampshires and the Dorsets, received 'Normandy' as a battle honour. The Dorsets, landing off the beach here, were out of range of the German guns at le Hamel and, covered by the CRABS and working in conjunction with a variety of AVREs, were off the beach within the hour, having cleared three exits. It was as they moved south-west towards the high ground behind Arromanches, their main objective, that they met members of No 47 RM Commando and encountered opposition from entrenched elements of the 352nd Division. However, by nightfall they had reached Ryes, three miles inland. A memorial surmounted by a metal Cross of Lorraine reproduces Général de Gaulle's message of June 1940. A black marble memorial with inscriptions in English, French and Welsh to the 2nd Battalion the South Wales Borderers who landed at Asnelles on 6 June 1944 was unveiled on 5 June 1994 by Brigadier Sir Nicholas Somerville Bt. [sic]. On the coast here (down a road to the left) is a significant bunker.

Continue along the D514 making particular note of the wet and marshy land between the road and the beach. At the small crossroads just after the sign indicating that you are entering Ver-sur- Mer, stop.

50th Anniversary Parade at the Essex Yeomanry Memorial, Le Hamel.

Memorial to the 2nd Battalion, SW Borderers, Asnelles.

• *KING Sector, GOLD Beach and Stan Hollis VC/24.5 miles*

The German defences here were mainly sited along the line of the road or just south (inland) of it on the high ground. Thus they overlooked the wet and marshy land below, which was mined and traversed by an anti-tank ditch. It was here that Hobart's Funnies really paid off. Without them the infantry might have been stuck, floundering in the soft ground under the eyes of the defenders and without a scrap of cover. The weather was so bad that the DD tanks were not launched, and they and the Funnies were landed directly onto the beach. This assault, scheduled for 0725 hours, was the earliest of the British landings. The small road leading to the sea was an exit from KING Beach where the 6th Battalion Green Howards landed on 6 June 1944.

The main enemy position here was known as the Fleury battery and consisted of four 150mm guns in concrete casemates on Mont Fleury. It was situated in what is now a new housing estate half a mile uphill from where you are and to the west of the exit. The casemates are still there today, though steadily being masked by new houses.

The assault of the 69th Brigade was led by the 6th Battalion Green Howards under Lieutenant-Colonel Robin Hastings. In his force for the landing he had a squadron of the 4th/7th Royal Dragoon Guards with DD tanks, two teams of AVRE and flail tanks (CRABS), one platoon of medium machine-guns of the 2nd Cheshire Regiment and a detachment of Royal Engineers. The front on which the force landed was some 900 yards long and, in addition to the Mont Fleury position, the Germans had half a dozen pillboxes with machine guns and at least one 105mm cannon. Colonel Hastings allocated different tasks to different companies within his battalion, though all had the general purpose of reaching the high ground of the Meauvaines Ridge on the skyline to the south of your present position. D Company was given the task of capturing Mont Fleury.

The Green Howards had boarded their transport ship, the *Empire Lance*, on 1 June and spent their time in physical exercise, cleaning their weapons, attending religious services on deck (General Montgomery's message to them, indeed to his whole force before the invasion, had said, 'Let us pray that "The Lord Mighty in Battle" will go forth with our armies...'), eating and sleeping. They also studied aerial photographs updated daily showing the beach obstacles. Their ship assembled with others of Force G for GOLD off the Solent and after the 24-hour delay everyone was relieved to hear the Navy announce over the Tannoy system at 1700 hours on 5 June, 'At 1745 hours this ship will weigh anchor and, in passage with the remainder of the armada, sail for the coast of France'. At 0315 hours on 6 June reveille was sounded and at 0500 hours seven miles offshore the battalion began climbing into the assault craft that the *Empire Lance* had carried under her davits. As everywhere else along the invasion coast the sea was rough. Very soon everyone was wet and almost everyone was sick. At 0730 hours the leading companies began their final approach to the beach. Overhead thundered the express train shells from HMS *Warspite*, accompanied by the smaller calibre fire of cruisers and destroyers. 25-pounders of the Royal Artillery, firing from landing craft, added their enthusiasm to the affair and in the last few yards came the dragon's roar of the rocket ships, 100 yards out, firing four salvos a minute of ninety rockets each.

The Green Howards had most of their casualties at sea on the run in, including some who drowned, unable to wade the last stretch to the shore after having been dropped too far out. But, despite heavy mortar and machine-gun fire, Captain F.H. Honeyman led 'A' Company across the beach to the sea wall, and there, in a grenade and sten-gun battle, aided by Lance Sergeant H. Prenty and Lance Corporal A. Joyce, cleared the beach of small arms opposition. All three were killed five days later and were posthumously awarded the Military Cross and Military Medals respectively for their action on the beach. Captain Honeyman is buried in the Commonwealth War Graves Commission cemetery at Bayeux.

'D' Company, meanwhile, had come up against mines and deep water and suffered casualties. The company commander, Major R. Lofthouse, rallied his men in conjunction with his CSM, Stan Hollis, and personally led them off the beach and up the road you can see, en route to their objective at Mont Fleury. He too was awarded the Military Cross. CSM Hollis, however, won the VC, the only man to do so on D-Day. His citation reads:

> In Normandy, on June 6th, 1944, during the assault on the beaches and the Mont Fleury battery, CSM Hollis's Company Commander noticed that two of the pill-boxes had been by-passed, and went with CSM Hollis to see that they were clear. When they were twenty yards from the pill-box a machine-gun opened fire from the slit, and CSM Hollis instantly rushed straight at the pill-box, recharged his magazine, threw a grenade in through the door, and fired his Sten gun into it, killing two Germans and making the remainder prisoner. He then cleared several Germans from a neighbouring

trench. By his action he undoubtedly saved his Company from being fired on heavily from the rear, and enabled them to open the main beach exit. Later the same day, in the village of Crépon, the Company encountered a field gun and crew, armed with Spandaus, at a hundred yards' range. CSM Hollis was put in command of a party to cover an attack on the gun, but the movement was held up. Seeing this, CSM Hollis pushed right forward to engage the gun with a PIAT [Projector Infantry Anti-tank] from a house at fifty yards' range. He was observed by a sniper who fired and grazed his right cheek, and at the same moment the gun swung round and fired at point blank range into the house. To avoid the falling masonry CSM Hollis moved his party to an alternative position. Two of the enemy gun crew had by this time been killed, and the gun was destroyed shortly afterwards. He later found that two of his men had stayed behind in the house, and immediately volunteered to get them out. In full view of the

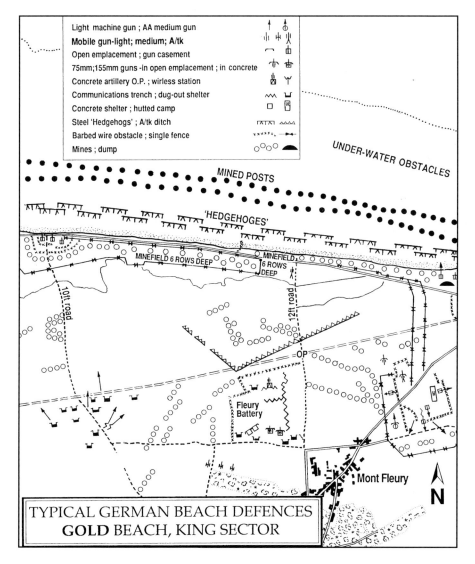

TYPICAL GERMAN BEACH DEFENCES
GOLD BEACH, KING SECTOR

enemy, who were continually firing at him, he went forward alone using a Bren gun to distract their attention from the other men. Under cover of his diversion the two men were able to get back.

Wherever fighting was heaviest CSM Hollis appeared, and in the course of a magnificent day's work he displayed the utmost gallantry, and on two separate occasions his courage and initiative prevented the enemy from holding up the advance at critical stages. It was largely through his heroism and resource that the Company's objectives were gained and casualties were not heavier, and by his own bravery he saved the lives of many of his men.

One of the authors, while at the Army Staff College at Camberley, was fortunate enough to accompany CSM Stan Hollis back to Normandy on a battlefield tour, and to hear at first hand what happened on the beach below you, on the road that passes you and on the ridge above. The citation gives the facts, but the following anecdote gives the man. We make no apologies for the language. This short gem is from Stan's own commentary and illustrates the indomitable spirit of the British soldier and his use of humour as a means of easing tension. We tell it like it was.

As 'D' Company made its way towards France the soldiers were busily arranging ammunition and other supplies into their landing craft.

CSM Hollis described the activities and then said - 'The Company Commander came to me - Major Lofthouse. He was a very good friend of mine. We had been through a lot of war together and had a good working relationship. He gave me a square box and he said, "Give one of these to each of the men Sergeant Major". So I opened it and it was a box of French letters, and I said, "What's to do? Are we going to fight 'em or fuck 'em?"'

CSM Stan Hollis died in the early 1970s and his VC was sold in 1983 for £32,000 (see Crépon entry below).

Continue on the D517 to the crossroads with the D112 in the centre of Ver-sur-Mer (la Rivière) and stop by the memorials.

• Ver-sur-Mer (la Rivière)/Admiral Ramsay's HQ/RA HQ and 2nd Battalion Herts Memorials/25.9 miles/10 minutes/Map B 4,5,6,7,8

This is KING sector, the extreme eastern end of GOLD beach. Here the East Yorkshire Regiment landed alongside the Green Howards, followed by the Hertfordshires.

The D514 continues into JUNO, Love sector. The road leading to the beach is Avénue Colonel J.R. Harper and on the corner is a memorial to the battalion he commanded, the 2nd Battalion Hertfordshire Regiment. Almost opposite, a few yards along the D514 towards JUNO, is a substantial house used by Admiral Sir Bertram Ramsay, Allied Naval Commander in Chief, as a headquarters and there is a memorial plaque on the gate post. An impressive memorial on the opposite corner commemorating the HQ of the Regiments of the Royal Artillery of the 50th Northumbrian Division was dedicated in September 1993. On the road overlooking the beach there is a huge German bunker now used as a sailing equipment store.

Turn right on the Avénue du 6 juin, the D112, direction Crépon. In Ver turn right

Memorial to the Royal Artillery, 50th
Northumbrian Division, Ver-Sur-Mer.

Memorial to the 2nd Battalion,
Hertfordshire Regiment, Ver-sur-Mer.

Memorial to the Green Howards, Crépon.

Detail of the Memorial to the 4th/7th
Royal Dragoon Guards, Creully.

following Centre Ville/Musée signs to the T junction. Turn left.
100 yards to the right at this junction can be seen a sign pointing to the left to
Résidence Les Loges. 100 yards along that road is a blockhouse of the Fleury
Battery.
*Continue and turn left to the America Museum on Rue America and stop in the
Museum car park in Place Amiral Byrd.*

• America-GOLD Beach Museum, Ver-sur-Mer/25.9 miles/15 minutes

The name 'America' refers to the first airmail flight of US airmen Byrd, Acosta,
Balchen and Noville from New York to France in June 1927. Thick fog over their
intended landing area at Paris forced them down at Ver-sur-Mer. Part of the
museum charts the days of the pioneer airmail service and continues with the
advances made in weather forecasting and radio communications. Despite the
logic behind the name, it is ironic that the only museum behind this British beach
is called 'America'. The GOLD Beach section concentrates on the information
gathered by the British Intelligence Services in preparation for the landings. It
commemorates the assaults by the 69th Brigade and the 50th Northumbrian
Division at Ver-sur-Mer.
Open: 1030-1330 and 1430-1730 every day July-August. May, June, September and
October closed on Tuesday. Entrance fee payable. Tel: (0)2 31 22 58 58.

In the square is a **NTL Totem** and in the garden in the centre is an anchor from a 1944
battleship, recovered in 1985.
*Return to the D112 and turn left following signs to Crépon. Follow signs to Centre
Ville and drive round the church to the figure of a seated soldier.*

• Green Howards Memorial/27.9 miles/ 10 minutes Map B29

The figure on this magnificent memorial is popularly supposed to be that of CSM
Stanley Hollis, the only man to win a VC on D-Day, but although a plaque on the
base of the statue tells the story of Hollis's VC, the figure is meant to represent a
soldier of the Green Howards on 6 June 1944 reflecting upon the events of the day.
The men behind the idea of the memorial were the then Colonel of the Regiment,
Field Marshal Sir Peter Inge, and Ian Homersham, who with his friend James
Butler, the sculptor (whose name can be seen inscribed on the figure's right foot),
saw the project through. The whole project cost in the region of £100,000, which
was greatly helped by a substantial donation by Sir Ernest Harrison the Chairman
of Racal Engineering. On 11 November 1997 Sir Ernest also generously donated
Stan's VC to the Green Howards' Museum and in return the Green Howards are
renaming the medal gallery as the Harrison Gallery. The memorial bears the
legend, 'Remember the 6th June 1944', and is dedicated 'To the memory of all the
Green Howards who fought and died in the Second World War'. Their names are
listed in alphabetical order on the pleasingly designed wall behind the statue. The
memorial was unveiled on 26 October 1996 by HM Harald V, King of Norway,

Colonel-in-Chief of the Green Howards. The regiment's connection with the house of Norway dates back to 1875 when Alexandra, then Princess of Wales and a daughter of the Norwegian Royal Family, presented them with new colours. They then became known as 'The Princess of Wales's Own' and their cap badge, designed by Alexandra, incorporated the Cross of Denmark. In 1942 Alexandra's son-in-law, King Haakon VII - a Prince of Denmark who became King of Norway - became Colonel-in-Chief. He was succeeded by his son, King Olav V, and in February 1992 by King Harald, a great-great-grandson of Queen Victoria. The impressive unveiling ceremony was also attended by the Colonel of the Regiment, Brigadier F.R. Dannatt MC, Members of the Green Howards Association, the Corps of Drums of the 1st Battalion, many local dignitaries and Stan Hollis's son and daughter. Built on a site provided by the people of Crépon, the memorial is one of the most beautiful in the whole Normandy area.

In the churchyard here are two RAF graves from 10 June 1944.

Continue on the D65, signed Creully, to the crossroads with the D12. Continue straight over, down the narrow road, and stop just before the bridge over the River Seulles. Look back to your right.

• *The Château at Creullet/30 miles/5 minutes/Map B24*

It was here on 9 June that General Montgomery parked his caravan and set up his Tactical HQ. He met Winston Churchill and Field Marshal Smuts in the grand salon of the château on 12 June, de Gaulle on 14 June and King George VI on 16 June, when they came here after landing at Graye on JUNO Beach. However, shortly after arriving from Portsmouth, General Montgomery found that his caravan lacked one essential item - a chamber pot. An embarrassed ADC was sent to the château, and came back with a small white pot, decorated with pink flowers. On 22 June Montgomery moved to Blay, six miles west of Bayeux, to be nearer the Americans. Presumably the ADC gave the *'vase de nuit'*, as Monty called it, back to Madame de Druval, the owner of the château.

The road that you have followed from Crépon, the D65, is the one taken by the 4th/7th Royal Dragoon Guards on D-Day after landing on GOLD Beach KING sector with the Green Howards. In the early evening the Royal Dragoon Guards lost four tanks on approaching the river and later 1st and 3rd Troops, carrying infantry on their tanks, arrived here just before the bridge over the River Seulles, and found a German Tiger blocking the way. However, the Tiger disappeared and the 4th/7th were able to drive on in cautious single file through the village of Creully without opposition.

Continue over the river and up the hill. Stop at the memorial on the left.

• *4th/7th Royal Dragoon Guards Memorial/30.1 miles/5 minutes/ Map B27*

In 1989 a group of four retired WW2 veterans of the 4th/7th Royal Dragoon Guards decided that there should be a memorial in Normandy to commemorate the part played by the Regiment in the liberation of France and those who gave their lives. After consultation with the French authorities, this site near Creully was chosen, four miles inland from the beach which the 4th/7th assaulted in their DD tanks at H-hour on D-Day. Creully was on the regimental centre line and was liberated by 'A' Squadron on 6 June after fierce fighting, although there was no fighting in the town itself. Sir Peter Shepheard, a past President of the Royal Institute of Architects, offered to design the memorial. Donations were sought from all past and serving members of the Regiment and the result was this fine memorial built with Norman stone by local craftsmen which was completed three years later. It includes the coloured Regimental Crest and the silhouette of a Sherman tank, both in relief, panels of dedication and explanatory notes, together with the story of the 4th/7th's contribution to the Campaign in N.W. Europe, throughout which it suffered 340 casualties, including 124 dead. It was formally unveiled on 6 June 1992 by HRH the Duke of Kent, Colonel-in-Chief, in the presence of 250 Old Comrades and 150 serving officers and men from Detmold, Germany. 'For a few hours the Regimental family was together at one of the scenes of the 4th/7th Royal Dragoon Guards' greatest triumphs', remembers General Sir Robert Ford, a member of the memorial committee and one of only two surviving officers of the 6 June landings.

Continue uphill (past the Old Mill on the River Seulles) and turn left by the French 'Poilu' World War One Memorial into the square in Creully.

• *Creully Château BBC Studio and Plaque/30.9 miles/15 minutes/ RWC/Map B25, 26*

The château was built in 1035, was taken by the English in 1356, reconstructed by Louis XI in 1471, and had a chequered history until bought by the council in 1946. Inside the *Mairie* is part of a Royal Engineers commemorative stone and a bronze plaque with the following inscription, 'During the critical days of June and July 1944, the world listened to news of the Battle of Normandy, broadcast by radio correspondents of many nations from the BBC studio in the tower of this castle.' The BBC set up its studio here on 19 June and it was used by American, Canadian and French broadcasters, the BBC broadcasting not only to the General Forces Programme and the Home Service but also on short wave to the Pacific and Africa. In preparing for its coverage of the invasion the BBC had committed £100,000 of equipment and resources and from 6 June each day the war news was broadcast under the title 'War Report' - more than 725 radio stations around America broadcast the 'War Report' of 6 June. 'War Report' continued until 5 May 1945 except for a short break between 4 February 1945 and 24 March when preparations were being made for the crossing of the Rhine. On D-Day BBC correspondents were distributed throughout the invasion force: -

On 5 June - at Harwell, Richard Dimbleby watching the first paratroops take off
At Supreme HQ - Robert Barr
In a glider - Chester Wilmot
With the paratroops - Guy Byam
On a minesweeper - Stanley Maxted
In a landing craft - Richard North

With the US Navy - Robin Duff
With the 1st US Army - Robert Dunnett

The tower may be climbed and it contains a small museum. You will probably have to ask at the *Mairie* office to be shown these memorials, so visit during normal weekday office hours. Tel: (0)2 31 80 18 65.

There are a couple of restaurants in this attractive little town and a useful supermarket. The church is historic and interesting.

Continue straight through Creully on the D93 towards Tierceville. On meeting the D12 turn right and drive about one hundred yards to the roundabout where there is a memorial.

• *Tierceville Eros/31.4 miles/5 minutes/Map B28*

This copy of Eros, made in cement, was constructed by 179 Special Field Company RE, on 23 August 1944. Owing to a heavy frost it lost a leg, but in 1971 members of the French Resistance restored it with the help of the *Comité du Débarquement*.

This area became an RE enclave from early in the invasion, as the engineers sought to clear roads, mend bridges, demolish obstacles and build airstrips. Some three miles south-east from here is the small village of le Fresne Camilly where it was planned to have a 5,000-yard strip by last light on D+6 (six days after D-Day). The work was the responsibility of 23rd Airfield Construction Group RE which began landing just east of Ver-sur-Mer on JUNO Mike on 7 June. Two officers then set off on bicycles to reconnoitre le Fresne Camilly in anticipation of the arrival of the remainder of the group over the next few days. On 8 June the 88th Road Construction Company staged here. On 9 June 250th Pioneer Company moved in and that evening Group HQ was established here and was immediately attacked by the Luftwaffe. Work on the airstrip had begun on 9 June and the site was completed on 17 June.

Eros probably commemorates the Royal Engineers presence in general and HQ 23rd Airfield Construction Group in particular.

• *End of Itinerary Three*

'Eros', Tierceville.

ITINERARY FOUR

JUNO AND SWORD BEACHES

• **Itinerary Four** starts near Carpiquet Airport, Caen, covers the 3rd Canadian Division's actions on JUNO Beach and inland to Caen and 3rd British Division's landings on SWORD Beach, finishing at Ouistreham.

• **The Route:** Carpiquet; Authie Nova Scotia Highlanders Memorial; Buron - Highland Light Infantry and Sherbrooke Fusiliers Memorials; Villons-le-Buissons - Hells Corner, 9th Canadian Infantry Memorial, Airstrip B16, Norwegian Forces Memorial; Cambes-en-Plaine - CWGC Cemetery; 2nd Battalion the Royal Ulster Rifles Memorial; Anisy Queen's Own Rifles of Canada Memorial; Anguerny Régiment de la Chaudière Memorial; Basly Maple Leaf Memorial; Bény-sur-Mer Régiment de la Chaudière Memorial; Douvres - Radar Station Museum, Blockhouses, CWGC Cemetery; CWGC Bény Canadian Cemetery, Cameron Highlanders Plaque; Reviers, Regina Rifles Memorial; Graye - *Comité du Débarquement* Monument, Churchill AVRE, Cross of Lorraine; Courseulles - Sherman Tank, German Anti-Tank Gun, Memorials to de Gaulle's Landing, Canadian Scottish, Regina and Royal Winnipeg Rifles Regiments and Destroyer *la Combattante*; Bernières - Comité du Débarquement Monument, War Correspondents' Plaque, Bunker with Régiment de la Chaudière, Queen's Own Rifles of Canada, 5th Hackney Battalion the Royal Berks Regiment, Plaques and Memorials; St Aubin - Bunker, North Shore Regiment, No 48 RM Commando, Fort Garry Horse, Duclos Memorials; Langrune - Colas 'Work of War', No 48 RM Commando Memorials; Luc-sur-Mer - No 1 Commando 1941 Memorial; Lion-sur-Mer - No 41 RM Commando Symbolic Sundial, 2nd Battalion Royal Ulster Rifles Churchill Tank, Roosevelt Quotation Memorials, No 1 RM Commando Square, Liberation and 77th Assault Squadron RE Memorials; la Brèche d'Hermanville - S Lancs Regiment, Allied Pioneers/Gooseberry, RA 3rd British Division Sign and Memorials, AVRE Churchill Tank, De Gaulle/Roger Weitzel Memorial; Colleville-Montgomery - General Montgomery Statue, First British Graves/Commandant Keiffer/Anglo-French Forces, Naming of Colleville-Montgomery Memorials: Riva Bella/Ouistreham - No 4 Commando, Commandant Keiffer and ten Commandos Flame Memorial, No 4 Commando Museum, Atlantic Wall Museum, Comité du Débarquement Monument, No 4 Commando Plaque.

• **Extra Visits** are suggested to: Carpiquet Liberation and North Shore Regiment

Memorials; Thaon Fort Garry Horse and Liberation Memorial; La Chaudière/Regina Rifles Memorial, Plaque on Church, Pumping Station, Fontaine Henry; Hermanville CWGC Cemetery, Plaque to Well, 3rd Division Plaque, Medical HQ plaque, Harold Pickersgill Tree; HILLMAN Bunker; Stained Glass Windows to the 51st Division and Commandos, Ouistreham Church.
• **Planned duration,** without stops for refreshments or Extra Visits: **6 hours, 30 minutes**
• **Total distance: 41.3 miles**

BACKGROUND TO JUNO AND SWORD BEACHES
The area covered by these two beaches is included in the same battlefield Itinerary. However, the background to each beach is first dealt with separately.

JUNO BEACH - 3rd CANADIAN DIVISION

Assault Time:	0745 hours
Leading Formations:	6th Armoured Regiment (1st Hussars) DD tanks
	The Royal Winnipeg Rifles
	The Regina Rifle Regiment
	10th Armoured Regiment (Ford Garry Horse)
	DD Tanks
	The Queen's Own Rifles of Canada
	The North Shore (New Brunswick) Regiment
3rd Canadian Division Commander:	Major General R.F.L. Keller
Bombarding Force E:	Cruisers: HMS *Belfast* (flagship)
	HMS *Diadem*
	Eleven destroyers including the
	FFS *Combattante* (French)
German Defenders:	716th Infantry Division
716th Division Commander:	Lieutenant General Wilhelm Richter

The Canadian 3rd Division had been selected to take part in the invasion in July 1943 and trained in assault landings in Scotland and in inter-service co-operation, particularly with the Royal Navy, in the Portsmouth area. Throughout training the 3rd Division worked closely with the 2nd Armoured Brigade which was equipped with DD tanks. On 26 May the Division was sealed into its concentration area and on 1 June 15,000 Canadians and 9,000 British, who together made up the Division, began to board at Southampton. Four days later they set sail for France.

The Plan (See Map 8)
JUNO Beach was divided into two sectors which, looking inland from the sea to the land, were right to left MIKE and NAN. The assault was on a two-brigade front with the 7th Brigade Group landing at Courseulles on MIKE sector and 8th Brigade Group landing at Bernières on NAN sector. Each brigade had DD floating tank support from the 6th Armoured and 10th Armoured Regiments respectively, plus fire support from the 107mm mortars of the Cameron Highlanders of Ottawa. 8th Brigade was to be

closely followed by elements of the 4th Special Service Brigade charged with mopping up, making contact with 3rd British Division Commandos and taking the German radar station at Douvres-la-Délivrande. The 9th Brigade, the follow-up brigade, was scheduled to land in either the 7th or the 8th Brigade areas according to the progress made.

The Canadians' objectives were the capture and clearance of the coastal villages and towns along JUNO Beach, particularly Courseulles, St Aubin and Bernières, and of specific villages inland. The Division had three objective lines, 'Yew', 'Elm' and 'Oak', which corresponded to three phases in their D-Day plan. The third phase was intended to be on 'Oak' which ran along the railway line just south of the N13 road from Caen to Bayeux (see the Holts' map). There the 3rd Division was to 'reorganise in preparation for further advance and to repel enemy counter-attacks'.

What Happened on D-Day
During the night of 5 June, and early morning of 6 June, RAF Bomber Command hammered likely German defence positions along the Normandy coastline. At dawn the US Army Air Force took over and continued the attack until, as everywhere along the invasion front, the Royal Navy joined in. Off JUNO Beach were eleven destroyers and support craft adding their weight to the bombardment including two Canadian destroyers, the *Algonquin* and the *Sioux*.

The crossing for the troops at sea was rough and the time for the assault was put back by ten minutes because the heavy seas had delayed some of the landing craft, but despite considerable opposition from entrenched German positions relatively unaffected by the air and sea bombardments, the Canadians got ashore.

By the end of the day they were practically everywhere beyond 'Elm', their intermediate objective line, and some tanks had crossed 'Oak', but, without infantry support, had withdrawn. General Keller's men had made the greatest gains of all on D-Day, in some places seven miles inland. On their right they had made contact with the 50th Northumbrian Division at Creully, but on their left was a dangerous gap between themselves and the British 3rd Division. Into that gap General Eric Marcks, Commanding the German LXXXIV Corps, ordered Major General Edgar Feuchtinger's 21st Panzer Division (the gap is clearly evident on the Holts' map). South of Caen, that evening, the leading elements of 12th SS Panzer Division began to arrive.

SWORD BEACH - 3rd BRITISH DIVISION

Assault Time:	0725 hours
Leading Formations:	8th Infantry Brigade Group
	13th/18th Hussars DD Tanks
	1st South Lancashire Regiment
	2nd East Yorkshire Regiment
3rd British Division	
Commander:	Major General T.G. Rennie
Bombarding Force D:	Battleships: HMS *Warspite*
	HMS *Ramillies*
	Monitor: HMS *Roberts*

Cruisers:	HMS *Mauritius* (flagship)
	HMS *Arethusa*
	HMS *Frobisher*
	HMS *Danal*
	ORP *Dragon* (Polish)
	13 destroyers including HNMS *Svenner* (Norwegian)
German Defenders:	716th Infantry Division

The 3rd British Division had last been in action at Dunkirk, and most of its soldiers had since then only served on the Home Front. In a way it was similar in its battle experience to the 4th US Division that landed at UTAH Beach. In its training the Division had concentrated upon D-Day, and on the breaking of the Atlantic Wall which it identified with the moment of landing. That moment, because of the variation in the time of the tides between UTAH and SWORD, came one hour after the Americans and ninety minutes after dawn. Therefore the Germans would be both alert to a seaborne assault and able to see the landing craft coming in.

The Plan (See Map 9)
In formulating his plan for 1st British Corps, Lieutenant General Crocker was acutely aware that the 21st Panzer Division was in or around Caen. His eastern flank was well defined by the Orne river and canal and they were to be secured by the Special Service Brigade, plus 6th Airborne Division, but if the 21st Panzer Division reacted quickly and 12th SS Panzer joined them, he would be much inferior in armoured strength and likely to be thrown back into the sea. Thus it was important that the extreme eastern division, the 3rd British Division, should break through the defence crust and move rapidly inland in anticipation of an armoured counter-attack.

The plan of the 3rd British Division Commander, Major General T.G. Rennie, was to attack on a single brigade front on White and Red sectors of QUEEN Beach. The 8th Infantry Brigade Group, the first to land, had a number of tasks: to secure the landing areas; to relieve 6th Airborne Division at Pegasus Bridge; No 4 Commando to clear east to Ouistreham; No 41 Royal Marine Commando to clear west to the Canadians at Langrune; and 1st Special Service Brigade to move east across Pegasus Bridge. Following up was the 185th Infantry Brigade Group. Their task was to pass through 8th Brigade and to 'seize Caen' - the most ambitious aim of all.

What Happened on D-Day
Naval Force S for SWORD gathered off the beach in the early hours of 6 June. Just before daylight a smoke screen was laid by aircraft between the ships and the coastal batteries at le Havre. In the morning gloom, thickened with smoke, four German E-Boats appeared, fired torpedoes and vanished. The *Warspite* and the *Ramillies* had narrow misses but the Norwegian destroyer *Svenner* was hit and sank. That was all that Admiral Ramsay's invasion fleet saw of the German Navy on D-Day.

The bombardment followed the pattern employed everywhere else, though SWORD probably had the most intensive attention of all of the beaches, and was concentrated on a strip 3 miles long and $1/2$ mile deep.

Despite the rough seas, the DD tanks of the 13th/18th Hussars and the LCT-borne 'Funnies' of the Engineer Assault Teams hit the beaches ahead of the LCAs of the infantry. Of the twenty-five tanks launched, twenty-one made the shore and these, together with the flail tanks of 22nd Royal Dragoons, gave immediate fire support to the infantry battalions.

Although the landing craft suffered considerable casualties from Teller mines on the beach obstacles, for almost five hours the landing sequence went pretty well to plan. The rising tide, however, reduced the beach to a width of 30 yards and this caused congestion and confusion so that follow-up landings had to be delayed.

The South Lancashire and East Yorkshire Regiments were off the beaches within an hour, though stubborn German resistance continued in la Brêche, the centre of the landing beach, until around 1030 hours. The 185th Infantry Brigade began coming ashore mid-morning and passed through the 8th Brigade, but enemy resistance on the Periers Ridge, between Douvres and Bénouville, prevented rapid movement inland.

By the end of the day the 2nd Battalion King's Shropshire Light Infantry, part of 185th Brigade, whose task it had been to ride on the tanks of the Staffordshire Yeomanry into Caen on 6 June, were still four miles short. Another forty-three days would pass before Caen fell.

THE TOUR

•*Carpiquet/0 miles*

Take the D220 Carpiquet/Authie exit from the N13.

Extra Visit to the Liberation and North Shore Regiment Memorials, Carpiquet (Map H14,15). Round trip: 2.4 miles. Approximate time: 15 minutes.

Turn right, direction Airport, and continue on the D14 over the traffic lights on Avénue Charles de Gaulle. Turn right at the second traffic lights, direction Tilly/Caen-Carpiquet. Continue towards the next traffic lights. Just before, on the right, is the

Monument dedicated to the memory of officers and men of the **North Shore "New Brunswick" Regiment, 3rd Canadian Division** and the **People of Normandy**, erected by the North Shore Veterans' Association in 1986. Beside it is a **NTL Totem,** with a comprehensive description of the action here by the Canadian 9th Brigade to take Carpiquet, and the fierce counter-attack of the 12th SS ('Hitler Youth'). It

---

Extra visit continued

also describes the action of Operation WINDSOR in early July when the 8th Canadian Brigade led the assault with flame-throwing tanks, support from 21st Artillery Regiment, Typhoon fighter-bombers and the guns of HMS *Rodney*. The airfield was defended by a squadron of Panther tanks and a company of 12th SS Grenadiers. During the fighting, which lasted until 8 July, the Canadians lost 377 men, including 117 killed.

Continue over the traffic lights for about 100 metres to the ruin of a stone arch on the right.

On it there is a black marble plaque to the **Fort Garry Horse** and below a brass plaque in memory of 4 July 1944 and expressing the homage of the Commune of Carpiquet to its **Canadian Liberators**.

Return to the N13 and rejoin the main itinerary.

Continue to Authie on the D220

On entering the town the white JUNO Itinerary sign with red lettering erected at the entrance to each town and village on the JUNO Routes (see the Holts' map where they are indicated by red maple leaf signs and red lettering) and the typical 'twinning' sign (with North Baddesley, Hampshire) are passed. The road here is dedicated to Henri Brunet, 1902-1943, Fusillé.

Continue to the memorial on the left opposite the Mairie.

•Nova Scotia Highlanders Memorial, Authie/1.1 miles/ 10 minutes/ Map H18

This memorial commemorates the Nova Scotia Highlanders who in fighting around the village on 7 June lost 84 men. In addition to the dead, the Nova Scotians lost 158 men wounded or taken prisoner. The Sherbrooke Rifles had 60 dead. 7 Citizens were also killed. Beside it is a **NTL Totem** describing the Canadians' progress from JUNO Beach to Buron on 7 June. Here in Authie leading elements of the Highlanders were attacked by Colonel Kurt Meyer's fanatical SS Units which pressed forward regardless of their losses. Meyer had taken over the Abbaye d'Ardenne, 1,500 metres south east of here and whose owners had been arrested the year before as members of the Resistance, as the HQ for his 25th SS Panzergrenadier Regiment of Fritz Witt's 12th SS (Hitler Youth) Panzer Division. He found its old tower an excellent vantage point from which to watch the Canadians moving inland from JUNO.

The severity of the losses was compounded by reports that Canadian prisoners had been shot by SS troops. These and other murders formed the basis for charges made against Meyer by a Canadian Military Court in December 1945. He was found guilty on three of five charges (on a charge of responsibility for twenty-three murders in the Buron area on 7 June 1944 he was acquitted) and sentenced to be shot. However, the sentence was commuted to life imprisonment and he was released in 1954. A chilling account of the shooting on 8 June of seven Canadian prisoners of war in the grounds of

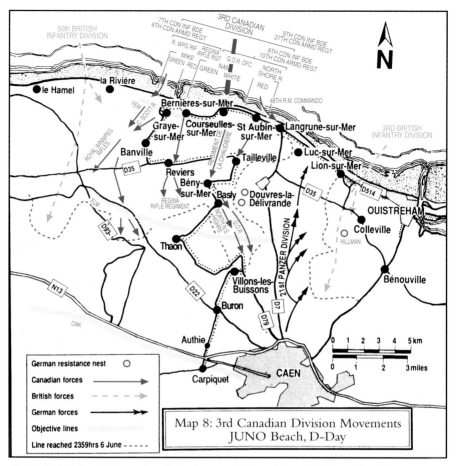

Map 8: 3rd Canadian Division Movements
JUNO Beach, D-Day

German resistance nest ○
Canadian forces
British forces
German forces
Objective lines
Line reached 2359hrs 6 June - - - -

Typical JUNO Route marker/Twinning sign, Authie.

Memorial to the Nova Scotia Highlanders, Authie.

the Abbaye was given at Meyer's trial. They were called out one by one by name, led into the garden and shot in the back of the head. They had guessed what was to happen to them and each man had shaken hands with the others as his name was called. However, the shooting of prisoners was not confined to the SS and there is no doubt that many SS were killed in that way which thus accounts for why so few ever turned up in the prisoner-of-war cages.

Continue on the D220 to the Mairie square in Buron.

•*North Nova Scotia Highlanders and Sherbrooke Fusiliers Memorials, Buron/2 miles/10minutes/Map H19,20*

The D220 road, down which you have driven, was a main axis for the Canadian forces moving inland from JUNO. It leads directly to the high ground at Carpiquet Airport three miles behind you which was the special visit at the start of this itinerary. Carpiquet was the objective of the follow-up, 9th Brigade Group. At the end of D-Day the Canadians had reached Villons-le-Buissons, $3^1/2$ miles north of here, and by around 0700 hours on 7 June the 9th Brigade, led by the North Nova Scotia Highlanders and the 27th Armoured Regiment (Sherbrooke Fusiliers), was advancing towards Buron. Just north of the village they came under fire from machine guns and anti-tank weapons, and a set-piece battle followed in which Canadians and Germans fought from house to house. It was not until midday that the village was secured. Meanwhile

Memorial to the Sherbrooke Fusiliers, Buron.

troops of the Highlanders and Sherbrookes not involved at Buron had pushed on to the edge of Carpiquet. The 9th Brigade was dangerously extended and, unknown to them, they were being watched by Kurt Meyer from the Abbaye.

At 1500 hours Meyer launched a counter-attack on Buron, hoping to drive to the sea in conjunction with 21st Panzer Division. Late in the afternoon the Canadians lost Buron and fell back to Villons-le-Buissons where they had begun the day. It had been a bloody struggle. The Highlanders had some 250 casualties and the Sherbrookes lost 21 cruiser tanks.

The battle for the high ground of Carpiquet was to be a long and hard one against fanatical troops of the 12th SS Panzer Division. It had been created in 1943 from elements of the 1st SS (Leibstandarte Adolf Hitler) Division and though it had not been in battle before it had a high proportion of experienced officers and NCOs from the Russian Front. The bulk of the soldiers were youngsters under 18 years old straight out of military fitness camps and full of Nazi ideology. In all, the division, which was initially commanded by Brigadeführer Fritz Witt, had about 20,000 men and 150 tanks. It was a formidable fighting force and it held on to Buron and Carpiquet for another month.

At 0420 hours on 8 July a combined five-phase British and Canadian assault was launched in the direction of Carpiquet, and once again the 9th Brigade advanced on Buron. As the second phase began the Highland Light Infantry of Canada and the Sherbrookes led off at 0730 hours and by 0830 hours were in the village. The 12th SS Panzer Division, now commanded by Kurt Meyer following Fritz Witt's death on 14 June, fought with the determination expected of them and it was not until early the following morning that the last SS man had been found and silenced. The Highland Light Infantry lost half of its attacking force in what had been its first real battle and it was to prove its bloodiest of the campaign with 262 casualties. The CO, Lieutenant-Colonel F.M. Griffiths, was wounded and later received the DSO for his actions on that day.

There are memorials to the Highland Light Infantry and to the Sherbrooke Fusiliers here. The area is known as the Place des Canadians, and the Highland memorial was dedicated on 21 July 1969. The Sherbrooke memorial explains the origin of the name: '...recruited from the city of Sherbrooke Quebec Canada'.

Continue on the D220 over the D22 crossroads and head north towards Villons-les-Buissons. At the first road junction left, just short of the village, stop.

•Hell's Corner/9th Canadian Infantry Memorial, Villons-les-Buissons/3.2 miles/5 minutes/Map H22

Here is the memorial to the 9th Canadian Infantry (Highland) Brigade that fought so determinedly between here and Buron from 6 June to 8 July. It was dedicated on 8 June 1984. As the Canadian 9th Brigade cleared Villons they captured a German 88mm gun and a six-barrelled mortar, something that they had not seen before. The small road leading to the left is the Rue des Glengarrians.

Continue to the Villons-les-Buissons village sign. Stop on the left.

•B-16 Airstrip Memorial, Villons-les-Buissons/3.5 miles/5 minutes/Map H23

This commemorates the British and Norwegian units of the 84th Group 2nd TAF who were based here. The memorial gives details of the layout of the airstrip. The Group was commanded by Air Vice- Marshal L. O. Brown and consisted of 10 Wings, two of which were Polish, one was Czechoslovakian, one French and one Norwegian. The Norwegian Squadrons, 331 and 332, flew Spitfires. In 135 Wing was a Belgian squadron and a New Zealand squadron each also flying Spitfires.

Continue into the village along the Rue des Sherbrooke Fusiliers and take the first turning right on rue des Cambes along the château wall towards the junction with the D79. Stop on the left just before the junction.

•Norwegian Memorial, Villons-les-Buissons/4.3 miles/5 minutes/Map H24

The Norwegian memorial has splendid bas relief panels representing the invasion and the naval action and is dedicated to the memory of the Norwegian fighters from 1940 to 1945. The only Allied naval casualty from attacks by German naval forces on D-Day was the Royal Norwegian Navy destroyer *Svenner*. Immediately prior to the initial bombardment on D-Day allied aircraft had laid a smoke screen between the bombarding warships of Force 'D' and the German batteries at le Havre. Out of that smoke screen at 0530 hours four German torpedo boats suddenly appeared - whether by design or by accident is not known. They fired torpedoes and then quickly turned back to le Havre. Two of the torpedoes passed between HMS *Warspite* and HMS *Ramillies*, HMS *Largs*, the HQ ship for SWORD area, avoided another, but a fourth hit the *Svenner* in the boiler room. There was a great cloud of steam, her funnel collapsed and she broke her back. Eye-witnesses recorded that her crew fell in on deck in perfect discipline before they had to jump for their lives.

Continue over the junction into Cambes-en-Plaine. Turn left at the first junction and continue to the Cemetery on the right.

• Cambes-en-Plaine CWGC Cemetery/5.1 miles/15 minutes/Map H25

This unusual cemetery has no enclosing wall or hedge as is traditional with CWGC Cemeteries and has a 'modern' yellow Caen stone entrance complex. More than half the 224 burials in this cemetery are of the North and South Staffordshire Regiments from the fighting of 8 and 9 July in the final assault on Caen. Many of the personal inscriptions here are almost unbearably moving in their simple expressions of close family grief at the loss of a dear one. The 6th North Staffords had passed through this area on 9 July having had 190 casualties (a quarter of their strength) in their first two days in action. Lieutenant Brown, second in command of the 6-pounder anti-tank platoon of 6th North Staffords, recalled his own entry into the combat:-

I came across a still smouldering Tiger Tank. Lying alongside was a boot with the foot

The unusual entrance to Cambes-en-Plaine CWGC Cemetery.

Detail, Hell's Corner Memorial, Villons-les-Buissons.

Memorial to the 2nd Battalion, the Royal Ulster Rifles, Cambes-en-Plaine.

Memorial to Basly's Canadian Liberators.

and stump of a charred leg still attached. Over all hung a most appalling smell, from the grotesque carcases of bloated cattle and horses lying in the fields. Then I came face to face with a steel-helmeted German, head and shoulders out of a slit trench, rifle pointing straight at me. In sheer panic, I fired several times with my revolver but when there was no reply advanced cautiously. I need not have worried, he had been dead for some hours. The poor fellow's intestines were hanging from a gaping hole in his stomach.

Continue to the T junction. On the right at the corner is

• 2nd Battalion Royal Ulster Rifles Memorial/5.2 miles/5 minutes/Map H33

The Battalion captured the village of Cambes-en-Plaine on 9 June and the memorial is a tribute to those who 'gave their lives in Normandy in the cause of freedom 6 June-19 September 1994.' It bears the regimental badge and the words, 'We will remember them'. Cambes was one of the strongest German positions on this part of the front and had repulsed a 9th Brigade attack on 7 June. The successful attack two days later was made in conjunction with the East Riding Yeomanry over some 1000 yards of flat open land while being mortared and machine-gunned. Although casualties were almost 200 and four tanks were lost, the village was taken, and later that day re-inforced by the King's Own Scottish Borderers. The taking of Cambes secured the junction between the British and Canadian forces.

The road here is called Rue du Lieutenant Lynn 8 juillet 1944.

Turn left up the small road and at the crossroads turn right signed Mathieu D220. After 200 yards stop at the memorial on the left.

• Queen's Own Rifles of Canada Memorial, Anisy/6.2 miles/5 minutes/Map H32

The stone memorial, with a cut-out maple leaf in the centre, remembers the members of the regiment who gave their lives to take and hold Anisy, their D-Day objective. It was unveiled on 6 June 1994.

Continue to the roundabout and turn left signed Anguerny. At the junction turn left on the D141 and continue into the village, past the church to the junction with the D141/D141A. Stop by the Mairie. On the left hand corner is

• Memorial to the Régiment de la Chaudière, Anguerny's Liberators/7.9 miles/5 minutes

The black marble plaque lists seven members of the regiment who died on 6 and 8 June 1944.

Turn right direction Basly on the D141A on rue Régiment de la Chaudière, 6 juin 1944. Continue to the junction with the D79 and turn right. Continue into the village and stop at the memorial by the Church.

• *Maple Leaf Memorial, Basly/9.5 miles/5 minutes/Map C30*

This was erected on 8 June 1991 by the citizens of Basly in gratitude to their Canadian liberators.

Extra Visit to the Fort Garry Horse and Liberation Memorial, Thaon (Map H30) and the Canadian Memorial and Plaque and Moulinaux Pumping Station, Fontaine Henry (Map C28,29). Round trip:15.6 miles. Approximate time: 50 minutes.

Take the D83 signed Thaon and enter the village past the château on the right and follow the winding road through the village to La Place de la Crié. Stop at the memorial, Place de la Crié.

The plaque on a small stone commemorates the liberation of the village by the **10th Armoured Regiment (Fort Garry Horse)** in support of the **8th Canadian Infantry Brigade** on 6th June 1944. In the same way that it is unwise to be dogmatic about battle casualty figures, whether of men or equipment, it is unwise to assert that a particular place, house or person was 'liberated' at a specific time. The French remain enthusiastically grateful for their Liberation in 1944-5 and a vigorous internal contest has developed between claimants to being the 'first'. Failing the possibility of being a contender for a 'first' the next best thing is to have been liberated on D-Day, 6 June. Thaon says 'thank you for Liberation on 6 June', while official Canadian records suggest that it was not occupied until 7 June.

The village is just south of 'Elm', the intermediate objective, and in the general line of advance of the 9th Infantry Brigade Group on 7 June. The Régiment de la Chaudière, part of 8th Infantry Brigade Group, came ashore at Bernières on NAN White just before 0830 hours on 6 June, supported by two DD squadrons of the 10th Armoured Regiment (Fort Garry Horse). By midnight the Chaudières had reached Bény four miles north of here and there can be little doubt that elements of their brigade had entered Thaon, but the main body of the force spent the night north of the village, i.e. nearer the landing beaches. The 9th Brigade had followed the 8th onto the beach at Bernières and pushed on early on 7 June into the actions at Buron.

Continue to the crossroads with the D170 and turn right direction Fontaine Henry. Continue to the church and stop on the left.

Above the parking area is a grey marble memorial with a flagpole behind to **'The First Hussars, La Chaudière, Regina Rifles, 13th RCA and RCEME:** Fontaine Henry remembers.' On the side wall of the church to the left of the entrance is a well-weathered plaque to the **Canadian Heroes who fell at Fontaine Henry. 12 are listed by name.**

Continue past the château on the right.

The 15th/16th Century Château here boasts the highest roof in France and the fact that it has never been sold. For visits apply to the owner, M. D'Ouilliamson. Tel: (0)2 31 80 00.

Extra visit continued

Continue to the T junction and turn left on the D141 signed Creully/Courseulles to the junction with the D170. Turn right signed Reviers and just before the exit sign to Fontaine Henry turn right past house No 14. Stop at the first small house on the right and ask permission to see

The Pumping Station, Moulinaux. Note that it is in private land. This stone structure was built to supply Airstrip B16 at Villons-le-Buissons. The signs *CARPE DIEM* and 'JULY 1944' can still be clearly seen on its walls. As early as December 1942 the selection of suitable airfield sites had begun. In the planning stage it was thought that more than 90 airfields would be needed to sustain the invasion over the first three months, 27 of which were to be in Normandy. By 30 June, 10 British and 7 American had been completed, the first being that at St Laurent behind OMAHA beach. Initially this was an 'ELS', the most junior of landing facilities of which there were, in order of ascending facilities, five types -

ELS - Emergency Landing Strip. A minimum length of 1,800 feet being just enough to enable emergency landings.

RRS - Re-fuelling and Re-arming Strip. A minimum length of 3,600 feet of compact surface with turning and marshalling areas.

ALG - Advanced Landing Ground. Similar to an RRS but with dispersal facilities and the ability to handle greater weights of traffic

Airfield - Similar to an ALG but with facilities that allowed squadrons to be based there, rather than operate on the 'fly-in, fly-out' system.

All-Weather Airfield. The same as an Airfield but with all-weather facilities and hard surfaced runways.

The distinction of being the first British squadron to land in France since Dunkirk is claimed both by 130 and 303 Squadron. They landed at B3, Ste Croix sur Mer in the Canadian sector behind Courseulles, at 1200 hours on 10 June. In 1994 a memorial was inaugurated there to mark the airfield.

Turn round and return to the junction with the D141 signed Colombey sur Thaon. Turn left and continue to the crossroads and turn left on the D83. Return to to Basly. Rejoin the main itinerary.

Continue on the D79 to Bény sur Mer. Stop in the Place de l'Eglise.

• *Régiment de Chaudière Memorial, Bény/10.6 miles/5 minutes/Map C32*

'Bény thanks the Canadians for Liberation on 6 June: *Reconnaissance aux soldats Canadiens du Régiment de la Chaudière qui Liberèrent ce village 6 Juin 1944. Bény s/Mer. Aleppo.'* Canadians and French agree about Bény and HQ 8th Brigade actually signalled the Chaudières at 1535 hours on D-Day: 'Understand you are in Aleppo'. 'Aleppo' was the codename for Bény. The Advanced Landing Ground B4 was in the area between here and the next stop and the first aircraft to use it was a damaged Spitfire which crash-landed on 12 June. The Rhodesian pilot finished most of the bottle of whisky belonging

List of Canadians killed at Fontaine-Henry, on church wall.

RCAF Memorial at Airstrip B4. Bény.

Radar Museum, Douvres.

to the CO of the RE unit building the strip. Two days later it was ready for full use. At the junction some 800 yards ahead and across the main road is a memorial to **401, 411 and 412 Squadrons of the Royal Canadian Air Force** who flew Spitfires from B4 as part of 126 Wing. (Map C31).

Turn round and go past the church, turning left immediately on the Route de Douvres. Cross the D404 and continue on the C301 to Douvres-Tailleville. At the junction with the D219 go straight ahead signed Douvres. Continue to a cart track to the left (11.9 miles). Stop.

At the end of the track are impressive bunkers. Ahead to the left are the twin spires of Douvres Church and to the right the radar dish of the Radar Museum can be seen.

You are in the centre of what was the **German radar station**. It was mainly manned by the Luftwaffe with about 200 men and 5 officers. The site covered a large area some 300 yards to your left and right. According to the time of year and state of the crops it is possible to see the remains of the northern blockhouses in the field to the left. There were two steel towers supporting the radar antennae, power coming from underground diesel generators. All-round defence was effected by minefields and barbed wire and the strong points were connected by tunnels. As can probably be seen, the position is on high ground and allows good observation over routes from the sea to the left and to Caen $7^1/_2$ miles away to the right.

The task of taking the radar station was allocated to the North Shore (New Brunswick) Regiment. It had reached the village of Tailleville, barely a mile north of here, on the night of 6 June but when it moved off at 0700 hours on 7 June it met heavy opposition in the woods on the far side of the field to the left (north). Late in the afternoon the attack was abandoned and responsibility passed to the 51st Highland Division. That evening the 5th Battalion Black Watch attacked the station but made no impression, but unfortunately it seems that the Black Watch and the New Brunswicks may have briefly fought each other.

Entrance porch, Douvres-la-Délivrande CWGC Cemetery.

The station position, stretched along the 50-metre contour line, is plumb in the middle of the gap that existed between the British and Canadian armies, (see the Holts' map - 'approx front lines midnight 6 June') the gap that the 21st Panzer Division had its eyes on. At 1500 hours on 6 June, Major General Edgar Feuchtinger's 21st Panzer Division, led by its Panzers, was advancing in two columns towards the beaches east of Douvres. Attentions from the British 3rd Division stayed the bulk of 21st Panzer but a small force of infantry and tanks reached Luc-sur-Mer to find their defences there still intact. The Canadians steeled themselves for a major assault as the Germans attempted to exploit the corridor separating the two divisions, but the follow-up armada of 250 gliders for 6AB Division arrived at 2100 hours and by the time that Feuchtinger had figured out where they had landed it was too dark to attack.

The radar station overlooked the corridor and General Dempsey, commanding the 2nd British Army, considered it essential that it should be taken so that his forces were not being watched and reported upon. On 7 June the 51st Highland Division tried again, supported by 80th Assault Squadron RE, but failed. On 11 June No 48 RM Commando had a look at it but moved on without making a full assault.

Eventually a combat group of one squadron of 22nd Dragoons, No 41 RM Commando and 26th Assault Squadron RE attacked uphill towards you from the village of Douvres ahead (with its twin church spires). Diversionary attacks were also made from the three other points of the compass. Four flail tanks led the way through the minefield, each followed by three AVREs. Heavy artillery gave covering fire. High explosive charges were laid against the blockhouses and the Commandos went in under cover of smoke. It was a short, furious battle, and the Germans raised the white flag. Eight tanks were damaged, but repairable, four AVREs were written off. Casualties were less than a dozen. Yet it was 17 June, almost 2 weeks after D-Day. The blockhouse Hillman (qv) also held up the Allies.

— Continue to the junction and turn right. Continue to the Museum parking area on the right.

• Douvres Radar Station Museum/13.1 miles/20 minutes/Map C33

The museum is housed in two remarkably well-preserved bunkers and charts the evolution of radar. In front of it are a **NTL Totem** and a red marble **plaque to M Raymond Laville**, 1923-1996, the instigator of the museum.
Open: during the season (April-September). Entrance fee payable. Tel: (0)2 31 06 06 45.

Continue to the D404 and turn left signed Caen. Continue to the roundabout and turn left signed Douvres. Continue to the CWGC Cemetery on the right. (There is room to pull in on the left, or more parking space round the corner to the right.)

•La Délivrande CWGC Cemetery, Douvres/15.2 miles/15 minutes/ Map C8

The cemetery contains 1,123 burials of which 927 are British, 11 Canadian, 3 Australian, 180 German, 1 unidentified and 1 Pole. He is Mat L. Grzestak of the Polish Forces, died 'August 1944'. His grave stands isolated from the rows of headstones.

From the pleasing design of the Caen stone entrance complex (covered in wistaria in the summer) a tree-lined central avenue leads to the Cross of Sacrifice.

Continue to the Rond Point de l'Europe.

The road to the left leads to the large square in front of the Post Office where there is an impressive local war memorial and a new memorial to Douvres' civilian dead of 1944. On the right of the roundabout is the conveniently placed Le Relais restaurant and pizzeria.

Go straight over the roundabout on the D7 and continue to the traffic lights. Turn left signed Langrune and follow the one-way system right around the church and turn right signed Bayeux and then keep left signed Tailleville. Continue to the roundabout. Go straight over on the D35. Continue. Enter Tailleville and continue to the square with a large local memorial in the centre.

• *Tailleville/17.8 miles*

The road you have entered on is the Rue de la Chaudière and the square is Place du Royal North Shore Regiment, named in honour of Tailleville's liberators.

This small village is at the end of the main exit road from NAN White at Bernières. When the 9th Brigade landing beach was chosen to be in the 8th Brigade area the only suitable spot was NAN White and the whole of the follow-up force had to come ashore there. The task of clearing Tailleville had been given to C Company of the North Shore Regiment but stubborn resistance by the 736th Grenadier Regiment, whose HQ was in the village, prevented its capture until 2010 hours on 6 June, thus delaying the deployment of the 9th Brigade.

Turn left at the T junction with the D35 towards Reviers, crossing the D79. Stop at the cemetery on the right.

• *Canadian CWGC Cemetery, Cameron Highlanders of Ottawa Memorial/Bény-sur-Mer/19.7 miles/20 minutes/Map C25,26*

This is the highest point for some miles around and there are two watch-towers from which excellent views may be obtained towards Courseulles and JUNO Beach. At the bottom of the left-hand tower is a memorial tablet to the Cameron Highlanders of Ottawa. There are 2,049 graves in the cemetery, 2,044 of which are Canadian, including 335 officers and men of the 3rd Canadian Division who were killed on D-Day. Among them are nine pairs of brothers - Blais, Boyd, Branton, Hadden, Hobbin, Mekin, Skwarchuk, Tadgell and White. There are three Westlake brothers - Rifleman T.L, of the Queen's Own Rifles of Canada age 33 and Rifleman A.N., age 26 of the same regiment, both killed on 11 June and buried side by side in Plot III Row D and Private George, of the Nova Scotia Highlanders, killed on 7 June who is in Plot VIII Row F12. The British and Commonwealth Forces did not at this stage have the same policy of trying to separate close relations as did the Americans (giving rise to the story of 'Private Ryan', qv). Also buried here is Lieutenant Edward Frank Mantle of the 5th Anti-Tank Regiment, RCA, killed on 2 August. His father, Major Alfred Mantle, was killed in the First World War on 26 September 1916.

Entrance wall, Bény CWGC Canadian Cemetery.

General view, CWGC Canadian Cemetery, Bény.

Headstones of two of the three Westlake brothers buried at Bény.

Plaque to the Cameron Highlanders of Ottawa, Bény CWGC Cemetery.

1939 1945

THIS PLAQUE COMMEMORATES
THE CAMERON HIGHLANDERS OF OTTAWA (MG)
WHO FELL IN THE LANDINGS ON D DAY
AND IN THE ENSUING BATTLES
FOR THE LIBERATION OF EUROPE

CETTE PLAQUE HONORE LA MEMOIRE
DES OFFICIERS ET SOLDATS DU REGIMENT
DES CAMERON HIGHLANDERS D'OTTAWA (MIT)
TOMBES AU COURS DU DEBARQUEMENT EN EUROPE
ET DES COMBATS QUI S'ENSUIVIRENT
POUR SA LIBERATION

Continue towards the village of Reviers and as the road enters the village there is a road junction to the left with a small memorial.

• Regina Rifle Regiment Memorial, Reviers/22.1 miles/5 minutes /Map C26

The small plaque and stone are to the Regina Rifle Regiment who liberated Reviers on D-Day. They and their fellow regiment of the 7th Brigade, the Royal Winnipeg Rifles, moved rapidly off the beach at Courseulles and by mid-morning were two miles inland. The Reginas had the specific task of seizing the crossings over the River Seulles which lie at the bottom of this hill. By 7 June they were astride the N13 at Bretteville-l'Orgueilleuse, west of Carpiquet. The following morning they had a head-on battle with Meyer's 12th SS Division at Bretteville when one of the German Panthers got to battalion HQ, where it was knocked out by a PIAT (Projector, Infantry, Anti-tank). Although they were over-run they held their ground and the Germans withdrew.

Continue on the D176/35 and immediately after crossing the River Seulles turn right towards Banville on the C1. In the village turn right onto the D12 signed Courseulles and at Graye-sur-Mer turn left just before the river. Follow signs to Centre Ville and Croix de Lorraine. (Do not take to the road to Courseulles). Turn right at the War Memorial following the Croix de Lorraine sign. At the junction with the D514 coast road go straight across towards the beach and a tank in the dunes, signed la Brèche de Graye/Croix de Lorraine along Avénue Général de Gaulle.

On the corner on the left is a **sign listing the VIPs who landed here.**

• Graye Churchill Tank/Comité du Débarquement Monument /Cross of Lorraine/26.2 miles/15 minutes/Map B1,2,3

By the *Comité du Débarquement* Signal Monument is a Churchill tank AVRE with a petard. Both are at the junction of the Green (left) and Red (right) sectors of MIKE Beach where the Royal Winnipeg Rifles came ashore together with elements of the 6th Canadian Armoured Regiment. They were to suffer 128 casualties, the second heaviest Canadian regimental casualties of the day. Accompanying the Canadians were the 1st and 2nd Troops of the 26th Assault Squadron Royal Engineers charged with clearing exits off the beach through the obstacles and the dunes. The leading AVRE touched down about 0755 hours, somewhat behind the DD tanks and assault infantry. Using flails and bridge-layers, the squadron began to work its way through the wire and the mines and between the bunkers whose remains can still be seen.

At this exit there was an anti-tank ditch and just south of it a flooded culvert connected to the River Seulles which barred the way inland. 2nd Troop's fascine tank dropped its bundle into the tank trap and 1st Troop went over it to the culvert.

This tank, commanded by Bill Dunn, slid down into the flooded culvert. Water poured into the tank, so the crew scrambled out and, escorted by another tank, made their way back to the dunes, where they lay down behind a sandbank. There they were hit by mortar bombs and Sappers Manley, Philips and Batson were killed. That afternoon the two survivors, Bill Dunn and Bill Hawkins, were evacuated to England. Six days later Winston Churchill landed here, followed by HM King George V1 on 16 June.

The sunken tank was incorporated into the exit road and there it stayed until 1976 when it was recovered by the citizens of Graye with help from British REs and REMEs and the 70-ton crane of Monsieur Desmezière, a local contractor. The ceremony inaugurating the tank as a memorial was attended by both survivors. Below the tank is a plaque, erected in 1994, describing the story of the tank, which is called 'One Charlie'.

In the dunes above is a large metal Cross of Lorraine, below which is a **NTL Totem** on the back of which is the story of the the the Ost truppen - an artillery unit of Russian troops who held out in the open air sanatorium here for 24 hours fom 6-7 June. It also describes how on 14 June General de Gaulle first went to see General Montgomery at Creully and then used the short journey to Bayeux and Isigny to assert the authority of the provisional Government of the French Republic.

1^1/$_2$ miles west, by the remains of a large German bunker, is the boundary between JUNO (where you are now) and GOLD Beaches.

Return to the D514 and turn left towards Courseulles. Cross the River Seulles and continue to the narrow swing bridge and immediately before it turn right following the one-way system around the harbour towards the Maison de la Mer. Three hundred yards later stop near a Sherman tank in Place Général de Gaulle.

• *Courseulles Memorials/27.5 miles/20 minutes/Map C20,21,22,23,24*

This seaside town where the River Seulles reaches the sea was the aiming point for the 7th Canadian Infantry Brigade Group. Its task was to clear Courseulles and move rapidly inland to gain the crossings over the River Seulles. In a leap-frogging operation, including the possible use of the 9th Brigade the follow-up force, the Canadians' target was the high ground around Carpiquet just south of the N13. The landing at Courseulles was complicated by the fact that there were reefs offshore and that in order to carry the landing craft over these a higher tide than desirable was needed if the obstacles were to be seen. The bad weather delayed the assault for some thirty minutes and most of the infantry landed ahead of the tanks, although the latter were launched only 800 yards out. The delay in the arrival of the tanks might have been greater but for the initiative of some of the DD tank commanders, like Sergeant Leo Gariepy of B Squadron, who launched on their own initiative. Gariepy was probably the first to land.

The assault battalion here, east of the Seulles, was the Regina Rifles and A and B Companies hit the shore about 0800 hours. They were immediately fired upon from concrete strongpoints apparently unaffected by the pre-invasion bombardments. The following companies lost many men as their assault craft hit mined obstacles some 200 yards out to sea and the Canadians had a hard struggle to get ashore. Operating to a detailed plan in which Courseulles had been divided up into twelve zones of responsibility, the Reginas, helped by the tanks of the 1st Hussars, (6th Canadian Armoured Regiment), forced their way through and around the town.

Churchill AVRE with troop of French Scouts and
Cross of Lorraine, Graye-sur-Mer.

Cross of Lorraine and NTL
Totem, Graye-sur-Mer.

Sherman tank, Courseulles.

Comité du Débarquement
Monument, Graye-sur-Mer.

Memorials to the French destroyer, La Combattante, Courselles.

Memorial to Général de Gaulle's landing on 14 June 1944, Courselles.

Plaque to 1st Canadian Scottish, JUNO Beach exit, Courselles.

German KWK 39 tank gun, Courselles.

A D-DAY MEMORY

Captain John W. Winckworth, Adjutant 7th GHQ Troop RE. Landed on JUNO beach.

"As I had no opportunity to sleep from daybreak on D-Day until 0800 on D+3, my memories are vague and confused.

I do clearly remember that sometime on D-Day I paused to wash my hands free of oil and sand in a small stream just inland from NAN Beach. A few hours later I found that I had lost the signet ring my wife gave me on our wedding day, and which I regarded as something of a mascot. This was a serious loss to me. On mentioning it to one of my Sappers he said he'd go and have a look for it. Half an hour or so later he returned triumphant having found it with the aid of a mine detector. I still wear it today."

Sergeant Gariepy's tank had passed a German coastal gun firing from a concrete bunker. Gariepy stopped, opened and shared a bottle of rum with the crew, then reversed and put seven rounds into the bunker. It stopped firing. At about 1200 hours the troops reached the area of Reviers and the Canadian War Cemetery visited earlier on this itinerary and by this time the Hussars had lost ten tanks.

In 1970 Jean Demota who owned the salvage rights off Courseulles recovered a Canadian Sherman DD from about three miles out at sea. Leo Gariepy had settled in France after the war and he, in conjunction with the Mayor of Courseulles, helped to raise money for the venture. Once on shore Canadian Army Engineers from Germany moved and restored the vehicle and in 1971 it was dedicated in the position it is in today. Leo Gariepy was present, although sadly he died a year later. The road behind the Sherman is named after him (Leo Gariepy, *Citoyen d'Honneur de Courseulles sur Mer.* 1912-1972.)

There are a number of memorials within walking distance of the Sherman, now named Bold (Audacieux), which has a notice board explaining its history. On the side of the tank is a row of regimental plaques: 12th Field Regiment, RCA; 6th Canadian Field Company Royal Canadian Engineers; 1st Canadian Para Battalion; 14th Canadian Field Ambulance; 5th Field Company, Royal Canadian Engineers Veterans; Canadian Provost Corps; 13th Field Regiment Royal Canadian Artillery; 19th Canadian Army Field Regiment (SP) RCA; 14th Field Regiment RCA (erected in 1944) and above them RCEME.

NTL Totem

Plaque describing the action on JUNO Beach.

German anti-tank gun KWK 39 used on 6 June 1944 and restored in 1994. Most of the coastal   defence weapons were provided by the German Navy but large numbers of this pivot-mounted 5cm weapon (made by Krupp) plus its other tank variants, 39/1 and 40, were used. The KWK 39 was the main armament of the German battle tanks used during the advance on Moscow.

A memorial commemorating de Gaulle's landing here on 14 June.

A plaque on one side of the beach entrance to the 1st Canadian Scottish Regiment erected on 6 June 1969.

A plaque on the other side of the beach entrance to the **458 officers and men of the Regina Regiment** who fell from 1939 to 1945.

A memorial to the French destroyer *la Combattante.* She was part of the supporting Bombardment Group and was built in 1942 at the Fairfields Yard in Glasgow. On 23 February 1945 she disappeared in the North Sea. Sixty-five French and two Royal Navy sailors were lost.

Walk some 200 yards to the west along the promenade to

'Little Black Devils', the Royal Winnipeg Rifles Memorial which is a huge memorial dagger, erected on 6 June 1964 by the Hon Roger Teillet, MP, Canadian Minister of Veterans' Affairs.

Another **plaque** was unveiled on **'D-Day plus 50 years'** by the mayor of Courseulles, J. de Mourgues, and Colonel the Hon Gildas Molgat CD Senator. On the seafront side is a coloured regimental badge.

Continue on the D514 following signs to Bernières and Ouistreham. As the road returns to the coast on entering Bernières there is a large clearing, Place du 6 juin, on the left with a Comité du Débarquement Monument. Stop.

On the right of the square is the Restaurant 'La-Bas'. Tel: (0)2 311 96 45 74.

A D-Day Memory

Sergeant Howard Roy (John) Clewlow. 13th/18th Hussars, Turret Gunner DD tank. Landed on SWORD beach.

"We had to do this DD training in Yarmouth and then right to the north in Scotland to Fort George. We did practice landings in these DD tanks. The problem was ... it was a bit of a hairy scary thing. We were sometimes under the submarine command ... we had to have Davis escape apparatus ... if the tank sunk we had to put on the Davis escape apparatus, a bottle on our front, we had the bag on our chest, we had a nose-clip where we took the oxygen in. The submarine lieutenant there said, 'It's only to give you a bit of buoyancy, if you sink in these things, you'll go down so fast you'll get the bends.' I think it was in Yarmouth that they stuck us in a big tank, a big pit, and the water just flowed in and the water came up your body that quick ... you had to put the Davis escape apparatus on. The water went all the way over you and went up about twenty or thirty feet and you had to get out. If you couldn't swim you were a bit panicky.

DD tanks were compulsory. The regiment I was in did the charge of the Light Brigade and that was it, the charge of the Light Brigade came all again - officers with big moustaches and they all thought they were charging at Balaclava... DD tanks were a bit weird. All it was was a canvas screen and that kept the tank afloat. There were about thirty-two air pillows. The canvas screen came up - there was a mesh that kept it up. So all there was between you and the bottom of the sea was this canvas screen. The drive from the engine was transferred from two propellers

A D-Day memory continued

at the back. You pulled a lever and it turned these two propellers and you went around 5 knots an hour and when you got heavy seas you really rocked...In training we lost about three crews up in Scotland, they went down in about three hundred feet of water and we never saw them again. It was a bit weird when you thought what might happen on D-Day, but we took it philosophically...

On D-Day there was a hell of a swell on ... we launched three miles out and the waves came up that high that we had to get out of the tanks and hold the canvas screen up, what a way to land... We were awash with water, we were sea-sick, we had the Davis escape apparatus on, we had the ear phones on, you'd got a mike, you'd got a Mae West on, you didn't know which to pull next.

The real panic came when the other stuff started to back up on us. We were supposed to be ahead of it but we were going that slow that the other stuff was catching up on us. If we got too close the landing craft just ploughed into you and sunk you. They didn't worry. Their idea was to get to the shore and if you were in the way that was just your hard luck. Being outside the tank instead of inside we could see these landing craft coming closer and the stuff was going over from the battleships, the fifteen inch shells, sixteen inch shells. The air force was flying around at about five hundred feet. You didn't know what to do and you were sick and you'd got all this gear on. People say, 'Were you panicky?' There was that much confusion you hadn't got time to feel frightened."

• *Comité du Débarquement Monument/Bunker and Memorials /First Journalists Plaque, Bernières/29.7 miles/20 minutes/Map C18,19,16*

This was the centre of the assault area of the 8th Canadian Brigade Group and the sector here is NAN White. The assault regiment was the Queen's Own Rifles of Canada and they had the largest D-Day casualties of any Canadian unit. The Germans had constructed a '*Widerstandsnester*', a resistance nest, with mutually supporting weapons and good fields of fire using concrete bunkers and connecting trenches.

The Queen's Own landed at about 0815 hours without tank support (it was too rough to launch the DDs), and some 200 yards east of its target - right in front of the *Widerstandsnester*. The leading company lost half its strength running over the beach to the sea wall, but, thanks to the support of a flak ship which came almost to the beach, the Germans were so effectively silenced that only snipers were active when the Régiment de la Chaudière began to land fifteen minutes later. The Canadians headed inland towards the D79 leading to Bény, but German 88mm guns and machine guns stopped the advance. The divisional commander, not aware of the hold-up inland, ordered the follow-up brigade, the 9th, to land at Bernières on NAN White, and by midday the whole area was packed solid with men and equipment. It was one huge traffic jam and the 9th could not get moving until around 1600 hours. Without the jam the 9th might have reached Carpiquet that night before the 12th SS, and the battle for

Detail, 'Little Black Devils'

Detail, Queen's Own Rifles of Canada Memorial.

Memorial to Royal Winnipeg Rifles ('Little Black Devils'), Courselles.

Memorials and plaques on or near the bunkers, Bernières.

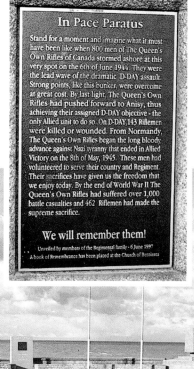

In Pace Paratus

Stand for a moment and imagine what it must have been like when 800 men of The Queen's Own Rifles of Canada stormed ashore at this very spot on the 6th of June 1944. They were the lead wave of the dramatic D-DAY assault. Strong points, like this bunker, were overcome at great cost. By last light, The Queen's Own Rifles had pushed forward to Anisy, thus achieving their assigned D-DAY objective - the only Allied unit to do so. On D-DAY 143 Riflemen were killed or wounded. From Normandy, The Queen's Own Rifles began the long bloody advance against Nazi tyranny that ended in Allied Victory on the 8th of May, 1945. These men had volunteered to serve their country and Regiment. Their sacrifices have given us the freedom that we enjoy today. By the end of World War II The Queen's Own Rifles had suffered over 1,000 battle casualties and 462 Riflemen had made the supreme sacrifice.

We will remember them!

Unveiled by members of the Regimental family - 6 June 1997
A book of Remembrance has been placed at the Church of Bernières

Caen *might* have been quite different.

On the beach here a sapper bulldozer driver silenced one pillbox by driving up behind it and filling it with sand and on 7 June Lieutenant Fairbrother RE won the George Cross for moving ammunition during an air raid.

The armoured car that stood here until 1997 has been sold.

From the Comité Monument walk 250 yards to the east along the promenade to the large German bunker.

There is a **NTL Totem** at the entrance to the draw. It is in an area called Place du Canada and on and beside it are memorials to the **Queen's Own Rifles of Canada** and **Le Régiment de la Chaudière**. The latter mentions the CO of the Regiment, Lieutenant-Colonel Paul Mathieu DSO ED, and 0700 hours as the landing hour. The official history says 'about 0830'. There is a bronze plaque to **8th Brigade 3rd Canadian Infantry Division** with a map of the Normandy campaign 6 June-18 August 1944 and European Operations 1944-45 and Rhineland Campaign 8 February - 27 March 1945. A plaque headed 'In Peace Paratus' bears the lines, 'Stand for a moment and imagine what it must have been like when 800 men of the Queen's Own Rifles of Canada stormed ashore at this very spot on 6 June 1944... We will remember them!' It was unveiled by 'Members of the Regimental Family' on 6 June 1997. It bears the information that a book of remembrance is held in the Church of Bernières. There is a plaque to the **5th Hackney Battalion the Royal Berks Regiment and No 8 Beach Group** who landed here with the assault troops and a memorial to the **Fort Garry Horse 10th Armoured Regiment** unveiled in 1994. On a separate bunker is a plaque to **the Régiment de la Chaudière** erected by the *Commission des Monuments Historiques de Québec*. General Keller, the Divisional Commander, left his HQ ship HMS Hilary at 1145 hours and by 1435 hours held his first conference in France in a small orchard outside Berniéres.

Return to Place du 6 Juin. Walk over the D514 to the road leading straight ahead.

The press had established themselves in the centre of Bernières even earlier - at 1030 hours - in the Hotel de Grave, now a private house, no. 288, the first on the left in the Rue du Régiment de la Chaudière. There is a **plaque** there to commemorate **'The first HQ for journalists,** photographers and moviemakers, British and Canadian from which the first reports destined for the press and the radio of the world were despatched.' One thing in particular surprised the local inhabitants. The 'Tommies' spoke French.

Continue on the D514 to St Aubin Plage keeping to the sea front and stop by the German bunker.

• *Fort Garry Horse, North Shore, No 48 RM Commando, Maurice Duclos Memorials, Bunker, St Aubin/31.1 miles/ 10 minutes/Map12,13,14,15*

The area to the east of here has no suitable beach for a major landing until la Brèche d'Hermanville is reached some four miles away. On this coast landed special forces such as commandos. No 48 RM Commando were to land at St Aubin and to move east, while No 41 RM Commando were to land at Lion-sur-Mer and move west. They were to meet at Petit Enfer two miles east of Langrune, which was a German strongpoint.

The North Shore Regiment of Canada under Lieutenant-Colonel D. B. Buell who landed here found that the German strongpoints were still in action despite the bombardment and it was thanks to their DD tanks, and AVREs using their petards, that they overcame the pillboxes. One bunker, silenced by a Royal Marine Centaur, had some seventy empty shell cases inside it as witness to the determination of the defenders. About four hours after landing the beach was clear except for one strongpoint and a number of snipers. The Commandos struck out to Langrune two miles east where they were held up until the following day by stubborn German opposition.

There is a **NTL Totem** here which describes the charge of No 48 Commando over the rocks and through the waves under heavy shellfire and the fact that a misdirected British bombardment 'killed and wounded the assailants who were forced to withdraw'. To the left of the bunker are memorials to the Fort Garry Horse, 5 Field Company RCE, 19 Field Regiment RCA; North Shore Regiment, No 48 RM Commando, civilian victims and to Maurice Duclos, a French secret agent code-named 'Saint Jacques' who landed here on 4 August 1940. One hundred yards to the right of the bunker, in front of the *Syndicat d'Initiative* **(Tourist Office, Tel: (0)2 31 97 30 41)** is a stone memorial to the 10th Canadian Armoured Regiment, Fort Garry Horse, erected in 1965. It was just below this point on the beach that a Thunderbolt crash-landed on D Day and it was this beach that members of the 4th Special Service Brigade had later to clear up. Lieutenant-Colonel James Moulton remembered what it had been like:-

> It was a shocking sight. Many corpses, some of them badly dismembered, were lying among the rest of the debris of the assault ...among all this several French women were walking about picking up what tinned food they could find - incredibly they had small children with them.

> *On leaving St Aubin turn left on rue Eugène Meriel Mère, signed Car Ferry, and turn right at the T junction, passing a splendid Casino on the right. Continue and stop in the open space on the promenade of Langrune near the Tourist Office. Tel: (0)2 31 97 32 77.*

•*No 48 RM Commando/Work of War Memorials, Langrune/32.7 miles/10 minutes/Map C11*

This seafront road and the parallel one behind it had been strongly fortified by the Germans. The sea wall was covered in barbed wire and there were trenches running along this road, while the parallel one inland had inset concrete machine-gun positions. Lateral roads were blocked, the windows and doors of all the buildings were bricked up and there were connecting underground passages. Coming in on the parallel road from St Aubin, the Commandos enlisted the help of a naval bombardment and a Centaur tank of the 5 (Independent) RM Armd Spt Bty to help them break through to the seafront. The Centaur ran out of ammunition and was replaced by another. That blew up on a minefield. Further efforts involved an anti-tank gun and a Sherman tank, which was also immobilised. It was a bitter hand-to-hand battle, which was not won until late on 7 June, when thirty-one German prisoners were taken, but the Commandos had over 100 casualties. The memorial stone commemorates No 48

RM Commando on one side and on the other, under the coat of arms of Langrune and the *Croix de Guerre,* it carries the command *'Souviens-Toi* [Remember]'. In front and to the left of the memorial is a dramatic cubic sculpture made out of compacted debris of war with the caption, 'This is a not a work of arts. This is a work of war 1944-1994. Never again.' It was presented by the sculptor, Dominique Colas.

Continue on the D514 to Luc-sur-Mer. Pass the Casino and **Tourist Office. Tel:** **(0)2 31 97 33 25** *and stop at the eastern end of the sea front near the Hotel Beau Rivage.*

• *First Commando Raid, 1941/Liberation, Memorials, Luc-sur-Mer/Petit Enfer/33.6 miles/10 minutes/Map C10*

This is the boundary between JUNO and SWORD Beaches, the town itself being in SWORD. It was to here that the small detachment of 21st Panzer advanced on the evening of 6 June to find the German defences intact, and it was the arrival of 6th AB Division's follow-up glider force that so stunned 21st Panzer's commanding general that by the time he recovered it was too dark to reinforce the advance. By the following day it was too late.

The memorial asks the passer-by to remember *'le premier commando allié en Normandie, 28 Septembre 1941'* - the first allied commando raid on Normandy 28 September 1941. At the foot of the memorial is a plaque to 'Capitaine Tom Gordon-Hemming'. The reference to Captain Hemming is a mystery because it does not seem that he was on the raid. He was certainly part of No 2 Commando employed during the Salerno landings in 1943 when 4th Troop, which Hemming commanded, took 35 prisoners.The raid referred to here was carried out on the night of 27 September 1941 by 5th Troop of No 1 Commando. Their intended landing place had been Courseulles but as they approached the shore their commander, Captain Davies, realised that they were heading for St Aubin and decided to go ahead anyway. As they landed, a machine gun fired at them and Davies led an assault over the sea wall. Two more machine guns

No. 288 Rue du Régiment de la Chaudière Bernières: First Journalists' HQ.

joined in and the commandos had to withdraw. Two commandos were missing and one was wounded. However, there is some confusion about where this took place and whether a German bicycle patrol had been involved. Whatever the truth, the memorial is here. It also commemorates the liberation of Luc on 6/7 June 1944.

On the southern approach to the town (on the D83 Douvres road) is a somewhat poorly maintained memorial to **General Leclerc and his French Armoured Division (Map C9).**

Continue on the D514 to Lion-sur-Mer. At the roundabout at the entrance to the town stop in the car park to the left. Walk back to the tank and memorials.

• Churchill Tank, No 41 RM Commando Sundial Memorial, Roosevelt Quotes Monument, Lion-sur-Mer/35.3 miles/10 minutes/Map C35

No 41 RM Commando landed here, having crossed the Channel in 'LCI(S)' - Landing Craft Infantry (Small) - and it was not until they had begun their far from comfortable journey that they found out their exact destination. At about 0845 hours they hit the sand some 200 yards out under intense mortar and shell fire and not exactly on target. Lieutenant-Colonel T.M. Gray, CO of No 41 RM Commando, sent part of his force to the east to make contact with the South Lancashire Regiment and part into the town. Three

Memorial group at St Aubin.

'Work of War' sculpture by D. Colas, Langrune.

41 RM Commando 'Sundial' with Churchill tank in background, Lion-sur-Mer.

tanks brought up in support were quickly knocked out. Between 1600 hours and 1800 hours destroyers fired upon German positions in the town, but the defenders were still there the following morning. Just before a set-piece attack by the 5th Lincolnshires supported by the Royal Ulster Rifles and No 41 Commando, a raid with anti-personnel bombs by three Heinkels killed the Forward Observation Officer and wounded the CO and 11 members of the HQ staff. The attack was successful, however, and that evening No 41 Commando moved on to Luc-sur-Mer to join up with No 46 Commando.

There is a **NTL Totem** here and the spectacular memorial to No 41 RM Commando is a symbolic sundial. The Churchill Tank was offered by General Sir Ian Harris who commanded 2nd Battalion The Royal Ulster Rifles. On a low plaque is a quotation from President Roosevelt of 6 January 1941 outlining the four essential freedoms.

Continue through the town and after 600 yards turn left signed to La Plage. Turn left to the square opposite the Mairie.

• *Place du No 41 Commando/Libération and Royal Engineer Memorials, Lion-sur-Mer/35.7 miles/10 minutes/Map C3,4,5*

The square has been named after the Commandos who landed here.

Continue to the parking area in front of the Hotel de la Plage and stop. Walk to the memorial on the promenade.

The **monument** was unveiled by General Sir George Cooper GCB MC on the occasion of the granting of the freedom of Lion-sur-Mer **to the Corps of Royal Engineers** on 10 June 1989 to commemorate the part played by 77th Assault Squadron RE in the liberation of the town 6 June 1944 and the continued links.

A D-DAY MEMORY

Lance Corporal P.L.M. Hennessey. A Sqn 13th/18th Royal Hussars DD tank. Landed on SWORD beach.

"My Regiment led the assault on SWORD Beach, at Lion-sur-Mer, in amphibious tanks, (DD), swimming in from 5,000 yards in a very rough sea. On the beach we dropped our canvas screen and opened fire. The tide was coming in and the water where we stood was getting deeper. We could not move further inland because the mines had not yet been cleared. A large wave swamped the engine, the tank was immobilised and was becoming flooded. We took to the rubber dinghy, but, hit by machine-gun fire we were sunk and obliged to swim for the shore, now some 300 yards away. Halfway there I clung to a post sticking up out of the water and glancing up I saw a large black Teller Mine attached to the top of it - I swam on.

We reached dry land where we lay wet and exhausted. One of our tanks came up beside us and the commander threw us a tin of self-heating soup, which we gratefully shared between the five of us. The beach was now an inferno of machine-gun, shell and mortar fire, but we reached the promenade behind it and met up

---

A D-Day memory continued

with some other unhorsed tank crews. Later we were directed to make for the village of Hermanville where we found the survivors of 'A' Squadron and our five remaining serviceable tanks."

Return to your car and continue keeping left of the turning to the beach. Continue on the D514 to the crossroads with the D60 to Hermanville-sur-Mer. On entering la Brêche fork left at the red British phone box and continue past the memorial square on the left to the parking area by the tank. Walk back to the square.

* La Brêche d'Hermanville Memorials to S Lancs Regiment, Royal Artillery Units/'Pionniers'/Gooseberry, Churchill AVRE/36.5 miles/15 minutes/Map D17,18,19,20

The upright memorial acknowledges a number of formations on either side:

> *'Pionniers alliés. Le 5 juin 2300 heures'.* Presumably this acknowledges the work of the two midget submarines X20 and X23 that marked the edges of the British beaches, though they were actually in position by 2300 hours on 4 June in anticipation of the original date for D-Day of 5 June.
> 3rd Division. 27th Tank Brigade. Royal Marine Commandos. 101st Beach Sub-Area. Commanded by Major General T.G. Rennie.
> Ships making up the Gooseberry off SWORD Beach including the *Courbet* (she had been part of the fleet that sailed in the Gallipoli affair in 1915) the *Centurion,* the *Durban* and the *Sumatra.*

To the left is a memorial to the S Lancs (Prince of Wales Volunteers) Regiment who lost 288 officers and men on D-Day and in the subsequent campaign. In the ground before the memorial is the triangular emblem of 3rd British Division in red and black and to the right a Royal Artillery memorial listing 7th Field Regiment (SP) RA, 33rd Field Regiment, 76th Highland Field Regiment and 92nd LAA Regiment RA.

In the **Tourist Office** building there are often D-Day exhibitions during the season. Enquire at the *Mairie* (see below) Tel: (0)2 31 97 20 15.

3rd British Division's task on D-Day was to capture Caen. Its landing beach had been divided into three sections which, west to east, were PETER, QUEEN and ROGER. QUEEN Beach, the area behind which you now are, stretched from the centre of Lion-sur-Mer to la Brêche. Each of these three main sections had been further divided into - once again west to east - Green, White and Red. The plan was to land on a one-brigade front in the centre of QUEEN Beach using 8th Infantry Brigade who were to secure the landing areas and the high ground of the Periers Ridge just inland. Then, by moving both east and west, it was to link up with 6th AB Division and the Canadians respectively. 185th Infantry Brigade, the follow-up force, was to pass through 8th Brigade and seize Caen eight miles inland. The assault brigade plan was to attack the beach on a two-battalion front astride the boundary between QUEEN White and QUEEN Red supported by DD tanks and with 77th and 79th Squadrons Royal Engineers in the vanguard.

Piper Bill Millin and friends on the beach where he landed at la Brêche.

3rd Division Insignia, with RA Memorial behind, La Brêche.

A D-DAY MEMORY

Lieutenant Commander Rupert Curtis RNVR Commander LCI (S)519. Ferried Lord Lovat's Commandos ashore onto SWORD beach.

"My mind concentrated on finding a path through the underwater obstructions. Fortunately at that state of the tide, the tops of many of them were still visible sprouting above the surface of the sea, many with lethal attachments.

Working completely by instinct ... I felt I could discern a clear path through the menacing stakes. It looked a bit of a zig-zag but I backed my instinct and took 519 through with rapid helm orders. We emerged unscathed and I called for more power from the engine room to thrust our bows hard on to the beach to ensure as dry a landing as possible. Then we kept both engines running at half ahead to hold the bows in position. At that moment we were hit by armour-piercing shells which zipped through the port Oerlikon gunshield but fortunately missed both gunners and our Commandos. 502 (Lieutenant John Seymour, RANVR) carrying the remainder

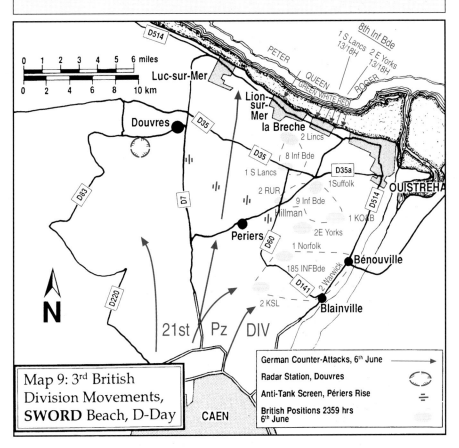

Map 9: 3rd British Division Movements, **SWORD** Beach, D-Day

A D-Day Memory continued

of Brigade Headquarters, beached very close on our port hand and as she did so she was hit by armour-piercing shells which penetrated four petrol tanks and hit the port engine and put it out of action. Perhaps I should explain that each of our craft carried 4,000 gallons of high octane petrol in non-sealing tanks just abaft the bridge. Had the enemy used incendiary or high explosive ammunition 502 would have blown up and disintegrated in a sheet of flame which would have engulfed them and us in 519. The Brigade would almost certainly have lost its trusted leader, Lord Lovat, and most of the Headquarters group. At the end of the day I estimated that half of the Brigade might not have got ashore but for the fact that the Germans used solid shot on us which was really meant for tanks.

I gave the order for our troops to land. The ramps were manhandled over the bows by our well trained ramp crew under Sub-Lieutenant Stephen Garrett, RNVR, and our Commandos began to land in about three feet of water as calmly as though on exercise. Each man carried some 80lb of weaponry and gear and clambering down our narrow landing bows on to a danger-laden strip of sand could have been no fun.

We bade goodbye to Lord Lovat and wished him good luck... as pipes gave heart and encouragement to all. Then we began the tricky task of coming off the beach stern first through the obstructions to make way for our second wave of LCI(S) to come in to land No 3 Commando and No 45 Commando Royal Marines."

You are now approximately in the centre of SWORD Beach, on QUEEN sector. As you face out to sea to your left is QUEEN White. To the right is QUEEN Red. The assault infantry on QUEEN White was the 1st South Lancashire Regiment, and on Red the 2nd East Yorkshire Regiment. The sight that faced the defenders in the early light of 6 June 1944 must have been terrifying. The sea was full of ships, the sky alive with aeroplanes. In the gap between flew hundreds of barrage balloons, while, driving rapidly towards the shore, were landing craft carrying the infantry. In front of them were the DD floating tanks of the 13th/18th Hussars.

SWORD Beach stretches for about $1^1/_2$ miles in each direction and it received the most concentrated pre-assault bombardment of all beaches, being drenched with fire from every gun available to the 3rd Division. The area between here and Ouistreham was thought to be under observation from the big guns at le Havre. Bomber Command destroyed the 16in guns before D-Day and the 11in guns were blanked off by a smoke screen out at sea. In the bad visibility, a group of LCTs lost their direction and cut across the main axis, hitting and sinking two DD tanks. Twenty-one DDs made it ashore, and it was these tanks, and the other specialised armour of Major General Sir Percy Hobart's 79th Armoured Division, that enabled major exits to be cleared from Red and White sectors within 2 hours. There were no minefields on the beaches here, though the lateral and exit roads were heavily mined. All minefields were clearly marked and many turned out to be dummy ones - probably one of Rommel's ideas. There was, however, a double row of ramps out at sea, and a large number of 'hedgehogs', many of which were mined. Following the initial landings just after a low tide, the sea came in rapidly, hiding the obstacles and making their clearance difficult. The water pushed those troops ashore up against the promenade where you now are, and they suffered heavily from enemy machine-gun and small-arms fire, particular on Red from the 3 o'clock direction. Into this turmoil at 0820 hours came No 4 Commando, complete with Piper Bill Millin, playing *Highland Laddie*, and stormed their way past the German shoreline defences, re-organised, then moved off to Ouistreham, which can be seen to the right. There the Free French of No 10 (Inter-Allied) Commando took the Casino, which was a German strongpoint covering SWORD Beach, and, with its capture, the assault infantry were better able to move off the beaches.

As the troops and equipment poured ashore, the incoming tide reduced the width of the beach available and shore and exits became jammed. Orders were given to delay the landing of follow-up units, but, before the congestion could ease, accurate German artillery fire began to fall. It was a puzzle trying to decide how the Germans were working out where to aim their guns. Suddenly someone realised that they were ranging on the barrage balloons, which were being put up on the beaches against low-level aircraft attack. The balloons were quickly lowered. They were no loss. The only significant air attack came from eight aircraft the following morning. One was shot down and crashed 300 yards away to the right from the beach exit. Slightly right of centre, 1,100 yards out to sea, was the wreck of the French Cruiser, the *Courbet*. She had last helped the British by covering their evacuation from Cherbourg in June 1940. The old ship, without engine or guns, and filled with concrete, had to be towed across the Channel to be sunk as a Gooseberry blockship to provide protection for craft landing on SWORD Beach. There she proudly flew the *Tricolore* and the Cross of Lorraine, making her a favourite target for the Germans, ignorant of her helplessness. She was shelled, bombed and attacked by human torpedoes. German radio on 8 July claimed that their attacks had driven the *Courbet* ashore. The illusion of her importance was fostered by other Allied ships, which fired from directly behind her cover. Each of the five invasion beaches was provided with a temporary harbour named a Gooseberry. The shelter was formed by sinking old ships in a line off the beach. Over sixty were sunk altogether. The majority were merchantmen, though a few warships were used - the cruiser *Courbet*, the British battleship *Centurion*, the cruiser *Durban*, and the Dutch cruiser *Sumatra*.

The order of landing of 8th Infantry Brigade Group from H-Hour at 0725 hours was:
1. A and B Squadrons of 13th/18th Hussars. DD tanks.
2. Eight Royal Engineer (77th and 79th Assault Squadrons) obstacle-gapping teams, each one made up of two flail tanks of 22nd Dragoons, three AVREs and one bulldozer.
3. Two obstacle-clearing teams, each of four flail tanks and four AVREs.
4. The assault infantry:
   QUEEN White - two companies of the 1st South Lancashire Regiment.
   QUEEN Red - two companies of the 2nd East Yorkshire Regiment.
5. At 0734 hours the HQ elements of the assault infantry plus their remaining two companies.
6. At 0810 hours HQ and C Squadron 13th/18th Hussars.
7. At 0825 hours the 1st Suffolk Regiment, the reserve battalion, plus 8th Brigade alternative main HQ.
8. At 1000 hours the 185th Brigade.

A D-DAY MEMORY

Piper Bill Millin. 1st Special Service Brigade. Landed on SWORD Beach.

"Lovat got into the water first ... I followed closely behind him ... he's a man about six feet tall and, of course, the water came up to his knees ... I thought it would be alright for me so I jumped into the water and it came up to my waist ... anyway I managed to struggle forward and then I started to play the bagpipes. I played Highland Laddie towards the beach which was very much under fire. At that time there were several ... three ... burning tanks, there were bodies, lying at the water's edge, face down floating back and forward. Some [men] were frantically digging in ... others crouched behind a low sea wall. No one could get off the beach. The road and the exits were under heavy fire. I made for cover at an exit ... a narrow road and I just got there behind a group of soldiers and they were all cut down ... about nine or twelve of them ... they were shouting and seeing me with the kilt and the bagpipes they shouted, 'Jock! Get the medics'.

Then I looked around and to my horror I saw this tank coming off a landing craft with the flails going and making straight for the road. I tried to catch the commander's attention ... his head was sticking out of the turret ... but he paid no attention and went straight in and churned all the bodies up. Then I saw Lovat and the Brigade Major standing at the water's edge. Everyone else was lying down. So I joined them. He [Lovat] asked me to play. That sounded rather ridiculous to me to play the bagpipes and entertain people just like on Brighton sands in peacetime. Anyway ... I started the pipes up and marched up and down. This Sergeant came running over, 'Get down you mad bastard. You're attracting attention on us'. Anyway I continued marching up and down until we moved off the beach."

Inevitably there was overlapping between the phases, but for over four hours the landings went to the timetable. Then, because of crowding on the beaches, a half-hour delay was ordered. However, despite the loss of the officer commanding the beach clearance who was killed on landing and over 50 per cent casualties to the armoured vehicles, nine beach exits were opened by 1130 hours. Meanwhile the German resistance on Periers Ridge (the strongpoint HILLMAN and the radar station at Douvres are on the ridge) was holding up movement inland, preventing the 185th Brigade from getting on towards Caen. There has been criticism of 3rd Division's performance following its successful landing. It has been suggested that their hearts and minds had been set on breaking the Atlantic Wall, and when that had been achieved relatively easily, the Division was left without a clear purpose. Troops accustomed to a defensive mentality in England since Dunkirk favoured digging in instead of aggressive forward movement. The German resistance on the Periers Ridge, at the strongpoints named Hillman and Morris, leeched away the armour strength needed for the drive to Caen, where the 21st Panzer Division was gathering itself to strike. General Bradley, commanding the United States First Army, expressed himself as 'keenly disappointed' at the performance of General Dempsey's Second British Army. In September 1944, lack of drive of the ground forces was said to have been one of the reasons why the 1st AB Division was cut off at Arnhem. General Dempsey was again the Army Commander.

Walk back to the tank.

The Churchill AVRE was presented to Hermanville on 6 June 1987 by 3rd British Armoured Division (it had originally come from the Imperial War Museum, Duxford). In September 1998 the tank was moved from its original position by the main memorials and soldiers of 6 HQ Squadron 22nd Engineer Regiment spent a fortnight refurbishing it. Beside it is a **NTL Totem** telling the story of Major General Rennie's 3rd Infantry Division.

Over the road is La Chapelle de la Brêche d'Hermanville, in which there is a colourful 4 metres high **stained glass window** which recalls the sacrifice of those who fought for the town's liberation. It depicts Christ on the Cross, surrounded by parachutes, aeroplanes and ships, with soldiers of June 1944 at his feet. The Chapel is often used for D-Day Landings and other exhibitions.

D-DAY MEMORIES OF ASSAULT ENGINEERS

Major C. H. Giddings, Troop Leader in 629th Field Squadron

'On going on deck as we approached the Normandy coast the first thing I saw was a destroyer which had been mined going down by the stern - and at that moment a Sten gun was let off accidently on the mess deck and three men were unfortunately killed. Not an auspicious beginning.'

Major W. Carruthers, Troop Leader 3rd Troop 77th Assault Squadron

'As I was to follow the flails through the gap I asked my gunner to lay the log carpet in the gap, but this and the turret had jammed and I had to cut it loose - the log carpet fell in a heap and formed more of an obstacle than a road. While I was doing this there was a bang, flash, red lights, blue lights etc., and I found myself lying on the sand, having been hit by a hand grenade thrown from the house alongside the tank. I was assured later by the flail commander that the thrower had a 90mm shell all to himself in return.'

Lieutenant I. C. Dickinson Second in Command 3rd Troop 77th Assault Squadron

'For the work done on D-Day, 77th and 79th Assault Squadrons between them won two DSOs, four MCs, two DCMs and three MMs'.

Extra Visits to Hermanville CWGC Cemetery (Map D21), 3rd Div HQ, Medical HQ (Map C1), Well (Map C2), Harold Pickersgill Tree. Round trip: 2.5 miles. Approximate time: 35 minutes.

Continue to the D514, turn right and then left by the church, signed Hermanville on the D60B on rue du 6 Juin. Continue into the village following Centre Ville and at the church drive into the square. Stop.

Extra Visits continued

On the left is a well with a plaque which explains that this was the well of the Mare Saint Pierre which is mentioned in British Army records as having supplied 1,500,000 gallons of water to the British Forces between 6th June and 1st July 1944.

Turn left along the narrow road signed Cimetière Britannique. Continue to

Hermanville CWGC Cemetery in Place des Combattants 6 juin 1944.

There are 1,005 burials in this beautiful cemetery, many of them from the 6 June actions in this area. There are 986 British, 13 Canadian, 3 Australian and 3 French. There is a pair of brothers, Lieutenant Alan Law Davis, 5th Battalion the W Yorks Regiment, age 24, Plot II Row O Grave 10, and CSM Norman Clave Davis, 5th Battalion the King's Regiment of Liverpool, age 28, Plot II Row O Grave 7, who were both killed on 6 June and *Croix de Guerre* winner the Rev Peter Francis Firth, Chaplain First Class to the Forces, age 33, killed on 7 June in Plot I Row J Grave 15.

Return to the square and continue 100 yards to the Mairie on the right.

On the left of the gatepost is a plaque commemorating 3rd British Infantry Division' HQ set up here on D-Day and on the right a plaque to an important hospital centre. Over the road in front of the Salle Polyvalente is a green plaque in front of a small oak tree which was planted in memory of Citizen of Honour Harold Pickersgill who died in 1998. In 1943 Harold worked on the highly secret exercise PINWE - Problems of the Invasion of North West Europe - making detailed maps of the Normandy area. Much of the information for the maps was supplied by members of the French Resistance. In June 1944 he insisted on landing at la Brêche (part of the coast whose defences he knew so well from his secret work) with his old regiment, the Reconnaissance Corps, 3rd Division. The regiment established its HQ in the house of the Lebret family in the village of Mathieu, where they were pinned down by the German tank divisions that barred their way to Caen. During their prolonged stay in the village, Harold Pickersgill fell in love with the daughter of the family, Marie-Geneviève, who was to become his wife after the war, and the newly-weds settled down in Mathieu. In 1946 Harold was attached to the Graves Registration Service, based at Luc-sur-Mer, and worked as an administrative officer on the sad task of re-interring his dead comrades and burying them in the newly constructed war cemeteries. It was not until twenty years later that Harold found out that his own doctor, M Sustendal of Luc-sur-Mer, had been one of the principal informants for PINWE, for which he was decorated with the Légion d'Honneur. Always active in liaising between his old division and the local authorities for commemorative events, Harold himself received an MBE in 1984. When he died on 31 July 1998 at the age of 76, this Scot by origin but Norman by adoption, gave his body to medical research. As he therefore had no grave, his friends and colleagues decided to plant an oak tree in his memory. The plaque was erected by the active HMS *(Histoire, Mémoire, Souvenir)* Association of Hermanville-sur-Mer, whose President is M J. Tirard.

Return to the D514 and rejoin the main itinerary.

Continue on the D514 for 300 yards to the junction of the 'Place 6 juin' on the left and 'Boulevard du 3me Division' on the right. Turn right and continue to the memorial on the left.

• Roger Weitzel Memorial/36.9 miles/5 minutes/Map D15

It was from this spot that Roger Weitzel, the captain of the *Courbet,* took a sample of French soil on 7 June which he later presented to de Gaulle.

Return to the D514 and turn right on rue Admiral Weitzel. Continue to the traffic light junction at Colleville-Montgomery Plage. Turn right on the D60A and stop in the square.

A D-DAY MEMORY

Major Patrick A. Porteous, VC. RA No 4 Commando. Landed on SWORD beach. "0600hrs, 6th June 1944. Reached lowering position - grey sky - sea very choppy - ships of every shape and size as far as the eye can see.

As my landing craft hit the water, we took a large wave over the side. A foot of water swilling round our feet. Get pumping - Damn! The bilge pumps not working, so get bailing with tin hats. Difficult in very cramped conditions on board, especially as some men being sick. Still making water as every wave slops some more in. Approaching the beach all hell going on but anything preferable to this horrible boat. As the front ramps went down, she finally sank in three feet of water."

• General Montgomery Statue, Anglo-French Forces/First British Graves, Naming of Colleville-Montgomery Memorials/37.7 miles/15 minutes/Map D22, 13,14

In the square is the bronze statue of General Montgomery sculpted by Vivien Mallock (qv), to which the statue in Portsmouth (qv) is identical. It was unveiled on 6 June 1996 by Prince Michael of Kent and was presented to Colleville-Mongomery by the Normandy Veterans' Association. The *Commune* of Colleville donated the land on which the statue stands. At night the statue is illuminated.

Walk over the road.

To the left on either side of the road leading to the beach - Avénue du No 4 Commando - are two memorials. One erected on 6 June 1945 commemorates the first British graves of 6 June 1944, the Anglo-French forces of General Montgomery and Capitaine Kieffer of No 10 (Inter-Allied) Commando and the decision of Colleville-sur-Mer to change its name to Colleville-Montgomery. On the other side of the road is another memorial to Commandant Kieffer and the French forces of No. 10 Commando.

Extra Visit to HILLMAN Strong Point, 1st Battalion Suffolk Regiment Plaque (Map H27, 28). Round trip: 4.6 miles. Approximate time: 15 minutes.

Continue inland on the D60A signed Biéville and drive to Colleville-Montgomery Bourg. At the crossroads with the D35A, go straight over, signed Caen, to the bunker complex on the right by a sign 'Rue du Suffolk Regiment'.

This strong defensive position covering 2,500 square yards protected by mines and wire and containing a concrete bunker and underground works was the HQ of the German 736th Regiment with an area strength of more than 150 men. It was taken by the Suffolk Regiment, aided by two troops of Shermans of the 13th/18th Hussars after a six-hour battle in which the Suffolks had 20 men killed. The way in which the position had to be approached was remembered by Lieutenant-Colonel R.M.S. Maude Commanding 246th Field Company Royal Engineers, one of whose detachments was involved:-

The position was approached from the north where the grass was sufficiently long to allow covered approach to the outer minefield area. It was decided to attack from this point and a mine clearance team was detailed to breach the minefield there. Lieutenant A. Heal led a party of four sappers. Working in two parties, each of two men with a mine detector, tracing tape and wire cutters, these parties, working on their stomachs in the long grass, and covered by fire from the infantry, cleared and marked two paths through the minefield. The inner wire was breached by Bangalore torpedoes placed by the infantry and the infantry (1st Battalion Suffolks) assaulted through these gaps with A Company. The Company, under Major G. Riley, captured the first concrete post but then found themselves under such intense fire that they were unable to maintain the position, and after the Company Commander had been killed they were forced to withdraw. It was then decided that the position could not be captured without the assistance of armour.

The plaque on the bunker commemorates all those of the regiment who fell in the liberation of Colleville, the capture of HILLMAN and later fighting in Normandy. It pays tribute to the Colleville family who in February 1989 made this site available so that future generations could recognise the bravery and sacrifice of the soldiers. On the right of the small parking area there is a coloured map of the strong point and a **NTL Totem**.

Return to the Montgomery statue and rejoin the main itinerary.

Hillman Blockhouse.

Local schoolchildren, Hermanville CWGC Cemetery.

Plaque to Harold Pickersgill, 'Citizen of Honour', Hermanville.

Statue of General Montgomery by Vivien Mallock, Collevile-Montgomery.

Continue on the D514 to the western edge of Ouistreham following signs to Casino and Musée. At the small roundabout by the splendid Hotel des Thermes Thalassotherapie Centre, Tel: (0)2 31 96 40 40, turn left and stop at the memorial on the right.

• *No 4 Commando, Keiffer Memorials, Musée du No 4 Commando, Ouistreham-Riva-Bella/39.2 miles/20 minutes/Map D10,11,12*

The central task of 1st SS (Special Service) Brigade was to land in the Ouistreham area, to clear the town and then to move on to link up with the airborne forces at Pegasus Bridge. The Brigade, under command of 3rd British Division, was made up of:

Brigade Commander. Brigadier The Lord Lovat, DSO MC
No 3 Commando. Lieutenant-Colonel P. Young, DSO MC
No 4 Commando. Lieutenant-Colonel R.W.F. Dawson.
No 6 Commando. Lieutenant-Colonel D. Mills-Roberts, DSO MC.
No 45 RM Commando. Lieutenant-Colonel N.C. Ries
No 1 and No 8 French Troops of No 10 Inter-Allied Commando. Captain Philippe Kieffer. In addition, No 41 RM Commando (Lieutenant-Colonel T.M. Gray) also came under command but had an independent role at Lion-sur-Mer.

No 4 Commando landed at 0820 hours on QUEEN Beach Red sector and came under heavy fire, suffering about forty casualties. Lieutenant-Colonel Robert Dawson was wounded in the leg and in the head but No 4 Commando reached the D514 and set off towards Ouistreham, led by Philippe Kieffer. A local gendarme whom they met on route gave them details of German strengths and positions and after a fierce fight ending with grenades and bayonets, in which both sides sustained many casualties, Kieffer's men took the Casino, an action that was made much of in the film *The Longest Day*. The casino building itself had been demolished by the Germans in October 1942 and replaced with concreted gun positions which were taken on by a Centaur prior to the final assault. No 4 Commando then moved on towards Pegasus Bridge.

Lord Lovat, SS Brigade HQ and No 6 Commando landed on QUEEN Beach Red sector at 0820 hours, piped ashore by Piper Bill Millin. Artillery and mortar fire was considerable and three of their landing craft were hit. They moved rapidly inland, heading for Bréville to the east of Pegasus Bridge, clearing two pillboxes on the way. As they approached the bridge they waved a Union Flag in order to establish themselves as 'friendly forces' and were met by Brigadier J.H.N. Poett, the Commander of 5th Parachute Brigade. 'We are very pleased to see you', said Nigel Poett. 'I am afraid we are a few minutes late sir,' was the reply. Lovat and his men then moved over Pegasus Bridge to the cheers of the paratroopers and attracted considerable fire from German snipers.

No 3 and No 45 RM Commando landed at 0910 hours and moved inland and across the bridges over the Orne river and canal. No 45 went on to Merville while No 3 formed a protection force at Ranville for 6th AB Division HQ.

By the end of the day the 1st SS Brigade had not occupied the high ground east of the Orne, but they had cleared Ouistreham and fulfilled their main task of linking up with the airborne forces. They had also found out that French civilians were not too enthusiastic about their shoulder patch, which said 'SS'. It was later changed.

On the dunes is a memorial to the memory of ten members of Kieffer's Commandos and to No 4 Commando. It is a symbolic flame erected in 1984 on top of a German blockhouse cupola. At its base is a bas relief memorial to Commandant Philippe Kieffer.

Continue to the junction, take the first left and turn left again. Continue to the Casino square and park by the Museum on the right.

By the Casino is the **Tourist Office**. Tel: (0)2 31 97 18 63.

The museum, now signed as *Musée du Débarquement* as well as of No 4 Commando, was organised by a group of citizens of Ouistreham who wished to preserve the memory of the events of the landings here. It has exhibits of arms, uniforms, badges and souvenirs. There is a film of the landings. Outside is a propellor from a Wellington which was recovered from the sea. There is also a **NTL Totem** which describes how 123 houses and villas were demolished by the Germans in the construction of the impressive defensive system here.

Open: Palm Sunday - end September every day 1030-1800. Entrance fee payable. Tel: (0)2 31 96 63 10.

Continue past the museum and take the road 'Boulevard 6 juin' straight ahead. 400 yards later stop by the large concrete building/museum on the left.

• *Musée le Mur de l'Atlantique/40 miles/20 minutes/Map D9*

This 52-feet-high concrete tower is the only major German work left in Ouistreham. It was a flak tower designed to control anti-aircraft defence of the harbour and was the German HQ in charge of the batteries covering the entrance of the River Orne and the Orne Canal. On 6 June the Franco-British commandos attempted to take the tower but were repulsed by machine-gun fire and stick grenades. It remained a threat until on 9 June Lieutenant Bob Orrell of 91st Field Company RE with three men placed explosive charges by the heavily armoured door which eventually burst open. The garrison of 2 officers and 50 men then surrendered. Since 1987 when it was fully restored the tower has been a museum in which one can see the generator room, the gas filter rooms, the machine gun emplacements, telephone exchange, radio transmission room and observation post. There are also many unpublished photographs and documents about the Atlantic Wall which employed over 2 million people in its construction. In September 1942 Hitler held a meeting with Speer (Minister for Armaments), von Rundstedt, Goering and others at which he specified a defensive coastal wall that would stretch from Norway to the Spanish border and consist of 15,000 strongpoints manned by 300,000 troops. In the grounds is a rare V1 and other interesting exhibits and a **NTL Totem.**

Open: daily from 12 February - 15 November 1000-1200 and 1400-1800 (from 1 June-30 September 0900-1900). Tel: (0)2 31 97 28 28 69.

*Continue straight on, passing on the left **the Ferry Terminal**. Tel: 08 03 82 88 28.*

In 1996 Maurice Hillebrandt, who served with **Combined Operations, RN,** during the war, noticed that there was no memorial in Normandy to the crews of the ships that supported D-Day. With Lieutenant-Commander R.J. Brend, RN, he formed a small

Museum of the Atlantic Wall, Ouistreham.

committee of which Prince Philip is the Patron, and is attempting to raise the £18,000 to have a memorial erected at the entrance to the terminal here. The projected design is that of a kedge anchor and Combined Operations badge on a 6-foot-high granite block with a text dedicating the memorial to the crews of landing craft, ships and barges, especially those killed on 6 June - VE Day. Inauguration date is planned for 6 June 2000.

On the right is the conveniently sited ***Hotel Mercure. Tel: (0)2 31 96 20 20.

On the harbour wall to the left can be seen a 'Maginot Line' type cupola and vestiges of two pontoons.

Continue to Place Général de Gaulle and park in the car park.

There is a variety of restaurants, newsagents and souvenir shops in the square, which makes an ideal lunch stop.

Extra Visit to Stained Glass Windows, Commandos/51st Highland Division, Ouistreham Church (Map D7,8). Round trip: 1.2 miles. Approximate time: 15 minutes.

From the square follow Centre Ville 12th Century Church signs. Continue to the church and park near the spendid Hôtel de Ville or La Poste.

In the church on the hill at the top are two beautiful stained glass windows. One is to the Commandos, offered by the Commando Association in memory of their dead and in recognition of the welcome of the people of Normandy. The other is to the 51st Highland Division, the follow-up formation in I Corps that was to have bloody battles east of the Orne in the fight for Caen. It has a fine Highlander and regimental badges.

Return to the Place Général de Gaulle and rejoin the main itinerary.

Stained glass window to the 51st Highland Division, Ouistreham Church.

Follow Autres Directions and continue to the roundabout.

• *Comité du Débarquement Monument, No 4 Commando Plaque/41.3 miles/5 minutes/Map I41,42*

In the roundabout is a *Comité du Débarquement Signal* Monument, which until 1987 stood on the harbour at Ouistreham. At the back of the memorial is a plaque to the French and British commandos of No 4 Commando.

* *End of Itinerary Four*

ITINERARY FIVE

THE BRITISH AIRBORNE LANDINGS

• **Itinerary Five starts** at Pegasus Bridge and covers the British and Canadian Airborne and Commando Operations, ending at Troarn.
• **The Route:** Bénouville - *Mairie* Plaque, 7th Light Infantry Battalion, Parachute Regiment, Café Gondrée, Pegasus Bridge, First Bailey Bridge, Oxs and Bucks Plaque, *Comité du Débarquement* Monument, Major Howard Bust, Glider Landings Markers, Centaur Tank, Cromwell Tank; Horsa Bridge Memorial; Ranville - 13th Parachute Battalion Memorial, General Gale Bust, CWGC Cemetery, Den Brotheridge Plaque, Airborne Forces Plaque, 8th and 9th Parachute Regiment Memorial Seats, 6th Airborne Division Cross, Piron Brigade Memorial, 13th Parachute Battalion Memorial; Amfreville - No 6 Commando Memorial, 1st Special Service Brigade Cross; Hoger No 4 Commando, Colonel Robert Dawson Memorials; Sallenelles - Belgian Soldier and Piron Brigade Memorials; Merville - Allied Soldiers and Civilians, Soldiers of the Piron Brigade, 9th Parachute Battalion Memorials, Battery and Museum; Bréville 6th Airborne, 12th Parachute and 12th Devonshire Regiment Memorial, CWGC Graves in Churchyard; Château St Côme 9th Parachute Infantry Battalion and 1st Canadian Parachute Memorials; Hérouvillette 2nd Airborne (Oxs & Bucks Light Infantry) Memorial; Manoir du Bois 8th Parachute Battalion Memorial; CWGC Grave, Touffreville Churchyard, Arthur Platt and Thomas Billington Memorial; Troarn 3rd Parachute Squadron RE; Major Roseveare Bridge Memorial; Captain Juckes Bridge Memorial; Bavent Cemetery - Grave of Brigadier Mills-Roberts; 1st Special Service Brigade Memorial.
• **Extra Visits are suggested to:** St Pierre de Jonquet Memorial; No 3 Commando Memorial, Petiville; 1st Canadian Parachute Memorial, Varaville; Memorial to Crash and Massacre at Grangues.
• **Planned duration,** without stops for refreshments or Extra Visits: **4 hours, 30 minutes**
• **Total distance: 31 miles**

The Germans had begun to organise airborne forces in 1936. The Americans are said to have considered an airborne assault in 1918 at St Mihiel. The British began their airborne forces in 1940 at the instigation of Prime Minister Winston Churchill, and the early paratroopers were volunteers from No 2 Commando. The first British paratroop action was Operation *Colossus* on 10 February 1941 when 35 men of 'X' Troop No 2 Commando were dropped into the Italian Apennines. The commander of 'X' Troop was Major T. A. G. Pritchard who was, much later, College Commander at Sandhurst for one of the authors. In May 1943 6th Airborne Division was formed under Major General R.N. Gale and, with 1st Airborne Division under Major General R.E. Urquhart, comprised the Airborne Corps commanded by Lieutenant General Sir F.A.M. ('Boy') Browning. Within the organisation, and an integral part of it, was the 38th Wing of the Royal Air Force.

As early as August 1943 COSSAC had proposed the use of airborne forces in the invasion. At that time a direct assault on Caen was being considered. General Montgomery's appointment brought drastic changes to the plan. His idea was to seal each end of the sea assault using airborne troops. Their prime task was flank protection.

There were two types of airborne soldiers, classified according to the way in which they landed - by parachute or by glider. Thus there were two types of zones in which they would come down - *dropping* zones [DZs] for parachutists and *landing* zones [LZs] for gliders. Parachute troops can be widely dispersed by wind, which is a considerable disadvantage, while glider-borne forces can be more readily directed or aimed at small targets and can bring with them heavy equipment like field guns and small vehicles.

Gliders, however, are more vulnerable to obstacles such as the poles, known as 'Rommel's asparagus', that the Germans were erecting on potential landing grounds along the French coast. Therefore, the mix of glider and parachute forces, and the tasks allocated to them, could decide the outcome of the airborne assault.

Six weeks before D-Day, over a three-day period, 6th Airborne Division carried out an airborne exercise. They did not know that it was a dress rehearsal for Normandy.

6TH AIRBORNE DIVISION LANDINGS

Drop Time:	0020 hours *coup-de-main* on Pegasus bridge.
	0050 hours 3rd & 5th Parachute Brigades.
Leading Formations:	3rd and 5th Parachute Brigades of 6th Airborne Division.
6th AB Division Commander:	Major General R.N. ('Windy') Gale
German Defenders:	716th Infantry Division
716th Division Commander:	Lieutenant General Wilhelm Richter

The Plan (See Map 10)
The airborne plan was scheduled to begin before the main landings, and in darkness, in order to achieve the maximum surprise. The earliest troops into Normandy were, where possible, to be paratroopers who would be less sensitive to obstacles than their comrades in gliders. The paratroopers were to clear landing areas for later glider landings. The tasks were distributed between two brigade groups on a geographical basis as follows:

5th Parachute Brigade Group (Brigadier J.H.N. Poett) comprising the 7th, 12th and 13th Parachute Battalions, D Company of the Oxfordshire and Buckinghamshire Light Infantry and supporting arms and services was to:

1. Seize the bridges over the Orne using six gliders manned by the Oxfordshire and Buckinghamshire Light Infantry and

2. Seize and hold the area of Pegasus Bridge and Ranville and clear the LZs north of Ranville for glider reinforcements. They were to land on DZ'N' with elements of the 7th Parachute Battalion on DZ 'W'.

3rd Parachute Brigade Group (Brigadier James Hill) comprising the 1st Canadian Parachute Battalion, 8th and 9th Parachute Battalions and supporting arms and services was to:

1. Destroy the Merville Battery $1^1/_2$ hours before the first landing craft were due and

2. Destroy a number of bridges (e.g. at Varaville, Robehomme, Bures and Troarn) over the River Dives and thus prevent the enemy from attacking Ranville from the eastern flank.

They were to land on DZ 'K' and DZ 'V'.

In each case the airborne brigades would be spearheaded by pathfinders scheduled to drop at 0020 hours on 6 June. The main troops were due to come in about thirty minutes later.

WHAT HAPPENED ON D-DAY

The leading planes of 38th and 46th Groups of the Royal Air Force carried men of the 22nd Independent Parachute Company whose job it was to mark the dropping and landing zones. With them went the RAF Commander, Air Vice Marshal L.N. Hollingshurst, and on time the pathfinders jumped out into the night sky. One of the first to land was Lieutenant de Latour who featured in a *Picture Post* story on 22 July as the 'first' Allied soldier to land in France. On 9 September the same magazine carried a sad postscript - a picture of de Latour's grave with a temporary wooden cross. He was killed on 20 June, then a captain, and is now buried in Ranville CWGC.

At the same time as the pathfinders flew over their objectives the *coup-de-main* party of Oxs and Bucks led by Major John Howard landed three of their gliders beside the Orne Canal, between the two bridges. In ten minutes Pegasus Bridge was theirs.

Thirty minutes later at 0045 hours the main bodies of the para brigades arrived and then, less than three hours after that, gliders brought in the heavy equipment and General Gale, the division's commander.

By the end of the day both Orne bridges were in Allied hands, despite German counter-attacks, Ranville and the DZs were secure, a link-up had been made with Lord Lovat's Special Service Brigade from SWORD Beach, bridges over the River Dives at Troarn, Bures, Robehomme and over a tributary of the Dives at Varaville had been blown and the Merville Battery had been put out of action, despite a bad start. Only seven of over 260 parachute aircraft used in the assault were missing, but twenty-two of the ninety-eight gliders did not reach their LZs. Some never made it to France due to broken tow ropes, and many landed in the wrong place. Of the 196 members of the Glider Pilot Regiment involved in the operation seventy-one were casualties. Some of the drops were very scattered so that only about 3,000 of the 4,800 men who landed fought as planned. 6th AB Division had achieved its objectives, but it was thinly spread. The 6 June may have been the longest day for the men of the airborne forces but there was another one tomorrow and the Panzers were coming.

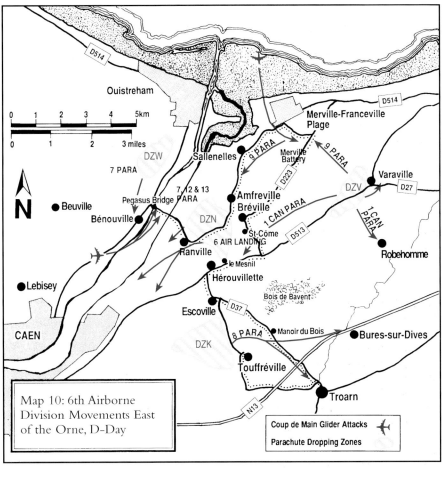

Map 10: 6th Airborne Division Movements East of the Orne, D-Day

Coup de Main Glider Attacks
Parachute Dropping Zones

THE TOUR

Pegasus Bridge may be found from the Caen ring road (Périphérique, N13) by following signs to Ouistreham and Car Ferry on the D515/D84, or from Ouistreham on the same road. Take the exit signed to Bénouville on the D514 (0 miles). Continue to the roundabout and park by the Mairie.

• *Bénouville/Mairie Plaque, 7th Light Infantry Battalion Plaque, Gondrée Café, Cromwell Tank, 1st Bailey Bridge Marker, New Pegasus Bridge, Oxs and Bucks Plaque, Comité du Débarquement Monument, John Howard Bust, Pegasus Trail Orientation Table, Glider Landings Markers/.8 miles/30 minutes/Map I31, 32, 25, 26, 27, 28, 29*

A D-DAY MEMORY

Brigadier Nigel Poett, Commander 5th Parachute Brigade who dropped with the pathfinders east of the Orne, said,

"My brigade task was to seize, intact, the bridges over the River Orne and the Canal de Caen at Bénouville and Ranville and establish a bridgehead.

As my small aircraft skimmed over the defences of the Atlantic Wall, not a shot was fired. The red light came on and then the green. I was 'out', seconds later a bump. It was the soil of France. The time some 20 minutes after midnight on the 5/6 June 1944. The darkness was complete; the silence unbroken except for the sound of my disappearing aircraft.

A few minutes later the sky to the west lit up - firing, explosions, all the sights and sounds of battle. It was John Howard's assault. He also had been timed to land at 20 minutes after midnight.

Now I must get to the bridges as quickly as possible and be able, if need be, to adjust the Brigade plan. Would the bridges be in the hands of friend or foe? Intact or damaged? Indeed Howard's Company had achieved a splendid success. The bridges were in our hands, intact. All was well!"

The bridge over the Orne Canal was captured by the British airborne forces on D-Day, and subsequently named after the emblem of the Airborne Division. 300 yards away to the east is a second, not original (which was built by Eiffel) bridge named 'Horsa'. Both were to be captured by a coup-de-main party of six gliders commanded by Major John Howard.

In 1942 one-time soldier and former Oxford policeman John Howard joined the airborne forces. He had been recalled in 1939, commissioned and posted to the Oxs and Bucks Light Infantry which was chosen to be glider-borne. In May 1942 he was promoted to major in command of D Company.

In late 1943 General Gale, knowing that the Orne bridges had to be captured by his airborne soldiers, and influenced by the German success at Eben Emael, decided upon a *coup-de-main* operation. He chose D Company of the Oxs and Bucks to carry it out and added two extra platoons to the normal complement of six. In the spring of 1944 training for the operation began, though neither Major Howard nor his men knew anything about Normandy and the task that was to be theirs. Night exercises were frequent and sixteen pilots were intensively trained to fly by moonlight and to land their Horsa gliders in a precise pattern.

In May 1944 John Howard found out what he and his company were being trained for - 'to capture and to hold the bridges over the Orne until relieved by the 7th Parachute Battalion', though he was forbidden to share this knowledge with any of his officers and men. He immediately began a detailed training programme on Salisbury Plain, using tapes to lay out a full-scale model of the bridge area. If the operation was to succeed the bridges would have to be captured in a few minutes, and that meant that the gliders needed to land almost on top of them. John Howard told his glider pilots that he wanted the leading machine to land within 50 yards of the canal bridge. Three gliders were to go for one bridge and three for the other. Howard himself was to be in the force attacking the canal bridge with a platoon of some thirty men in each glider. His plan there was that the platoon in No 1 glider, commanded by Lieutenant Den Brotheridge, would silence the pillbox and weapon pit at the eastern end of the bridge and then dash across the bridge to seize the other end. The platoon in No 2 glider, commanded by Lieutenant David Wood, was to clear enemy from trenches on the east bank and No 3 glider, under Lieutenant Sandy Smith, was to do the same for the west bank. All the while men were to shout out 'Able', 'Baker', or 'Charlie' to identify themselves as friendly and hence avoid being shot up in the darkness by their own side.

Final training took place at Tarrant Rushton where the Oxs and Bucks studied aerial photographs of the bridge defences. The steady increase in the erection of Rommel's asparagus in the fields around the bridges was worrying evidence of the Field Marshal's influence on the state of readiness of German defences. Howard confided his concern to Jim Wallwork, the pilot of his glider. To Howard's surprise, Wallwork was pleased. The poles, he said, would help the gliders to stop.

On 3 June General Montgomery visited Tarrant Rushton, had a look at the gliders and talked to John Howard. On 4 June the attack was postponed for 24 hours but at 2256 hours on 5 June the little armada, towed by Halifax bombers, took off. In glider No 1, flown by Jim Wallwork, John Howard sat beside Den Brotheridge and they all practised the code words meaning that the bridges had been captured - 'HAM' for the canal bridge and 'JAM' for the river bridge.

The journey over was uneventful and some seven miles from the bridges the tugs released the gliders. Now it was up to the pilots, and this is how John Howard remembers what happened from then on:

I was behind Staff Sergeant Ainsworth but could see Jim Wallwork in profile and could see the beads of perspiration on his forehead and face as he struggled to maintain control of that damned great monster he was driving. I knew that the arrester parachute in the tail would operate any moment now to help slow down the glider as it hurtled in to touch down at anything around 100mph. Everybody had automatically carried out the landing drill soon after we had done our second turn. This was to link arms down each side of the glider with fingers locked into what was known as a butcher's grip. Legs up under your chin to avoid breakages when the floor disintegrated, as we expected it to on that bumpy field. Then all you could do was pray to God for a safe landing. My thoughts were many. Firstly the damned poles. Would collision with one of them cause just one of the many primed grenades we were all carrying to explode and everything else in the glider go up through sympathetic detonation - it had happened many times in Sicily! Were the enemy standing-to and perhaps reinforced with Mgs [machine guns] trained on the landing zone? Where would the other gliders land? It was all flashing through my mind as we experienced the first terrific bump! The glider seemed to take it well because we were momentarily airborne again - crash again but this time on skids because the wheels had gone - this was a lot noisier and damaging as the skids seared through the ground and sent up sparks as the metal skids hit flints and it looked like tracer fire flashing past the door causing inevitable thought of surprise lost. Airborne again and suddenly there was to be the last searing God Almighty crash amidst smashing plywood, dust and noise like hell let loose, followed by sudden silence as we came to a halt. The dazed silence did not seem to last long because we all came to our senses together on realising that there was NO firing. There WAS NO FIRING, it seemed quite unbelievable - but where were we? Everyone automatically released safety belts and felt their limbs for breakages. I realised that everything around me had gone very dark and my head was aching. My God I can't see! I clutched at my helmet and found that I must have hit the top of the glider during that last helluva crash and all that had happened was that my battle-bowler had come down over my eyes. What a relief! I quickly pushed it up and saw that the cockpit and door had telescoped and we would have to break our way out. I could hear the Gps [glider pilots] moaning and knew that they must be hurt, but they seemed to be breaking out of the front and in any case the drill was to get the hell out of it before any machine guns had time to get into action. Everyone was doing the same and considering the situation, commendably quietly. I did not know whether Den was out before or after me. All I can remember was as I stood clear of the mangled glider I saw the tower of the canal bridge no more than 50 yards away, and the nose of the glider right through the enemy wire defences - precisely where I had asked the GPs to put it during briefing. To cap it all there was NO enemy firing. The sense of complete exhilaration was quite overwhelming! I automatically looked at my watch, it had stopped at 0016 hours.

As I experienced that never-to-be-forgotten moment, the leading section moved quietly up the small track leading to the bridge to their vital task of putting the pillbox out of action. As I moved up myself I heard the dull thud of the phosphorous bomb and saw the greenish cloud of smoke which the section quickly dashed through to lob short-fuse HE [high-explosive] grenades through the gun slits of the pillbox. In the meantime Den was moving up to the near end of the bridge with the rest of his platoon at his heels and as he and his men charged across the bridge we heard three or four ominous thuds inside the pillbox indicating that the grenades had done their stuff.

Then the battle really started, enemy firing came from all directions but the first shots were from the direction of the Gondrée café, clearly aimed at Den and his platoon as they came off the far end of the bridge. Our chaps replied with gusto, no doubt running and firing guns from the hip. I simultaneously heard two more crashes which sounded like gliders pranging and I could hardly believe my ears. Within a very short time it seemed David Wood came steaming up from the landing zone with his platoon hard on his heels and I straightaway confirmed task No 2. As soon as he got into the trenches enemy firing started from several new directions. A runner came from the other side of the bridge with the sad news that Mr Brotheridge had been seriously hit in the neck during the opening burst of enemy firing as he came off the bridge and he was lying unconscious. I was just about to go over when Sandy Smith arrived with his platoon. He said his glider had had a very bad landing and there were several casualties. I then noticed that one of his arms was hanging limply and tucked into his battle-dress blouse. He was also limping badly. He assured me that he was fit enough to bash on so I confirmed No 3 task and as Den was out of action said he was to co-ordinate things on the other side of the bridge until I could arrange a relief. So off he went and skirmishing went on all round the bridge. Very soon after I learnt that David Wood, his Sergeant and radio operator, had all run into enemy MG fire and were out of action the other side of the pillbox. They had apparently caught a German laying booby-trap mines in the trenches. I thus had only one of my three canal bridge platoon commanders on his feet and he had an injured arm and leg.

Apart from the firing going on a great deal of noise emanated from platoons shouting code-names to identify friends in the dark and there was an unholy rabble of Able-Able-Able, Baker-Baker-Baker, Charlie-Charlie-Charlie, and Sapper-Sapper-Sapper, coming from all directions; on top of automatic fire, tracer and the odd grenade it was hell let loose and most certainly would have helped any wavering enemy to make a quick decision about quitting.

The most spectacular operation of D-Day had lasted barely 10 minutes. Total casualties were two killed and fourteen wounded. The airborne had taken Pegasus Bridge and the Germans never re-took it.

A D-Day Memory

Lieutenant D.J. Wood, 24th Platoon Commander, D Company, 2nd Battalion Oxfordshire and Buckinghamshire Light Infantry. Coup-de-main group for Pegasus bridge.

"We were seated, arms interlocked, facing each other in silence, lest the enemy below were alerted by our voices. Not a sound, except for the swishing of air rushing past the open door of the Horsa glider, flying through the night at 90mph over Normandy just after midnight on the morning of D-Day. Without warning, the pilot shouted, 'Christ, there's the bridge!' The glider's nose tilted sharply down and sparks, which we thought were enemy tracer, flew from the skids as they struck the ground. A series of violent bumps and the sound of splintering wood, followed by my being ejected through the side of the aircraft. Relieved to find I was still in onepiece, still holding the sten with its bayonet fixed and gratified that none of the extra grenades, which I was carrying in my camp kit canvas bucket, had gone off. Pulled myself together, collected my platoon and doubled off to report to my Company Commander."

On the *Mairie* is a plaque commemorating it as the first *Mairie* to be liberated. Gallic enthusiasm insists that liberation came at 2345 hours on 5 June *'par les parachutistes anglais'*.

On the corner diagonally opposite the *Mairie*, at the foot of a religious stone memorial, is a plaque in memory of 7th Light Infantry Battalion of the Parachute Regiment. The 7th, the scheduled reinforcements for John Howard's men at Pegasus Bridge, were scattered by the strong winds and shot at by the Germans as they dropped but their CO, Lieutenant-Colonel Pine-Coffin, using his bugler who dropped with him, rallied a force of about 200 and by 0300 established a defence perimeter around the bridge.

Continue on the road (which is named 'Avénue du Commandant Kieffer') from the Mairie to the bridge. Park on the right.

In the grounds of the old museum (see below) is a **NTL Totem**.

Pegasus Café. As Den Brotheridge led his men over the bridge, George and Madame Gondrée, the owners of the café, looked excitedly out of the top windows. They may well have been the first French people to greet the Allies on French soil. In the fire-fight that followed between the airborne troops and men of the company of

736th Grenadier Regiment of 716th Infantry Division, guarding the bridge, several soldiers remember George Gondrée shouting loud encouragement. Within the first hours of D-Day, the Café quickly became a first aid post, with Therese who was a trained nurse helping the two doctors in the Café and Georges digging up 99 bottles of champagne which he had hidden in the garden. Much celebrating and 'reporting sick' went on. After the war the Café became a focal point for the veterans and their families and took the name of 'Pegasus Café', with the Gondrées and their three daughters, Georgette, Arlette and Françoise being a vital feature of every pilgrimage visit. The walls were covered with momentos and all veterans signed a 'Book of Honour'.

Madame Thérèse Gondrée outlived her husband to see the ceremonies of 40th Anniversary of D-Day in 1984 but died on 2nd July of that year. Sadly, following her death, the sisters disagreed on the future of the Café and its garden which resulted in the youngest sister Françoise asking the Court in Caen for its sale by auction in 1988. Supported by donations from veterans' organisations, British national newspapers and well-wishers, including the authors, Georgette backed up Arlette to secure the Café and its garden for £160,000 (probably five times its value as real estate).

By Normandy custom, bids were allowed to continue while three candles burned. Françoise's lawyer unsuccessfully appealed against the sale, claiming that the candles had not completely burned out when Arlette made the 76th and final bid. Arlette who was almost four years old at the time of its liberation on 5/6th June 1944, has maintained the Café as a place of pilgrimage for veterans and future generations. The Airborne Assault Normandy Trust, formed by General Sir Richard Gale and the Normandy Veterans' Association, support the retention of the Café as a memorial and although the French Authorities have recognised the Café as of 'historical importance', it has been owned and run by the Gondrée family since 1934 when George and Thérèse bought it. Since the auction, it has been run, maintained and cared for by Arlette. When Georges died in April 1969, Therese and her three daughters wished that the unfinished building in the Café garden should be used as a museum because of their love of the 'Red Berets'. The *Comité du Débarquement* was granted a 25-year lease of the museum building which was opened on 5th June 1974 by General Gale. Then relations between Arlette and the *Comité du Débarquement* deteriorated because she claimed that the museum building was in dire need of repair with a roof which was a danger to the visiting public. She won her case and the museum closed.

She hopes to reopen it shortly as an annexe to the Café and to serve as a memorial hall and conference room in memory of Georges and Thérèse, adding her recollections as a young child of the events of 5/6th June 1944 and up to the present time.

Over the road is a Centaur A27M Cromwell tank of 5 (Independent) RM Armd Spt Bty. It came ashore at la Brêche d'Hermanville, where it was put out of action. It was recovered in November 1975, brought to the Pegasus Bridge area in June 1977 and was originally sited on the opposite bank.

Walk 400 yards up the path by Pegasus café [Sentier GR 223/E0 Ouest walking trail].

There is a small **memorial stone** on the canal bank **at the site of the first Bailey pontoon bridge** built in France, named 'London 1', which commemorates the 17th, 71st and 263rd Field Squadrons RE. It was completed by 0100 hours on D+3.

Return to the café.

To the right of the bridge is a fine painted Pegasus Bridge sign, renovated in 1996 by the Airborne Assault Normandy Trust.

Continue over the new bridge and park beside the memorials along the opposite bank.

The original bridge was replaced in April 1994. The new bridge is essentially the same shape and design as the original but is longer and wider. Much debate about the future of the old bridge took place. In February 2000 it was moved to a site adjacent to the *Chambre de Commerce et d'Industrie du Port de Caen* area where the *Comité du Débarquement*, in conjunction with the Communes of Ranville and Bénouville are planning to open a **new Airborne Museum,** with all the original exhibits, in the year 2000. The new museum is designed by Charles de Sèze and will occupy a space of 900m², with 500m² of exhibit space and an audio-visual theatre and will overlook the bridge. The museum is being energetically backed by the venerable M Triboulet (qv) who, when it was announced in October 1998, called upon the *Département* and the *Région* to help finance this expensive project. Prince Charles has already given his support and an important opening ceremony is envisaged.

On the bank of the Canal, known as the 'Esplanade John Howard', is a complex of memorials to the events of 5-6 June. On the side of the impressive new bridge is a **plaque to** commemorate the action of the **2nd (Airborne) Battalion Oxs and Bucks** who captured Pegasus Bridge in the night of 5-6 June 1944, erected by their heirs the Royal Green Jackets in recognition of the first Allied Unit victory on D-Day. On the bank is a German 50mm anti-tank gun where there was a Tobruk-type emplacement in June 1944. Beside it is a *Comité du Débarquement* Monument and an Orientation Table installed by Brittany Ferries as part of their old 'trail', which had a self-guiding cassette tape but which is no longer in operation. The bronze bust of John Howard was sculpted by Vivien Mallock (qv) and presented to the mayor and citizens of Bénouville by the Oxs and Bucks Light Infantry Association and the Airborne Assault Normandy Trust in June 1995. Further along the bank is the viewing area for the *Son et Lumière show* over Pegasus Bridge that takes place at nightfall from mid-May to early September each year on Tuesday-Saturday. Tel: (0)2 31 44 62 01. Fee payable.

In the low ground behind are three lectern-like glider markers. They were unveiled in June 1977 by General Gale. They show exactly where each of John Howard's gliders landed, and give details of their crews and passengers, and precise time of landing.

Face the Gondrée Café and take that direction as 12 o'clock.

From this point UTAH Beach, effectively the other extreme end of the invasion area, is 47 miles away in a straight line at 12 o'clock. Major Howard's glider PF800 landed at 0016 hours, where the first marker stands at 7 o'clock. It is 47 yards from the bridge. The leading section moved up, past where you are now standing, and threw grenades into a pillbox, which was located beside the bridge across the road from you at 3 o'clock.

Despite troublesome snipers in the woods, General Gale, Brigadier Poett, (who had dropped with the pathfinders at 0020 hours and was therefore the first general officer to land in Normandy) and Brigadier Kindersley (commanding 6th Air Landing Brigade) crossed the bridge (coming from 6 o'clock) on a tour of inspection around 0930 hours.

There were more snipers in the large building seen at 10 o'clock across the canal. It seemed likely that there was an artillery observation officer there too, because accurate mortar fire was coming down. However, it was thought that the building was a maternity hospital, and the paratroopers were forbidden to return the fire. To the right of the building, at 11 o'clock, there was a water tower, from which snipers were also operating, and, around midday, Major Howard agreed that one shot could be fired at the tower, using the 50mm German anti-tank gun on the riverbank. It scored a direct

5TH/6TH JUNE 1944
Just after midnight on 5th June, the first paratroopers and gliders land.
Seaborne commandos led by the piper of their Brigadier Lord Lovat link up
with the paratroopers on the afternoon of 6th June.

Panel 17 of the D-Day Tapestry, showing the action at Pegasus Bridge.

Plaque over the doorway of the Café Gondrée, the First House to be Liberated.

New Pegasus Bridge in raised position, showing the Café Gondrée on the left.

Bust of Major John Howard, coup-de-main Commander, Pegasus Bridge.

Sound and Light at Pegasus Bridge.

The original Pegasus Bridge languishing nearby in 1999.

hit and everyone cheered. An even stranger sound was heard later, when Lord Lovat and No 6 Commando arrived, led by Piper Bill Millin, en route to Amfréville, the village over the rise at 5 o'clock. He had piped them off from Spithead at 2100 on 5 June, and over the Ouistreham beaches at 0820 hours that morning, though he stopped playing as they crossed the bridge. For many years after the war Major Howard accompanied many student officers of the British Army's Staff College on their annual battlefield tour (including one of the authors). One of the innumerable stories which he told so well was of the two Italians that were taken prisoner near the bridge. Their job had been to put up the anti-glider poles in the fields. 'I didn't have the time to deal with prisoners,' he said, 'so I let them go. Do you know what they did? The silly sods went back to putting up the poles!'

A radio message was sent to John Howard to tell him that the river bridge had been captured intact and at almost the same time Howard learned that an inspection had shown that there were no explosives under the canal bridge. The first part of his task was complete. He ordered his men to take up defensive positions and despatched a patrol to secure the landing zones. Then he sent out the radio signal for success, 'Ham and Jam - Ham and Jam.' "As I spoke", he said, "I could hardly believe that we had done it."

Just before daylight three German tanks rounded the corner by the *Mairie*, at 12 o'clock, and headed slowly towards the bridge. The paratroopers' PIAT (Projector Infantry Anti-Tank) destroyed the first tank, which burst into flames and started exploding like fireworks. The noise it made probably persuaded the enemy that it was too dangerous to counter-attack until daylight. Some time after this a German motor cycle and car approached at speed from behind you along the road. They were shot up by Lieutenant Tod Sweeney and his men on the river bridge, and crashed in the ditch between the bridges. An officer in the car turned out to be the bridge commander, Major Hans Schmidt, who asked to be shot, because he had 'lost his honour'. Whether his loss was related to 6th Airborne's capture of the ridges, or to the ladies' lingerie and perfume found in the car, was never established.

Brigadier Peter Young once wrote, 'Much of what passes for military history is little more than fiction'. In the continuing struggle to achieve recognition as the 'first' to have done something or the 'first' to have been liberated some stories 'improve' with time. In a letter to the authors, Brigadier, later General, Sir Nigel Poett wrote, "Pegasus Bridge was the first engagement of D-Day. This is beyond dispute". That at least we can be certain of but it would be unwise to be dogmatic about timings.

Continue on the D514 to the bridge over the river and stop on the left.

• *Memorial to the Horsa Bridge Glider Landings/2.5 miles/5 minutes/Map I33*

The memorial, in French and English, tells the story of the capture of the bridge. It was erected by the Glider Pilots Association and was unveiled on 6 June 1989 by their President, Major Ian Toler. The bridge was then named 'Horsa' after the gliders used by the airborne forces. The enemy defending it had run away leaving their weapons behind. The first glider carrying the three platoons for the assault on the river bridge came down at 0020 hours about 190 yards away from it and, led by Lieutenant Fox, rushed it. Little more than a minute later Lieutenant Tod Sweeney's platoon landed some 400 yards away and he too led his men directly to their objective.

One of those who jumped into Normandy that morning was Richard Todd who landed just before 0100 hours. Both he and Lieutenant Sweeney told the same story about how they met each other on Pegasus Bridge on 6 June. Lieutenant Sweeney's version was, 'I met this chap on the bridge and he said, "Hello, my name is Todd and they call me Sweeney", so I replied, "Hello, my name is Sweeney and they call me Todd"'. Richard 'Sweeney' Todd went on to become a very well known actor while 'Tod' Sweeney, who later took part in the assault on Hamminkeln during the Rhine Crossing, became the head of the Battersea Dogs' Home and the subject of a *This is Your Life* programme in the 1980s.

Continue to the roundabout and take the D37 signed to Ranville. Take the next turning right on the rue de la Vallée and then immediately left heading for Ranville

A D-DAY MEMORY

Lieutenant H.J. ('Tod') Sweeney. 2nd Battalion Oxfordshire and Buckinghamshire Light Infantry. Coup-de-main group for the Orne river bridge.

"As the glider in which I was travelling broke through the clouds I saw clearly in the pale moonlight the River Orne, the Caen canal and the two bridges we had to capture - exactly as on the model we had studied so carefully over the last few weeks. The glider pilot called out, 'There's the bridge straight ahead, better strap up.' But I had one more task to carry out before I sat down and strapped up - to open the door for a quick exit. I struggled with the door for a few seconds and then it shot up. As it did so, to my horror, the glider made a final bank to the left and I found myself peering down at the fields and cattle 100ft below. Luckily my batman grabbed my belt and clung on to me until the glider righted itself and I was able to get into my seat. A minute later we were bumping over the fields of France towards the bridge over the River Orne. We had arrived, and for me and my platoon the invasion had started."

church. Drive just beyond the church to the Commonwealth War Graves Commission Cemetery. Stop on the left. There are a number of visits that can be made on foot:-

• *Ranville CWGC Cemetery, Airborne, Piron Brigade and other Memorials, General Gale Bust/3.4 miles/20 minutes/Map I 10, 11, 12, 13, 14, 15, 16, 17*

The capture of the Ranville area was the responsibility of the 13th (Lancashire) Parachute Battalion of Nigel Poett's 5th Brigade. First they had to improve and protect landing strips on DZ'N' in anticipation of the arrival of the glider waves at 0330 hours and of the 6th Airlanding Brigade at 2100 hours, and then move on to Ranville. Accompanying them, in order to remove the anti-landing poles and to prepare the landing strips, were sappers of the 591st Parachute Squadron RE, who dropped at 0030 hours. The first landing strips were cleared by 0330 hours and resistance by the 125th Panzer Grenadier Regiment of 21st Panzer Division was over by 0400 hours.

The cemetery was begun by Royal Engineers of 591st Parachute Squadron RE, who put up wooden crosses, which remained until after the war. Captain Davidson, the squadron second-in-command, was taken prisoner by the Germans and later rescued by the Commandos. By 21 June there were twenty-seven graves, left in the care of a 9-year-old French boy called Claude, who promised the Sappers that he would look after them. Today there are 2,563 burials, including 323 Germans. In it is buried Captain T.R. Juckes, MC who commanded 2nd Troop 3rd Parachute Squadron Engineers which blew one of the bridges over the River Dives, now named after him (see below). To the left of the War Stone almost in the centre of the cemetery is a stone cross bearing a bronze plaque with the emblem of the Airborne Forces on it and remembering simply,

Memorial to Horsa Bridge Glider Landings.

Grave of Lieutenant Den Brotheridge, Ranville churchyard.

Plaque to Ranville, the first village liberated, and 13th Battalion Parachute Regiment.

Bust of General Sir Richard Gale, Ranville library.

'June 1944'. This was erected in September 1944 by Royal Engineers of 1st AB Division. The chains surrounding it are glider lashing chains and the shell-like supports are brake fluid casings. At the multi-denominational inauguration were the Count and Countess de Rohan-Chabot. Inside and to the left of the gateway is a **memorial seat to 9th Parachute Battalion.** On the other side of the gateway is a **memorial seat to 8th Midland Counties Parachute Battalion,** dedicated on 5 June 1988. The **seat** by the entrance to the local churchyard was presented by the **Thanet Branch of the Airborne Forces Association** in June 1986. It matches one they presented to the Airborne Cemetery at Oosterbeek in Holland.

Also buried in Plot IIIA, Row L is the poet Major William John Fletcher Jarmain, of 193 Battery 61st Anti-tank Regiment, RA, 26 June. Like fellow poet Keith Douglas (qv) Jarmain served in North Africa. The night before he was killed he spent working through the records of his unit, assessing each man. Also like Douglas, he had a premonition of his death. Against advice he went on a recce into Ste Honorine la Chardonnerette (to the north of Ranville) and was killed by a German mortar bomb. One of his best known poems - although written at El Alamein - seems appropriate to be read at his grave:

At a War Grave
No grave is rich, the dust that herein lies
Beneath this white cross mixing with the sand
Was vital once, with skill of eye and hand
And speed of brain. These will not re-arise
These riches, nor will they be replaced;
They are lost and nothing now, and here is left
Only a worthless corpse of sense bereft,
Symbol of death, and sacrifice and waste.

Those for whom the sacriifice was made do not consider it mere waste.

Also buried here are the men who were killed in the disaster and massacre at Grangues (qv).

Stand squarely in front of the main entrance to the cemetery and take that direction as 12 o'clock.

Next to the cemetery is Ranville church. The old ruined tower is to the left of the main building. Following the immediate shock of the invasion, the Germans reacted quickly. The town of Colombelles (known to the troops as 'steel city' because of its tall metal chimneys) some two miles away at 6 o'clock, became a forming-up area for German counter-attacks. On D+5 naval spotters were sent up the tower to direct the fire of HMS *Belfast* (now floating on the River Thames near Tower Bridge in London) onto Colombelles and the shells could be heard whistling overhead here. The Germans replied with 88mm artillery fire onto the church, which was badly damaged. The civilian cemetery was destroyed, and so the first soldiers' graves were dug in the field, which is now the CWGC Cemetery. To allow access to the graves from the church, a hole was knocked in the boundary wall. Today the hole is a gateway between the two. Around the inside of the wall on the far side of the church there are also some war graves, including one German and two French soldiers and Lieutenant Den Brotheridge, who was killed at Pegasus Bridge. Behind Brotheridge's headstone is a commemorative plaque placed by the Gondrée family acknowledging him as the first Allied soldier killed during the landings. In the cemetery is buried Bombardier H. Hall whose date of death is given as 5 June 1944, presumably because he - and so many others - were killed at sea or in the air on the way over the Channel.

The general area outside the church is known as the 'Place General Sir Richard Gale'. Immediately opposite the entrance to the CWGC Cemetery is a low wall on which is a map and a concise summary of the airborne operations in the area, erected by 1 Field Squadron RE which lists the units involved in the actions. In the field beyond the wall, which faces the *Mairie,* Sergeant Ken Routman of the 591st Squadron organised a football match against the 13th Parachute Battalion on 9 June. The result is not recorded. Beside it is a stone tower on which is a **plaque in memory of the Belgian Piron Brigade** which formed an 'Allied' element of the 2nd British Army together with a Czech armoured brigade, a Netherlands brigade and a Polish armoured division. Between the two is a **memorial to Major Charles Strafford MBE** of HQ 6th AB Division, 1914-1993, erected by his comrades of the Airborne Forces and his many friends in France. Major Strafford, who lived for many years in Ranville and was a knowledgeable and active member of the Association, has no grave - he left his body to scientific research.

General Gale, the Airborne Division Commander, had arrived at about 0330 hours by glider and moved with his HQ to an area just to the west of the village of Ranville called le Bas de Ranville. On route he commandeered a white horse and many soldiers remember him riding it. Later it saved his life by being between him and a mortar shell. The area of le Bas de Ranville, which was being defended by the 12th (Yorkshire) Parachute Battalion, came under intense German counter-attacks, and when Lord Lovat's Special Service Brigade arrived at Pegasus Bridge at 1300 hours the leading Commando was diverted from its main task and sent up here. In the garden of the Mairie, in front of the Bibliothèque (Library), is a striking **bust of General Sir Richard Gale,** 1896-1982, sculpted by Vivien Mallock. It was presented in June 1994 by the Airborne Assault Association and the Normandy Trust and was unveiled by Prince Charles during the 50th Anniversary comemorations. Below it is an old plaque proclaiming that Ranville was the first village liberated at 0230 on 6 June 1944 by the 13th (Lancashire) Battalion the Parachute Regiment. This is the original of the plaque next visited, replaced because, when it was made in 1944, the badge upon it was painted, not carved, and therefore did not weather well. When the new plaque was erected, the old plaque was presented to the mayor and he placed it here.

Drive down the road past the Mairie to the first crossroads in the village.

Here on the wall is another **memorial,** which has in bas relief an Airborne Division cap badge, and asserts that Ranville was the first French village to be liberated, and gives the time as 0230 hours, by the **13th (Lancashire) Battalion.** Paratroopers re-visiting the area often discuss which was the first Mairie to be liberated, or the first house to be liberated, or the first village, or the first town, but the most enthusiastic conversation always centres around the first Frenchwoman they liberated. Whoever it was, and wherever, the ties between the local people and the British paratroopers remain very strong. The first Airborne Division pilgrimage here was led by Brigadier James Hill in June 1946 and the 29 June issue of *Illustrated Magazine* carried a full photographic report.

Turn left on the D223 following signs to Amfréville.

The road bisects DZ'N' on which the 5th Parachute Brigade and later the 6th Airlanding Brigade landed. The pathfinders of the Independent Parachute Company had had a scattered drop and were unable to set up their markers properly. One section operated its beacon thinking that DZ'N' was DZ'K' and attracted a number of 3rd Brigade units before the mistake was discovered. Therefore, as the Horsa gliders began to come in at 0330 hours, many pilots were unable to locate their correct strips or even be certain about which way they were supposed to land. One Sapper who was working on the landing strips remembered that "the gliders came from all directions ... some passed within thirty or fifty feet of each other going in opposite directions."

A D-DAY MEMORY

Major (later General) Tony Dyball, commanding D Company Royal Ulster Rifles, 6th Airlanding Brigade, who landed east of the Orne.

"I had a most unfortunate experience when we got into the gliders. If you can imagine - they were all lined up astern down the runway with the tug aircraft and then the glider. When we were about 100ft off the ground the tow rope broke and so we had to land - an emergency landing - on the grass. We just sat until some kind person brought round a tractor to drag us back and there we were at the end of the queue. Now perhaps you should understand that in those days we had six gliders for one company. At that particular time I was commanding D Company of the Royal Ulster Rifles. I had six officers and 128 riflemen. Anyway there I was and half an hour later I got off with another tug aeroplane. Well you can imagine what was going through my mind. What am I going to do? They've all gone there. I'm going to arrive. I don't know if I've got a company or anything at all. So I talked to the tug aeroplane and said 'Could you catch up?' He said, 'Well, I'll do my best. I'll slide down 400ft and I'll give full throttle.' So there we were chugging over Brighton, everybody waving away like mad. Then he said "We've got to get up a bit because I've got to let you off over Ouistreham." There were a few puffs of anti-aircraft fire but nothing serious. We got up and released and landed exactly where I'd shown the pilot on an aerial photograph that I'd wanted to be. There was the Company all lined up and ready to go. The Second in Command came up to me and said, "What kept you?"

Continue to the first crossroads and turn left and then left again on the C10 to Amfréville. On entering the village turn left, signed Sallenelles on the D37 and continue to where the road divides either side of a green in the centre of which is a church. Stop just before the division by a memorial on the right.

• No 6 Commando Memorial, Amfréville/6.1 miles/5 minutes/Map I34

Beyond the memorial to No 6 Commando is a **NTL Totem**.

The bridgehead established by the Airborne Forces and reinforced by the 1st Special Service Brigade (re-named No 1 Commando Brigade in June 1944) was under constant counter-attack for almost two months.

No 6 Commando led the way over Pegasus Bridge and their objective was the high ground over which you have driven. The road behind you leads to Bréville, not to Ranville, and also runs along the feature attacked and captured by No 6 Commando on the morning of 7 June, though since the whole Commando Brigade was involved in fighting in the area it is impossible to be absolutely certain about who was where. The area taken formed a salient into enemy lines pointing back in the direction from which you have come and at the tip was the village of Bréville, still held by the Germans. The commandos took heavy casualties from artillery fire over the coming days.

The farm buildings to the right of the memorial belong to farmer Bernard Saulnier who, during the fighting around Amfréville, was asked by Lieutenant-Colonel Peter Young of No 3 Commando to lop branches off some of the trees so that his soldiers would be able to see the Germans more clearly. Peter Young, who called himself a '3D' soldier because he served at Dunkirk, Dieppe and on D-Day, went on to become a brigadier, a renowned military historian and to found the 'Sealed Knot' a 'Cavalier and Roundheads' re-enactment organisation. He died in 1988.

On 12 June a major offensive was launched through Amfréville's commando positions by 12th Parachute Battalion and elements of the Devonshire Regiment in an attempt to capture Bréville. Lord Lovat was seriously wounded by a high explosive shell and Bernard Saulnier carried him into one of his cowsheds.

Originally, and for some 20 years, the town of Ouistreham held a day's open house for the commandos and provided free drink and meals with accommodation being offered by local people. Bernard took over the affair and on the 40th anniversary of D-Day in 1984 had about 700 people in his barn, 'Commando Farm'. In return the Commando Association presented their old friend with an especially commissioned cut glass decanter and glasses worth over £1,000 bearing the Commandos' insignia.

When Lord Lovat was wounded, Lieutenant-Colonel Mills-Roberts took over the brigade and commanded it for the rest of the war. He died in 1980 and in 1988 his ashes were transferred to Normandy and buried by Bernard Saulnier in Bavent (see below).

Continue left of the church to the memorial on the right.

• 1st Special Service Brigade Memorial/6.2 miles/5 minutes/Map I35

The white cross, with explanatory plaques each side, behind which are flagpoles, commemorates 1st Special Service Brigade's part in the action here.

Follow the road around the green.

It is known as the 'Le Plain Place du Commandant Kieffer' and there is a sign over the entrance to the *Mairie* to that effect.

Take the north-eastern exit from the green, the D37b signed to Sallenelles, and immediately before the road sign indicating that you are leaving Amfréville, turn left along rue Patra. Continue to the memorial at the end.

Memorial to No 6 Commando, Le Plain, Amfréville.

Memorial to 1st Special Services Brigade, Le Plain Amfréville.

Place Colonel Robert Dawson, (Lieutenant-Colonel RWF Dawson, commanding No 4 Commando).

• No 4 Commando Memorial, Place Colonel Robert Dawson, Hoger/6.3 miles/5 minutes/Map I36, 37

Since 1944 many place names in Normandy have changed or been amalgamated with others. In British accounts of actions the Anglicised versions of French names are often used offering yet another spelling to confuse the reader. The village here, now awash with new houses, was known in 1944 as 'Hauger' to the British.

This area is also known as le Hoger and on 10 June particularly intense fighting here involving No 4 Commando led to one troop losing all its officers. German counter-attacks on the high ground of Hoger - Le Plain - Amfréville had begun on the afternoon of 6 June and continued incessantly for four days.

The memorial cairn to No 4 Commando is in Place Colonel Robert Dawson (named on a memorial plaque). Colonel Dawson commanded No 4 but was twice wounded while landing on the beaches. On 7 June he rejoined the Commandos but on 9 June the medical officer ordered him to the rear. The château over the wall was, for a time, the No 4 Commando HQ and originally the memorial was in its grounds, but because it was difficult to get to, it was moved to its present site. The first Allied occupants of the château had been Lieutenant-Colonel Terence Otway and the remnants of the 9th Parachute Battalion who made their way here having taken the Merville Battery. They stayed until late on 6 June, suffering under heavy sniper fire, until relieved by men from No 3 Commando. No 3 then moved on to Le Plain handing the château over to No 4 Commando.

Return to the D37b, turn left and continue to Sallenelles. Stop on the right, just beyond the Sallenelles sign, near house No 23.

• 4th Special Services Brigade HQ Memorial/6.9 miles/5 minutes/ Map I38

The memorial commemorates Nos 41, 46, 47 and 48 RM Commandos whose headquarters were here from June- August 1944.

Continue into Sallenelles and turn right on the D514 signed to Merville and continue some 50 yards to house no 13-15.

• Edouard Gérard, Belgian Memorial/7.4 miles/5 minutes/Map I39

On the gate post of the house is a plaque to the memory of Edouard Gérard of the 1st Piron Brigade. He was the first Belgian soldier to be killed in Normandy - on 16 August 1944. The plaque was erected by his place of birth, Dinant.

Continue to the memorial on the junction on the left just before the Sallenelles exit sign.

• Piron Brigade Memorial/7.5 miles/5 minutes/Map I40.

The memorial commemorates the Belgian and Luxembourgois Brigade of Colonel Jean Piron, 14 August 1944.

Continue on the D514 following signs to Merville-Franceville-Plage.

A bunker (Map D6), now a brightly painted disco, is passed.

Continue to the traffic lights in Merville and turn right at the sign for la Batterie de Merville and stop immediately on the right by the group of memorials.

• *No 45 RM Commando, Liberators/Civilians, Piron Memorials, Merville/9 miles/10 minutes/Map D4,5*

On the left of the group is a new black marble memorial to the 35 soldiers of No 45 RM Commando killed in Merville on 8 June 1944. Beside it is the cream stone Merville-Franceville memorial to their dead and their liberators and a grey marble memorial to the 'Allied Soldiers and the Civilians of Merville-Franceville' who fell during June and July 1944 erected by the D-Day Commemoration Committee. On the right is a grey marble memorial to two sergeants and two soldiers of the Piron Brigade killed on 18 August.

Continue following signs to the Merville Battery and stop by the main gate.

• *Merville Battery/Museum/9th Parachute Battalion Memorial, Colonel Otway Bust/9.7 miles/20 minutes/Map D1,2,3*

At the entrance to the battery is a memorial to 9th Parachute Battalion and beside it a **NTL Totem.** At this spot the diversionary action was made and there are a number of notice boards and diagrams explaining what happened.

Inside the grounds is a bust to Lieutenant-Colonel Terence Otway sculpted by Vivien Mallock (in a similar style to that of John Howard at Pegasus bridge) and presented by the officer commanding 9th Parachute Battalion on 7 June 1997. The capture of the battery at Merville was one of the tasks of the 3rd Parachute Brigade. The other tasks, mainly the blowing of bridges over rivers, were widespread and far less concentrated than those of the 5th Parachute Brigade. The capture of the battery here was given to the 9th Parachute Battalion under Lieutenant-Colonel T. B. H. Otway whose planned DZ was two miles away near Varaville to the south-east.

In the planning for D-Day great care was taken to identify those aggressive elements of the Atlantic Wall that could threaten the invasion force as it came ashore - its most vulnerable moment. The concrete emplacements of the Merville Battery were thought to house four 150mm guns capable of bombarding the beaches on which 3rd British Division was due to land. It was deemed vital therefore that the guns be silenced by the airborne troops before the sea-borne forces arrived.

The area around the guns had been evacuated by the Germans and the villages of Franceville Plage and Gonneville were used as billets for German soldiers. In the weeks before D-Day the RAF bombed the area several times, but with no damage to any of the casemates. The 130 men of 716th Regiment who manned the battery not only had concrete to protect them from aerial attack but any assault on the ground had to penetrate a minefield between two barbed wire fences. On the north-west of the position, which was lozenge-shaped and some 800 yards by 500 yards, was a partially completed anti-tank ditch. Within the barbed-wire compound were a number of machine-gun positions. To the planners it had the appearance of a fortress and they planned to attack it as if it was.

In April 1944 Major Terence Otway was promoted to lieutenant-colonel and appointed to command the 9th Parachute Battalion. In a farmhouse near Netheravon he learned that his battalion had the very special task of neutralising a German battery on D-Day. In the farmhouse was a scale model of the battery with diagrams and aerial photographs, but it was some days before Otway learned where the guns were. It was some weeks before he learned when D-Day would be.

Very quickly Otway decided that the only way that a workable plan could be developed, and that he would be able to train his men to carry it out, was to build a full-scale model of the battery. A 45-acre site was found near Newbury and Royal Engineers with bulldozers worked for seven days and nights reproducing the anti-tank ditch, the paths, the gun emplacements (with steel girders covered with sacking) and the minefield areas. In 1993 a marker was erected on Walbury Hill to mark the site.

The plan was complex. The battalion was to divide into two groups. The first, smaller, group, was to prepare a rendezvous for the arrival of the main body and also reconnoitre the battery. An attack by a hundred RAF Lancaster bombers was scheduled

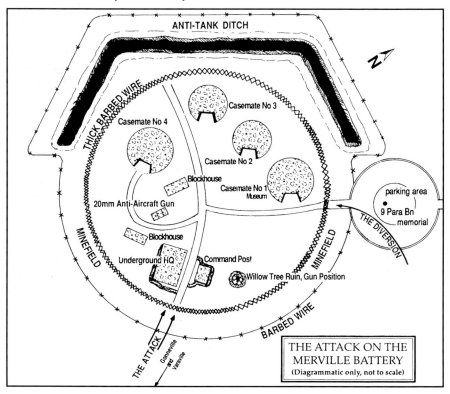

ANTI-TANK DITCH

N

THICK BARBED WIRE

Casemate No 3

Casemate No 4

Casemate No 2

Blockhouse

Casemate No 1
Museum

parking area

9 Para Bn
memorial

20mm Anti-Aircraft Gun

THE DIVERSION

MINEFIELD

Blockhouse

Underground HQ

Command Post

Willow Tree Ruin, Gun Position

MINEFIELD

THE ATTACK

Gonneville
and
Varaville

BARBED WIRE

THE ATTACK ON THE
MERVILLE BATTERY
(Diagrammatic only, not to scale)

for 0030 hours and Otway wanted to know the resulting damage before launching his assault. The first group was to jump at 0020 hours and the main body at 0050 hours. The main body comprised most of the battalion, including 'B' and 'C' Companies. 'B' Company was given the job of breaching the first wire barrier and clearing a path through the minefield. 'C' Company was the assault force, while the remainder of 'A' Company was to hold a firm base from which the others could begin the assault. 'C' Company was to rush the gap in the minefield and split into four parties accompanied by sappers of 591st Parachute Squadron. Each party was to capture and blow up a casemate. The plan did not end there. Timed to arrive as 'C' Company made its charge through the battery defences, three Horsa gliders were to crash-land inside the perimeter. This party, named like John Howard's force at Pegasus Bridge, as a *'coup-de-main'*, consisted mainly of A Company personnel and a number of sappers. Then, if all else had failed, HMS *Arethusa* was standing by to pound the battery with her 6in guns at 0550 hours.

Bust of Lieutenant-Colonel T Otway, Commander 9th Parachute Battalion, Merville Battery grounds.

Otway trained his men very hard. He was sparing with his praise and quick to find fault. They rehearsed over and over again - all except the gliders. He could not get gliders to crash land into his dummy battery, so he arranged that the RAF would fly in low as the practice attacks went in. However, the fifty or so paratroopers of 'A' Company had to be retrained as glider troops. They flew over Salisbury Plain and practised accurate landings at Thruxton. Then, finally, the colonel declared himself satisfied and a few days later the battalion was sealed into its pre-invasion camp near Broadwell in Berkshire. There were over seven hundred men, ready, trained and anxious to go.

The first small group took off from RAF Harwell at 2310 hours on 5 June in Albemarles, and dropped accurately and to time at 0020 hours, despite the fact that the aircraft had an uneasy reputation for losing its tail in mid-air. The officer in charge of the rendezvous to which the reconnaissance group and then the main body were to report was Major Allen Parry and on landing he used his 'Ducks, Bakelite' (a whistle device that made a sound like a duck, and the British equivalent to the Americans 'cricket') to locate a friendly face. There was no one about, so he set off alone to the rendezvous, hearing, en route, the explosions from the Lancaster raid on the battery. It was well off target. Reaching the rendezvous Parry set up his Aldis lamp to guide in the paratroopers and waited for the main body. When they came the aeroplanes seemed to be spread out and as their engine noise faded away he began to flash his Aldis signal. But two hours after the drop only 150 men, including Lieutenant-Colonel Otway, had arrived. It was less than 25 per cent of those that had set out. There were no Royal Engineers and, apart from sidearms, they had only one Vickers machine gun and twenty Bangalore torpedoes between them. Otway decided to make for his objective and at 0250 hours set out, reaching the firm base area 500 yards from the battery at about 0420 hours. Parry, originally in charge of the rendezvous, was given command of the assault party and divided his allocation of fifty men into four units in imitation of the original plan. Now they would wait for the *coup-de-main* party. When that arrived as planned into the middle of the battery, then they would attack.

A D-DAY MEMORY

Paratrooper Les Cartwright, 9th Parachute Battalion. Dropped for the Merville Battery.

"I think I should tell you first quickly who we were. Now we were the 9th Para Battalion. We were formed out of the 10th Essex Battalion and we were designated as a Home Counties Battalion therefore most of us came from the Home Counties - Middlesex, Surrey, Essex. That's who we were. The actual boys and myself, the Paras, the average age was 19 to 21. No older. Our officers were a bit older. Our NCOs were a bit older, because 'Windy' (if I speak of Windy that means General Gale) - Windy had nicked a lot of NCOs from the 1st Division who had experience to put in amongst us so as to give us that bit of backing and a bit of experience. Anyway, the first thing we knew about this was we knew something was up, 'cos if you remember we had these little exercises and it always seemed to be guns we were after - up the hill and down the valley, and then one day a little while before Normandy they marched us out and we stopped at the Battalion and the Colonel told us what the job was. Well after that we went down on the plains and the Colonel found a position practically like this (the Merville Battery) and we built a battery and we attacked it night and day for a week. The idea was that first of all to drop would be our pathfinders, then some of the lads would drop and they'd make for the battery, make sure it was alright and then we get to the RV and we do the approach march which was approximately about a mile and a half across the fields. And then when we got here we had three gliders coming in with twenty paras in each who had volunteered to go in, those gliders, to actually crash land in the battery when we put the attack in. That was at the same time that one party came up here to the main gate. They would attack from that position. Well we were to come through and blow the wire in four positions. 'C' Company was the attacking Company. Then once through those four positions we had to take a gun each and blow it. And everything we done just dovetailed, and it was beautiful. We were so confident that we could do it, he'd brain-washed us too much. So anyway, a couple of weeks later, three o'clock in the morning, lights go on in the barrack room. 'Right - get up, get your kit - OUT'. And when we walked out on the square there were all these transporters. Into the transporters, and I think we drove around for about 8 hours, changing drivers here and there, and the last thing we knew there was all these tanks, all the barbed wire round it. In we went, they shut the gate and said, 'You stay there'. And we'd had a big mosaic made of the battery itself, and we had to study that and an officer could stop you any time and say, 'Where is so-and-so in the battery?' And if you didn't know, mate, you were back in there and you were stuck in there an hour, and you had to explain everything to

A D-Day memory continued

him. So everybody knew exactly what the other chap was doing and exactly what was in there, and it looked a perfect plan. But come the night, 5 June, we took off just after midnight and we dropped just before one. It was a beautiful flight across till we hit the coast, and we hit the coast and you've never seen anything like it in your life. It was just like going into a firework display and the old duck was going five ways at once andeverybody was saying, 'Let's get out of this so-and-so thing'. Anyway eventually the Pilot says, 'Go', and puts the light on, and on our way we go. And as I dropped, obviously you look round and I could see other 'chutes coming down and I hit the deck and out of my 'chute, got my sten out, everything going, look round - couldn't see anybody. But there was one thing that got implanted in my mind - we must get to that RV. And the Colonel's orders were 'You were to have no private fire fights. You get to the RV AND THAT IS IT'. And I checked around a bit. I found the road that runs in front of the rendezvous. I didn't know which way to go - right or left - but I heard a fire fight going on up to the left so I thought I'd go up to the right. And I just got along the side of the road looking, and away in the distance I could just see this red light twinkling. And it was one of the officers got up the tree with an Aldis lamp and was flicking this right round in circles to bring the lads in. As soon as I saw that I knew where I was to get. I could see the tree across the fields and I saw a bod just in front of where I knew the RV was and I yelled the password out and he yelled it back and I looked at him and it was the Colonel. He was standing there waiting to bring the lads in. He tapped me on the shoulder and he said, 'Well done, lad. What company?' 'C Company.' 'Down there.' I went down there and ... I dropped down beside my Lieutenant (Jackson) and had a little word with him, you know. At the time I thought, well there don't seem many of us here, but you know most of us thought that but we didn't say it. 'Cos there's 100 of us in the company. It didn't look 100, but you didn't say anything because you didn't want to upset anybody. Any rate we was sitting there and we knew the timetable, knew we ought to be moving now. We ought to be moving and eventually the Colonel said 'Move', and it wasn't until years afterwards I found out that out of the 550 who jumped in our battalion, only 150 got to the rendezvous."

Things went wrong again. One of the three gliders broke its tow rope just after take-off, the second landed several miles east of the battery and the last one, although it actually flew over the battery, crashed in an orchard about 100 yards away to the south-west having been hit by anti-aircraft fire. The third glider did, however, distract the attention of some German machine gunners who had been causing casualties from their position outside the defended perimeter as well as intercepting a German patrol that was moving up to reinforce the battery. Otway decided to get on with the job. Without engineer support or any mine-clearing equipment it was a case of charging both the wire and the minefield. The paratroopers went forward firing their sten guns from the hip, using the gaps in the wire and minefield caused by the bombing and blowing two more gaps using the Bangalore torpedoes. At the main gate a small party opened fire, hoping to cause a diversion. The Germans fought well, coming out of their bunkers to counter-attack. It was a short and bloody scrap in which Allen Parry was wounded. The cost to the battalion was heavy - seventy officers and men killed or wounded. The battalion was down to eighty. The German garrison was reduced to twenty-two prisoners, all the rest were killed or wounded. When the fighting had stopped Sergeant Eric Bedford turned to one of his soldiers and said, "Blimey, Sid, here, take a look around. This is the 9th Battalion, mate. Looks more like the 9th Platoon to me." Bedford also laid claim to a 'first' - the first German flag captured in the invasion which he had found in Casemate 1. He stuffed it up his smock.

When the casemates were examined the guns were found to be old French 75mm weapons on wheels. The anticipated heavy weapons had not been installed. Nevertheless the guns were put out of action and the victory signal was made both by pigeon and by smoke flares just thirty minutes before 0530 hours when the *Arethusa* was due to begin her bombardment. The 9th Parachute Battalion had not finished its task, however. Now they had to head for the high ground around Amfréville. Otway led his men off and later in the day a combat group of the German 736th Grenadier Regiment regained Merville only to lose it the following day to an assault by two troops of No 3 Commando. Once again it was a fierce battle in the casemates and in the tunnels that linked the different bunkers, but the Germans were overcome. Almost immediately the enemy counter-attacked using self-propelled guns and drove the commandos out and back to Le Plain.

9th Parachute Battalion never collected all of its men. The initial drop which was supposed to have been contained within an area of $1^1/_2$ square miles was spread over 50 square miles. There were a number of reasons for this: the aircrews carrying out the drop were inexperienced, having only been formed into a Group (No 46) in January 1944: the leading aircraft of each formation did the navigating and signalled to the others when to drop so that single aircraft, when disorientated by trying to avoid flak on the way over, led groups of others to the wrong place, while others confused the Rivers Dives and Orne. Hundreds of men were dropped into the flooded areas of the Dives and many were drowned.

The museum here was established on 6 June 1982, thanks to the energy and enthusiasm of General Sir Nigel Poett, who, as Brigadier Poett, commanded the 5th Parachute Brigade on D-Day. It is partly funded by Airborne Assault Normandy, a charitable trust established to commemorate the 6th Airborne Division's achievements in Normandy. Like other museums in the area, this museum has suffered from a number of thefts, and it is kept tightly closed during most winter months. The ground, however, and the casemates themselves are always accessible.

Open: 1 April-30 September 1000-1300 and 1400-1900. Entrance fee payable. Tel: (0)2 31 24 21 83

Return to the T junction and turn right continuing in the original direction of travel to Descanneville. There turn right on to the D223 signed Bréville. Drive to the crossroads with the D37b in Bréville and the memorial on the right-hand corner opposite the Mairie.

• 12th Parachute/12th Devonshire Regiment Memorial, Grave of Captain Ward, Bréville/ 13 miles/10 minutes/Map I23

To best understand the importance of Bréville and its high ground, the traveller is advised to consult the Holts' map and Map 10 and to ascertain the general direction of Amfréville/Le Plain/Hoger and the château of St Côme.

During one of his inspection tours, Rommel had visited Bréville, planning his defence of the high ground from a viewpoint at the crossroads where you now are. That defence was formidable and, despite the best efforts of the commandos, paratroopers and 51st Highland Division, the Germans held on, giving ground reluctantly and at great cost to themselves and their attackers. Even by the start of Operation GOODWOOD on 18 July, some six weeks after D-Day, the British front line extended no further south than Bréville and GOODWOOD itself moved the line forward only to the southern edge of the Bois de Bavent, which is passed later on this tour.

The capture of the high ground on which Bréville and the other villages such as Le Plain, Hoger and Amfréville sit, was one of the tasks set for the 6th Airborne Division and General Gale allocated it to Brigadier James Hill's 3rd Parachute Brigade. The ground, and the bridges across the Orne which it overlooked, controlled German routes into the landing bridgehead from the east. It was vital, therefore, that it was quickly captured and then held.

On D-Day, after completing their primary tasks, the 9th Parachute Battalion (whose first task was to destroy the Merville Battery) and the 1st Canadian Parachute Battalion (whose first task was to destroy bridges over the River Dives) headed for the high ground. (See Map 10.) 9th Battalion got to Hoger, which you passed earlier, and the 1st Battalion reached le Mesnil, which you pass later. Meanwhile No 4 Commando dug in at Hoger and No 6 established themselves between Le Plain and Bréville. The Germans held Bréville. It was a patchy situation. The German defence was cellular, strong here and weak there, and this, combined with the independent nature of the specialist commando and airborne forces moving against them, produced a confused and irregular battlefield with opposing forces jumbled together.

The German formations in this area were the 346th and 711th Infantry Divisions and for three days after D-Day they mounted heavy counter-attacks against the lightly equipped airborne forces on the high ground. General Gale knew that his forces were tiring, and although the 1st Special Service Brigade had come under his command once they were ashore, he desperately needed fresh troops. But he also had to secure the high ground and to him that meant that he must capture Bréville. The General told Lord Lovat that Bréville must be cleared and towards midday on 7 June No 6 Commando supported by the No 1 French Commando, under Commandant Kieffer, attacked the village. The No 6 account claims that the village was taken and that a number of field and machine guns were captured and subsequently used by themselves in the defence at Le Plain, but it must have been a temporary occupation ended by a German counter-attack because on the fourth day after D-Day Bréville was still in German hands.

On 10 June Gale received three battalions of the 51st Highland Division as reinforcements and the 5th Battalion The Black Watch was moved to the château of St Côme to prepare for an assault. The château is some 500 yards south-east of where you are down the D376 to your left. It is next on the itinerary. At 0430 hours on 11 June, after a preliminary bombardment by five regiments of artillery, the Black Watch set off towards you on their first action in Normandy. It was over very quickly. The Germans opened up a barrage of mortar, assault and anti-aircraft guns and the Black Watch retired with some 200 casualties to where they had started. The morale of the 51st Division at that time was not good and the divisional history admits it. It had been troops of the Division that had mutinied on the beaches at Salerno the year before. A calculated assessment of British infantry divisions' performance against that of the Germans and the Americans suggests that they were short of combative senior commanders who could inspire and lead. Within two months Major General W.R.J. Erskine, commanding the 51st Highland Division, was sacked by General Montgomery.

General Gale, despite the failure of the Black Watch and being down to his reserve formation, the 12th Parachute Battalion, determined to try again. He strengthened the paratroopers with a company of the 12th Battalion the Devonshire Regiment and a troop of Sherman tanks of the 13th/18th Hussars and ordered an attack for 2200 hours on 12 June. So confused was the general situation that accounts of the attack cannot agree upon whether it was 'B' or 'D' Company of the Devonshire Regiment that was involved. The mixed formations gathered around and in the church in Amfréville (where you were earlier, some 750 yards north-east up the D376) and awaited the preliminary bombardment by the five field and one medium artillery regiments in support. At about 2100 hours the barrage began, but not all of it reached Bréville where you are. Some fell short onto Amfréville near Bernard Saulnier's farm and it seems highly likely that the shell burst that injured Lord Lovat was 'friendly fire'. Also injured by a shell at about the same time was Brigadier Hugh Kindersley of 6th Airlanding Brigade of which the 12th Devons were part.

The paratroopers and the Devonshire Regiment pushed on through the commandos holding Amfréville and advanced astride the D376 towards you. This time resistance was less determined but still heavy. Artillery had devastated the defenders and their defences. Damaged German equipment and dead and wounded soldiers were mixed amongst the carcasses of animals killed and left unburied over the last week. A pall of smoke hung over all and the flames from burning houses licked the gathering darkness into a scene of overwhelming horror.

As the paratroopers and the Devons captured and then conferred in the village to co-ordinate their defences, the bombardment began again. The Royal Artillery repeated their earlier barrage, churning the area where you are into a shapeless mass of earth and rubble and destroying churchyard and church. The codeword to start the barrage had been confused with another over a crackly radio. It was what those present called 'a bloody shambles'. But Bréville was captured, though the price was a high one - the Devons had had heavy casualties as they formed up to attack, possibly from our own artillery, losing thirty-five soldiers and their company commander. The paratroopers lost their CO, Lieutenant- Colonel A. P. Johnston, seven officers and 133 soldiers. The next day the small force handed Bréville over to the 1st Battalion Royal Ulster Rifles.

The memorial is to those who died here, with captions in English and French. It reads:

6th British Airborne Division.
In Memory of the Inhabitants of Bréville who died in 1944 and also to the men of the
12th (Yorkshire) Parachute Battalion, the 12th Batalion the Devonshire Regiment and
other detachments who on the evening of 12 June 1944 assaulted Bréville through the
No1 Commando Brigade positions from the direction of Amfréville and drove out the
German force.
162 men of the Division died. They lie in the Ranville Military Cemetery.

Beside it is a **NTL Totem.** The area is called *Carrefour* (crossroads) Airborne Division.
On the wall of the churchyard opposite is the small white on green Commonwealth
War Graves Commission sign that is placed on civilian cemeteries where British and
Commonwealth soldiers lie buried. Inside is a headstone for Captain H.W. Ward of the
53rd (Worcestershire Yeomanry) Airlanding Light Regiment RA who was killed on 12
June 1944, and Private Masters of 12 Para Battalion.

*Turn left on the D37b signed Troarn for about 500 yards and stop on the left at the
small track that leads to the Château St Côme.*

• *9th Parachute Infantry Battalion Memorial/13.4 miles/5 minutes/Map I20*

The Canadians, part of 3rd Parachute Brigade, dropped at DZ'V' in the area of
Varaville, some 5 miles to the north-east of here. Their main task was to destroy the
bridges over the River Dives in the region of Varaville and Robehomme. Despite being
scattered over a wide area the Canadians blew the bridges and then moved as shown
on Map 10 through Château St Côme to a position at le Mesnil which is next on our route.

The memorial here records in English and French what it calls the 'Battle of the Bois
des Monts and the Château St Côme 7-13 June 1944', and describes the actions of the
9th Parachute Battalion, the attack by the Black Watch on Bréville and the involvement
by the 1st Canadian Parachute Battalion until the force was relieved by the 52nd
Battalion Oxfordshire and Buckinghamshire Light Infantry.

*Continue to the junction with the D513. Go straight over, signed Troarn, and stop
immediately on the right in the car park by a grassy area.*

• *1st Canadian Parachute Battalion Memorial, Place Brigadier James Hill, l'Arbre Martin/14.2 miles/10 minutes/Map I19*

Beside the memorial to 1st Canadian Parachutists, which reads, 'In tribute to all ranks
of the 1st Canadian Parachute Battalion dropped into Normandy in the early hours of
'D'Day June 6 1944 who upon this ground successfully defended a vital approach to the
east flank of the allied landings', is a stone with the sign to 'Square Brigadier James Hill'
(Brigadier Hill, DSO and two bars, MC).

Return to the crossroads and turn left on the D513 signed Hérouvillette.
After some 250 yards is the area of le Mesnil, the rendezvous point for the 1st Canadian
Parachute Battalion and other elements of 3rd Parachute Brigade whose task was to

destroy bridges to the east around Varaville.

Continue to the layby on the right.

• 6th Airborne Table d'Orientation, le Mesnil/15.3 miles/5 minutes

This Orientation Table is part of the old Brittany Ferries trail which is now defunct.

Continue to the next village, Hérouvillette. After the church turn immediately left onto the rue de la Paix. Continue 100 yards to the new cemetery entrance and stop.

• 2nd (Airborne) Battalion Oxfordshire & Buckinghamshire Light Infantry Plaque, Hérouvillette/15.6 miles/10 minutes/Map I18

On the left of the entrance is the CWGC *'Tombes de Guerre'* (War Graves) sign and on the right a marble stone memorial originally dedicated on 6 June 1987 which says in English (and then in French):

'In Memory to those who fought at Pegasus Bridge, Escoville, Hérouvillette, Bréville les Monts and to the Seine and to the many brave French who helped us.'

In the cemetery are twenty-seven graves of airborne troops including Army Air Corps, RASC, the 12th Parachute Battalion and men of the Oxfordshire and Buckinghamshire Light Infantry.

This village was captured by the Oxs and Bucks Light Infantry and the 1st Royal

Memorial to 8th Parachute Battalion, le Manoir du Bois.

Memorial to Brigadier Alastair Pearson, le Manoir du Bois.

Ulster Rifles on 7 June. They then went on the same day to attack Escoville, but were unsuccessful. Two days later the 21st Panzer Division counter-attacked Hérouvillette, but were driven off, after losing forty dead and four tanks and armoured cars.

> *Return to the D513, turn left and at the end of the village turn left again onto the D37 signed Troarn. Continue to Escoville and stop in front of the church in Place Six Juin 1944.*

• *Memorial to British Liberators, Escoville/16.5 miles/5 minutes/Map I9*

This commemorates the liberation in July 1944. In the churchyard is buried Private Wilkins of the Oxs and Bucks, who was killed on 7 June 1944.

> *Continue towards Troarn over the junction with the D37b and some 250 yards later on the left is a track leading left to the Manoir du Bois. Some 50 yards further on beside the road on the left are two memorials.*

• *8th Parachute Battalion, Brigadier Alastair Pearson Memorials, Manoir du Bois/18.2 miles/10 minutes/Map I8*

The parachute memorial is a simple polished stone that says: 'In memory of all ranks of 8th Parachute Battalion 6 June-August 1944.'

The 8th Battalion had an unfortunate arrival. One of the pathfinder parties was dropped on DZ'N', three miles north of here, instead of being on DZ'K' a mile west (see Map 10). Thus the main body, which arrived at about 0050 hours, was split between the two zones. On DZ 'K' the battalion commander gathered about 160 men and formed a firm base. On DZ'N' Major J.C.A. Roseveare RE, who commanded 3rd Parachute Squadron Royal Engineers, gathered a force of about forty sappers and RE officers and some thirty paratroopers (who were reluctant to take orders from a non-paratroop officer). Collecting six trolleys, high explosives and a jeep Major Roseveare set off at about 0230 hours towards the bridges at Bures and Troarn that were his target. He followed the route which you have driven via Hérouvillette and Escoville. At the road junction of the D37 and D37b, just short of the 8th Parachute Battalion Memorial, he stopped. It was 0400 hours. There the paratroop infantry were left to form a defensive position. The main body of sappers was sent off to blow the Bures-sur-Dives bridges (both blown by 0930 hours). Major Roseveare plus one other officer and seven sappers jumped into the solitary jeep and, with a trailer of demolition equipment, set off for the bridge at Troarn. The second memorial here was unveiled on 5 June 1996 and is to Brigadier Alastair Pearson, CB, DSO (3 bars), CBE, MC, TD, 1915-1996, who commanded 8th Parachute Battalion. It was erected by the Veterans and Friends of the Battalion, Members of the Parachute Regiment Association and the local *Communes.*

> *Continue on the D37 and after 400 yards take the first small turning right signed to Touffreville. Continue into the village and fork right on the rue du Centre.*

In the village churchyard (reached by forking left here) is the grave of Corporal E.

O'Sullivan, killed 6 June 1944, age 22, of 8 Parachute Battalion. The church square is named after him.

At the next crossroads turn right on rue des Jardins. Continue on the C2, past the Touffreville exit sign and continue to the small memorial on the right.

• Arthur Platt/Thomas W Billington Memorial/19.9 miles/5 minutes/Map I7

The memorial marks the spot where the bodies of the two men of 8th Parachute Battalion were found on 10 June 1944. In 1976 Platt's son, William J. Lewis (Private Platt's wife married again), himself a paratrooper with the 2nd Battalion from 1958 to 1969, began a quest to find out what had happened to his father. With the help of the 8th Battalion Association and the wife of the Secretary of the *Anciens Combattants'* Association in Touffreville he established the place of his father's death. He also discovered that Private Platt had been shot in the back of the head and probably while a prisoner of war of the SS. The *Commune* of Touffreville raised the memorial and it was inaugurated on 6 June 1988. Private Platt is buried in Ranville Commonwealth War Graves Commission Cemetery. His photo, taken with General Montgomery in March 1944, used to be in the museum at Pegasus Bridge.

Return to the crossroads. Go straight across on the D227 to Sanneville, rue du 8th Parachute Battalion 6 juin 1944. At the junction with the N175 turn right signed Démouville and continue to the parking area on the left.

• Banneville-la-Campagne CWGC Cemetery/21.7 miles/15 minutes/ Map I2

The cemetery contains 2,175 burials - 2,150 British, 11 Canadian, 5 Australian, 2 New Zealand, 5 Polish and 2 unidentified graves. They are mostly from the fighting of mid July-end August 1944 when Caen was captured and the Falaise Gap was closed.

Turn round and continue on the N175, direction Troarn, going under the motorway. In the town continue to the Syndicat d'Initiative on the right. Park in the square (named after Resistance hero Paul Quelbec) *behind the office.*

• 3rd Parachute Squadron RE Memorial, Troarn/24 miles/10 minutes/RWC/Map I3

On the wall of the **Tourist Office,** Tel: (0)2 31 39 14 22, is a plaque erected by the population of Troarn in honour of the officers and men of 3rd Parachute Squadron RE who, at dawn on 6 June 1944, on information obtained from the Resistance, destroyed the bridges over the Dives in order to protect the left flank of the landings.

Return to the N175 and turn right downhill to the bridge over the Dives at St Sampson.

• *Major J.C.A. Roseveare Bridge Memorial, River Dives/24.9 miles/5 minutes/Map I4*

In the early hours of 6 June Major Roseveare, coming from the Manoir du Bois, drove down the D37 to the N875 junction in his jeep. At that time the D37 crossed a railway line before the town and the jeep ran into a barbed-wire knife rest guarding the crossing. The guard fired one shot at it and disappeared but it took twenty minutes to get free. At the N175 junction Roseveare's party met and shot a German soldier which roused the town. "We made the mistake of silencing him with a Sten instead of with a knife", said Roseveare. All the party then jumped into the jeep and trailer and Roseveare drove as fast as he could through the town. At about where the tourist office now is, in Major Roseveare's words, "The fun started, as there seemed to be a Boche in every doorway shooting like mad. However, the boys got to work with their Stens and Sapper Peachey did good work as rear gunner with the Bren. What saved the day was the steep hill down the main street. As the speed rose rapidly and we careered from side to side of the road, as the heavy trailer was swinging violently, we were chased out of the town by an MG 34 which fired tracer just over our heads."

When they got to the bridge (over the Dives on the N175 to St Samson) at the bottom of the hill it was found to be unguarded but they discovered that they had lost their Bren gunner. Five minutes later they had blown a 20ft gap in the masonry structure. It was not yet 0500 hours. Roseveare ditched the jeep north of Troarn and the party navigated their way on foot to le Mesnil which they reached at 1300 hours. The bridge is now named the Major J.C.A. Roseveare Bridge and the memorial was erected by the Commune on 5 June 1986 to commemorate the bridge crossing at dawn on 6 June 1944.

> *Return to Troarn and just before the Place Paul Quelbec turn right and take the D95 direction Bures. Turn right into the village along rue du Capitaine Juckes, fork right at the village war memorial and continue downhill along rue du Port to the bridge over the River Dives.*

• *Captain Juckes Bridge Memorial, Bures/27.3 miles/5 minutes/Map I5*

The memorial commemorates the destruction of this bridge and the railway bridge to the north, by 2nd Troop, 3rd Parachute Squadron of the Royal Engineers commanded by Capt T. R. Juckes MC. Juckes and his men arrived unopposed at the bridges at around 0630 hours and both were blown by 0930 after which they settled down for a well-earned breakfast. Sadly Capt Juckes was injured later in the campaign and died of wounds on 28 June 1944. He is buried in Ranville CWGC.

> *Return to the D95 and continue under the motorway to Bavent. Turn left on the D236 and in Bavent turn right at the junction past the church.*

In the churchyard is the grave of Lieutenant Haig-Thomas of No 4 Commando, 'naturalist and explorer', who was killed on 6 June 1944.

> *Turn left on the rue des Champs to large wooden gates on the left to the local cemetery extension. Stop. Walk into the top left-hand corner of the cemetery.*

Memorial to Captain Juckes, Bridge over the River Dives, Bures.

Grave of Brigadier Mills-Roberts, Bavent churchyard.

Memorial to the crash site and massacre, Grangues.

Memorial to Arthur Platt and Thomas Billington, shot by the SS, Touffreville.

Architect Philip Hepworth's serpentine path, Banneville-la-Campagne CWGC Cemetery.

Memorial to Major J.C.A. Roseveare, Commander 3rd Parachute Squadron RE, Dives Bridge.

• Grave of Brigadier Mills-Roberts CBE, DSO & Bar, MC, Légion d'Honneur, Croix de Guerre, Bavent Churchyard/30.6 miles/10 minutes/Map I20

The ashes of the Irish Guards commander of No 1 Commando Brigade who liberated Bavent on 17 August 1944 were interred here after his death on 1 October 1980.

Return to the T junction and turn right. Continue past the church and stop at the pond on the right, Place Alexandre Lofi, French Officer of No 4 Commando.

• 1st Special Service Brigade Commando Memorial/31.00 miles/5 minutes/Map 121

The 40th Anniversary tribute board tells the story of the 'Liberators of Bavent and Robehomme' from their landing at Colleville to 17 August 1944.

Extra Visit to the Memorial to the Massacre, St Pierre de Jonquet (Map J1). Round trip: 7.5 miles. Approximate time: 20 minutes.

Return to Troarn and take the D78 to St Pierre de Jonquet. Stop at the memorial by the church.

The dramatic memorial is to the memory of twenty-eight civilians shot for aiding their liberators.

Return to Bavent.

Extra Visits to No 3 Commando Memorial, Petiville,(Map 147) 1st Canadian Parachute Battalion, Varaville (Map I46) and Grangues Crash/Massacre (Map E2) Memorials. Round trip: 18 miles. Approximate time: 30 minutes.

Continue to the junction with the D5B and turn right direction Varaville. Continue on the D95 to Petiville and continue to the memorial by the cemetery and the Mairie.

The pink marble memorial was inaugurated on the 50th Anniversary by a delegation of Commandos and veterans. It honours **No 3 Commando and Brigadier Peter Young.** In the *Mairie* is a photograph of the Brigadier and a Commando dagger that were presented that day.

Continue to Varaville to the memorial at the entrance to the town on the right.

The grey marble memorial to **1st Canadian Parachute Battalion** was erected on the 50th Anniversary. At the bottom is a bronze plaque unveiled in June 1997.

Continue and take the next right signed A13 Honfleur on the D27, through Periers en Auge. Turn left on the D45B signed Grangues and continue (for what seems an awfully long time) along the narrow road to the church on the left.

Beside the church is a large open parking area and just inside the churchyard on the right is a flat memorial stone. Its caption is headed, 'In Memoriam 6 June 1944' followed by a list of 52 casualties. It summarises how 2 Stirling parachute transport aircraft (Nos EJ 116 and EF 295 of 620 Squadron RAF) were shot down close to Grangues Château near this site. The Stirlings had taken off from Fairford at about 2340 hours on 5 June. EJ 116 carried 14 men of 7th Para Battalion and 5 men from 6th Airborne Reconnaissance Regiment. The paras were to secure the area around the River Orne and the Caen Canal bridges. The Recce Regt was to find and secure a tank harbouring area. EF 295 was flown by the distinguished RCAF pilot, Sqn Leader W.R. Pettit, OBE, DFC. It carried 15 men of 591 Para Sqn RE, including Major Andy Wood, the Squadron Commander, and 2 members of an advance party from HQRE, the Intelligence Officer, J.S. Shinner and Sapper Peter Guard. The 591 Squadron men had to clear the glider landing strips on the DZ of the obstruction poles and the Sappers were carrying bicycle inner tubes filled with plastic explosives for this task. The Stirlings made the wrong landfall and EJ 116 was hit and crashed in a field about 400 metres from the Château. All 6 aircrew and 19 parachutists were killed, the wreckage burning fiercely for a day because of the explosives it carried, during which time no-one dared approach it for fear of further explosions. EF 295 was approaching the coast and her parachutists had received the instruction 'Running in' when one of the explosive sausages she was carrying was hit by tracer and there was a blinding flash inside the cabin. Her engines were also hit . Four men, including Major Wood, were able to jump. He landed in the field next to the 4-gun Light AA battery at Gonneville-sur-Mer that had hit his plane and spent the next 20 hours in hiding. As the plane crash-landed and ploughed on for

Extra Visits continued

more than 100 metres, the 4 Aircrew at the nose and 4 parachutists were killed, most of the other occupants were badly injured. The plane ground to a halt about 500 metres from the Château, which was occupied by the Germans, who were soon on the scene and rounded up the survivors. They were taken to a stable block and some primitive first aid was permitted for the injured. A wounded survivor, J.S, Stirling, describes how he was - perfectly correctly - interrogated and told he would be attended by a British RAMC Officer. Meanwhile the gliders were due to arrive from 0320 hours and two Horsas crashed in the grounds of the Château. One carried a party from 6th Airborne Division HQ, including Captain John Max (GSO 3) and five divisional HQ signals specialists. Captain Max and the co-pilot were killed in the crash, the remainder, including the pilot, Staff Sergeant D. Wright, were taken prisoner. The second Horsa came down vertically onto trees and all its occupants were killed. They included 3 men from division HQ and a Forward Observation party, consisting of an RA Officer and two RN telegraphists, who had been due to direct the fire of a cruiser offshore. A third Horsa landed with little damage in a field just to the north but the occupants have never been identified.

All French civilians in the vicinity had been confined to quarters so they could not witness what happened next. But from the evidence of a Red Cross worker in the Château, Mlle Thérèse Anne, it is clear that Staff Sergeant Wright and 7 of the Sapper survivors of EF 295 were shot. She was told there had been an attempted break-out and was shown the spot where the men were killed. The men were buried in a trench and were finally identified by a British medical team in 1945.

In all, 44 soldiers, sailors and airmen died or were mortally wounded and 8 survivors were shot. "These young men were all volunteers whose belief in the cause of freedom was such that they were prepared to give their lives in this dangerous mission. Let this peaceful place preserve a lasting memory of their names" are the very moving final words of the inscription. Grangues, a tiny, idyllic village with its XIIIth Century Church, is indeed a beautiful site for the memorial to this tragedy of war. The victims of the crashes and the massacre are buried in Ranville CWGC Cemetery. That they were able to be buried together was due to the fact that the owners of the Château had an Irish nanny who was so upset by what had happened that she went out and, using a wheelbarrow, collected all the bodies.

The memorial was dedicated in June 1994 in the presence of about 400 people, including several relatives of those who died, who had not known until recently what happened to their men. The funds for it were raised by veterans of the units and next of kin involved in the incident.

Return to Bures.

• End of Itinerary Five

ALLIED & GERMAN WARGRAVES & COMMEMORATIVE ASSOCIATIONS

THE AMERICAN BATTLE MONUMENTS COMMISSION

The Commission was established by the United States Congress in March 1923 for the permanent maintenance of military cemeteries and memorials on foreign soil. Their first task was to build cemeteries for the American dead of World War I.

After World War II, fourteen overseas military cemeteries were constructed, including the St Laurent Normandy Cemetery. They contain approximately 39 per cent of those originally buried in the region, the remaining 61 per cent were returned to the USA.

The ground on which each cemetery is built was granted by the host nation, free of rent or taxes. A white marble headstone marks every burial (Star of David for the Jewish, Latin cross for all others, whether they be Christian, Buddhist, agnostic or of any other belief). Memorials bearing the names of the missing, a non-denominational chapel and a visitors' room containing the register and visitors' book are standard in all cemeteries. All are open to the public daily.

The cemeteries are immaculately maintained by a superintendent (normally American) using local gardeners. He will supply photographs of the cemetery and the individual headstone for the next of kin and arrange for cut flowers to be bought locally and placed on the grave.

The Commission now maintains 24 permanent American burial grounds on foreign soil, in which there are 124,913 U.S. War Dead: 30,921 of WWI, 93,242 of WWII and 750 of the Mexican War.

For full details of the Normandy American Cemetery and Memorial, see Itinerary Two above (Map U10). Other Americans who died in Normandy are buried in Saint James (Map Y10), south of Avranches on the N798 to Fougères. Called 'The Brittany Cemetery', it contains 4,410 burials and the names of 498 missing.

The Battle Monuments Commission offices are at:
UNITED STATES. Room 2067, Tempo A and T Streets SW, Washington, DC 20315.
FRANCE. 68 rue 19 janvier, 92 Garches, France.

There is a new AMBC Website on htp://www.usabmc.com/abmc5.htm

CANADIAN CEMETERIES

The Canadian cemeteries at Bény-sur-Mer and Bretteville-sur-Laize are maintained by the CWGC and are described below. Although primarily Canadian they both include some British and other nationalities. Canadians are also buried in Bayeux (181), Ryes (21), Tilly (1), Hottot (34), Fontenay (4), St. Manvieu (3), Brouay (2), La Délivrande

(11), Hermanville (13), Ranville (76), Banneville (11), St Charles de Percy (3), and St Désir de Lisieux (16).

COMMONWEALTH WAR GRAVES COMMISSION

The story of the foundation of the Commonwealth War Graves Commission (CWGC) and its work after the Great War of 1914-18 is told in *Major & Mrs Holt's Battlefield Guides to the Ypres Salient* and *to the Somme*. After the Second World War, the Commission's task was two-fold: to restore the maintenance of the First World War Graves and to take on board the new task of commemorating the fallen from WWII. Conditions for the returning WWI gardeners, who had fled the invading Germans in 1940, were horrendous in war-torn Europe - often there was no housing, no food and the pay was pitiful. The story of the struggle is vividly told in Philip Longworth's *The Unending Vigil*. The inspiration and leading light of the Commission, Fabian Ware, was aging and ill. In November 1947 he resigned as Chairman, stayed on as theoretical Vice-Chairman, retired in June 1948 and died in April 1949 at the age of 80. There was no-one with his vision, practical experience and political acumen to succeed him. Ware is commemorated by a memorial plaque in the Warrior's Chapel at Westminster and in the naming of the principal ring-road around Bayeux (qv). Morale was at an all-time low as old problems were tackled anew and new ones emerged. Opinions as to the best way forward were mixed amongst the participating allies. New shaped headstones (examples of most of which can be seen in the polyglot Bayeux Cemetery) had to be designed for the Czechs, the Poles, the French, the Norwegians, the Greeks, the Dutch, the Italians and the Belgians. The New Zealanders still refused to allow a personal

Register and Visitor's Book, Bény CWGC Cemetery.

message at the foot of the standard headstone. The Australians were loath to charge families for the inscription as had been the British policy after WWI. But by April 1946 all the old cemeteries in France and Belgium had been taken over once more and priority could then be given to the design and construction of the new cemeteries and memorials. The Army exerted pressure to create the new cemeteries as quickly as possible. By 1947 the existing staff proved inadequate for the task of tending 212,000 new graves. Work had begun in Normandy, where a CWGC representative was posted in February 1946. The area was devastated, premises impossible to find. The Graves Registration Unit was operating from Bayeux and eventually they found some derelict garages on the coast. From there, operating from a solitary table, orange boxes for filing cabinets and a shell-case for boiling tea, the CWGC representative started his monumental task. Through Normandy came all the new headstones - it was now estimated that 350,000 would be required and at first it was thought that it would take 15 years to complete the carving of them on the favoured Portland stone. A special factory was set up, with templates for each regimental badge and machines that could cut four headstones a day. The stones were to be set in concrete beams, four kilometers of which were needed to set the Normandy headstones alone. By 1948 spacious premises were acquired in Bayeux, the horticulturist was joined by an architect and a quantity surveyor, administrative and drawing offices were added and the old stables were converted into a garage, the garden became a plant nursery. As the number of staff increased a wing was converted into a hostel for single workers, run by a motherly French lady. The first Cross of Sacrifice of WWII was erected in Chouain cemetery (qv). The first five Normandy cemeteries were built by the end of 1950 and by spring 1955 all eighteen had been completed, works and horticultural staff working in harmony to produce the pleasing and comforting cemeteries we see today. The Duke of Gloucester, then President of the Commission, unveiled the Bayeux Memorial in June 1955. The principal architect in Normandy was Philip Hepworth, a WWI veteran and Member of the Royal Academy Planning Committee for the rebuilding of London after the war. Hepworth was a draughtsman of the classical mould in the tradition of Lutyens and Baker - as can be seen in his gabled, barrel-vaulted entrance at Brouay (qv) and the watch-towers at Bény-sur-Mer. Hepworth always consulted the horticulturalists when designing his cemeteries, one of the most pleasing outcomes of the collaboration being the serpentine approach path at Banneville-la-Campagne (qv).

As time went on, staff were systematically reduced as the cemeteries were completed and machinery took over from manual labour. The policy of recruiting ex-Servicemen continued as far as possible, and for many years Ranville was attended by an officer who had landed there on D-Day and who helped bury some of his fallen comrades there. Sons and then grandsons of the original WWI gardeners continued the tradition, although today many local gardeners are employed. The cemeteries remain places of extreme peace and beauty, thanks to the dedication of the men who continue the standards set by the exceptional founder of this exceptional organisation, Fabian Ware.

The dedicated work of the Commission and its gardeners, who keep the cemeteries so beautifully, cannot be praised too highly. Please make sure to sign the Visitor's Book and to record your comments. Your visit is appreciated by those who tend the cemeteries.

CWGC Cemeteries in Normandy, with numbers of burials/names and Holt Map Reference

Banneville-la-Campagne	2,175	I2
Bayeux Cemetery	4,648	A11
Bayeux Memorial1,	808	A10
Bény-sur-Mer Canadian	2,049	C25
Bretteville-sur-Laize Canadian	2,958	N4
Brouay	377	G22
Cambes-en-Plaine	224	H25
Douvres la Délivrande	1,123	C8
Fontenay-le-Pesnil	519	G8
Hermanville	1,005	D21
Hottot-les-Bagues	1,137	G9
Jerusalem (Chouain)	47	F7
Ranville	2,562	I17
Ryes (Bazenville)	979	B22
St Charles de Percy (still open)	800	L5
St Désir (+ 4 WW1)	598	I45
St Manvieu (Cheux)	2,183	G10
Sequeville-en-Bessin	117	G17
Tilly-sur-Seulles	1,222	F5

Plus many graves in local churchyards - look for the green CWGC *'Tombes de Guerre'* sign at the cemetery entrance.

CWGC HEADQUARTERS
UK: 2 Marlow Road, Maidenhead, Berks SL6 7DK. Tel: 01628 634221
France: Rue Angèle, 62217 Beaurains. Tel: 00 33 (0)3 21 71 03 24

CWGC Website.
In 1995 the CWGC undertook the formidable task of scanning the details of 1.7 million casualties onto a computer database, the better to respond to the 50,000 or so annual enquiries they were receiving. In November 1998 they made this information, accessed by the criteria of family name, regiment or home town, available on the Internet, on www.cwgc.org. The site was opened on 9 November 1998 and during the first two weeks they had the extraordinary number of 4 million hits [the name given to one access of the information]. In the beginning of 1999 hits were running at an average of 55,000 per day!

Polish headstone Douvres-la-Délivrande showing the effect of weathering on the stone.

POLISH CEMETERY/BURIALS

The poignant Polish cemetery at Grainville-Langannerie, on the N158 south of Caen, (Map N1), contains 650 burials. It is maintained by the French Ministry of Anciens Combattants, rue de Bercy, Paris 12.

There are also Polish burials in Bayeux (25), Ryes (1), Douvres-la Délivrande (1), Ranville (1) and Banneville-la-Campagne (5). See the CWGC listing above.

VOLKSBUND DEUTSCHE KRIEGSGRÄBERFÜRSORGE

(The German War Graves Welfare Organisation)

The organisation is similar in function to the Commonwealth War Graves Commission and the American Battle Monuments Commission in that it maintains the war cemeteries and memorials to the German dead from World War I onwards.

In 1956, the organisation, with the help of volunteer students, started re-interring the German war dead, then buried in 1,400 sites in Normandy, into the six large cemeteries which exist today.

La Cambe is described in detail on Itinerary Two above (MapT18). Other German cemeteries in Normandy are:

Champigny-St André, between Evreux and Dreux, 19,795 burials

Huisnes-sur-Mer, near Mont St Michel, 11,956 burials

Marigny-la-Chapelle, near St Lô, 11,169 burials (Map Y7)

Orglandes, near Valognes, 10,152 burials (Map P1)

St Désir-de-Lisieux, 3,735 burials (Map I44)

There are also German burials in many CWGC Cemeteries. The address of the organisation is:

Volksbund Deutsche Kriegsgräberfürsorge, Werner-Hilpert-Strasse, 3500 Kassel, Germany.

Database at German Cemetery, la Cambe.

A wonderful facility exists at the Information Centre outside the German Cemetery at la Cambe. There is a freely available computer with a database containing the place of burial of all soldiers, sailors, airmen and others buried in war cemeteries in Normandy.

ORGANISATIONS FOR EX-SERVICEMEN AND REMEMBRANCE

As the veterans of the Normandy campaign reach retirement age and have more time to spend on meeting old comrades and on thinking back, membership of veterans' associations is growing. They include:

THE AMERICAN LEGION

They also have information about the many strong American divisional and other ex-servicemen's associations. Head Office: PO Box 1050 Indianapolis, IN 46206, USA. French Office: 49 rue Pierre Charron, Paris 8ème, France.

AIRBORNE ASSAULT NORMANDY TRUST

A trust to preserve the history of 6AB's assault into Normandy. Membership open to veterans and interested associate members. Regimental Headquarters, The Parachute Regiment, Browning Barracks, Aldershot, Hants, GU11 2BU, UK. Contact Major Jack Watson. Tel: 01252 349620.

D-DAY AND NORMANDY FELLOWSHIP

Formed in 1968, this is open to men and women of all armed forces and merchant navies who took part in the D-Day and subsequent operations in Normandy, to their relatives and those closely associated with or interested in the events of 1944. There are over 2,000 members. The President is General Sir Philip Ward, KVO, CBE, LL. Contact: Mrs L.R. Reed, 9 South Parade, Southsea, Portsmouth, Hants, PO5 2JB. Tel: 01705 812180. Mollie Reed has been the faithful secretary of the Association for over 25 years.

MOTHS (Memorable Order of Tin Hats)

Similar to the RBL, one has to have seen active service to belong to this organisation which was started in South Africa after World War I. They are still expanding and have seven 'Shell Holes' (branches) in the UK and have many Normandy veterans among their members. Contact: Mr Harry Turner (Senior 'Old Bill'), 3 Millicent Fawcett Court, Tottenham, London N17 6SH. Tel: 0181 808 8933.

THE NORMANDY VETERANS' ASSOCIATION

The association was formed in April 1981 in Grimsby by thirty-four dedicated Normandy veterans, whose energetic committee, with publicity officer Arthur Flodman, wrote to every local newspaper in Great Britain. By May sixteen other local branches had been formed. Arthur Flodman became the first national secretary, but sadly died in 1985. By 1994 there were eighty-nine active branches, including international branches in France (Normandy), Holland, Belgium, New Zealand, Nova Scotia, Australia and West Germany. The members of the 68th branch, 'Calvados', fought with the Maquis.

Representatives from the ten British regions form a national council. Funds are raised for the benevolent and welfare section through the sale of the NVA's own Commemoration Campaign Medal and other items.

The President is Colonel Sir Peter Hilton, MC and Bars, and the Duke of Gloucester, KCVO, is the Royal Patron. The association has its own chaplain and national standard.

Parades and services are held each year on the Sunday after 6 June and the association parades on Remembrance Sunday at the Cenotaph. Many branches run pilgrimages to Normandy each 6 June.

The purpose of the association is 'comradeship' and membership is open to all who took an active part in the assault on the beaches of Normandy, including all Auxilliary Services, WRENS, Nursing Services, ENSA and NAAFI. There are now over 100 branches and more than 10,000 members.

The Normandy Veterans, together with the D-Day and Normandy Fellowship (qv) commissioned Vivien Mallock (qv) to sculpt the statue of Field Marshal Montgomery at Colleville-Mongomery and contributed to the one at Portsmouth.

Contact: Mr E.S. Hannath, Hon Gen Secretary, 53 Normandy Road, Cleethorpes, N/E Lincs, DN35 9JE. Tel: 01472 600867.

ROYAL BRITISH LEGION

Their Pilgrimage Department arranges pilgrimages for war widows and families to CWGC cemeteries in Normandy. Their head office is RBL, Pall Mall, London SW1 and the Pilgrimages Department, run for many years by the enthusiastic Piers Storie-Pugh, is at the Royal British Legion Village, Aylesford, Kent ME20 7NX. Tel: 01622 716729.

ASSOCIATION FRANCE-GRANDE BRETAGNE

Comité de Caen, 9 Place Jean-Letellier, 14000 Caen. Contact: Mme Joan Boyer.

This extremely helpful association has been providing assistance for many years to Royal British Legion pilgrims and others wishing to visit the CWGC cemeteries around Caen, but who have no transport.

COMITÉ DU DÉBARQUEMENT (D-Day Commemoration Committee)

After the landings, the first 'Sous-Prefet' to be appointed in France was Monsieur Raymond Triboulet, OBE. He operated from Bayeux, the first French city to be liberated, and became Ministre des Anciens Combattants in 1958. He was also appointed Chairman of the 'Comité du Débarquement', set up in May 1945, which is dedicated to preserving the sites and the memory of the invasion and the landing beaches. The Comité is responsible for the siting of ten 'Monuments Signaux' - great stone markers commemorating the landing at, or Liberation of, Bénouville, Ouistreham-Riva-Bella, Bernières, Graye, Port-en-Bessin, Les Moulins (St Laurent), Isigny, Carentan, St Martin de Varreville and Ste Mère Eglise, as well as other memorials.

It also set up, or supports, the museums at Arromanches, Ste Mère Eglise, Cherbourg, Ste Marie-du-Mont (UTAH), Ouistreham, Merville Battery and the Mémorial Museum at Caen. The indefatigable Monsieur Triboulet is leading the campaign for the new Airborne Museum at Ranville. The Comité liaises with British regimental and ex-servicemen's associations to participate in ceremonies of remembrance in Normandy. Its head office is at Place aux Pommes, Bayeux.

SOUVENIR FRANÇAIS

This association was founded in 1872, after the Franco-Prussian War. Its aim is to keep alive the memory of those who died for France, to maintain their graves and memorials in good condition, and to transmit 'the flame of memory' to future generations. Head Office is at 9 rue de Clichy, 75009 Paris.

THE *SOUVENIR* JUNO COMMITTEE
This committee is the inspiration of its energetic President and Founder, M. Bernard Nourry, 44 rue 20ième Siècle, Caen. Tel: (0)2 31 86 2096. Its main aim is 'to perpetuate the memory of the liberation fight in June, July and August 1944, to worship the memory of the Canadians fallen dead on our ground during this time'.

Sixty *Communes* on the Canadians' liberation route have joined the Association and many of them have erected, or plan to erect, memorials with the date of their liberation and the name of the Canadian unit which liberated them.

Three itineraries have been marked with, at the entrance to the *Communes*, a red-on-white Souvenir Juno road sign carrying a Maple Leaf (see Holts' Map).

Route 1	Route 2	Route 3
Gray/Bernières	St Aubin/Courseulles	Caen
Reviers	Bény	Fleury
Fontaine-Henry	Tailleville	St André-sur-Orne
Thaon	Basly	St Martin-de-Fontenay
Bretteville l'Org	Anguerny	May-sur-Orne
Rosel	Anisy	Fontenel-le-Marmion
Rots	Villons le Buissons	Laize-la-Ville
Bretteville-sur-Odon	Cairon	Cintheaux
Putot	Buron	Soumont
Norrey St Contest	Authie	Potigny
Baron-sur-Odon	Carpiquet/Louvigny	

FRANCO-AMERICAN 9th US AIRFORCE NORMANDY AIRFIELDS ASSOCIATION
The dedicated founder is the assiduous researcher Madame Beatrice Bouvier-Muller, Neuilly-la-Fôret, 14230 Isigny-sur-Mer. Tel: (0) 2 31 22 82 05. In liaison with American archivists, veterans and local participants of the Landings and Battle for Normandy, Madame Bouvier-Muller has identified and marked, all the 9th USAAF 1944 airstrips in Normandy. They are (starting from Cherbourg, progressing towards Bayeux):-

A23	-	Querqueville (D45. North-west of Cherbourg)
A15	-	Cherbourg Airport. (D901. Near Maupertus)
A7	-	Fontenay-sur-Mer (D14-D214)
A24	-	Bénouville (D126)
A6	-	Beuzeville (D17/D115)
A8	-	Picauville (D69. North of Les Buts Dores)
A25	-	Bolleville (D903)
A14	-	Nr Coigny (D223/D138. North-east of Château de Franquetot)
A20	-	Lessay (D900. Near Aerodrome)
A26	-	Gonfreville (D140. Between Gorges and Gonfreville)
A17	-	Méautis (D443/D223)
A16	-	Brucheville (D424)
ELS	-	UTAH Beach, Pouppeville
A10	-	Les Veys (N13/D89)
A11	-	St Lambert (D19. Neuilly-la-Fôret)
A18	-	Le Dezert (N174. Near St Jean-de-Daye)

A3	-	Cardonville (D119/D199A)
A2	-	Cricqueville en Bessin (D194. La Grande Lande)
		La Cambe (Les Vignets)
A4	-	Longueille (Off N13)
A1	-	Englesqueville la Percée (seashore path above D514)
ELSA21	-	OMAHA Beach (Off D517. Les Moulins)
A22	-	Russy (West of D97. Château Rouge)
A13	-	Nr Vaucelles (N13)
A5	-	Cartigny-Epigny (Small road above D15)
A9	-	Le Molay Littry (D145/D191)
A19	-	Couvains (D92/D448)
A12	-	Lignerolles (Below D13)

The Association was also responsible for locating at Tournières General Eisenhower's 'First Command Post on the European Continent'. See Extra Visit, Itinerary Three.

WINGS OF VICTORY OVER NORMANDY ASSOCIATION

An organisation started and researched by the dedicated M. Michel Bréhin, inspired by his contact with the downed British Pilot, Peter Roper, in June 1944, and supported by the RAFA and the Comité du Débarquement. Their most important achievement is the striking memorial in Noyers Bocage (designed by M. Triboulet) to the 150 Typhoon pilots killed in Normandy, May-August 1944. In 1994 the names of the pilots were added. Airstrip/Squadron markers are in the following Communes:

Noyers Bocage	-	Typhoon pilots memorial (D875)
Martragny	-	Memorial to 438, 439, 440 Canadian Squadrons (D82)
Lantheuil	-	Memorial in Mairie (D93)
Coulombs	-	Cully-180 Squadron (D126)
Bény	-	401, 402, 422 Squadrons (D79)
Bazenville	-	Plaque on cemetery (D87)
St Croix-sur-Mer	-	(D112)
Plaque in Bayeux Museum		
Le Fresne	-	Camilly-B-6. Plaque on wall (D22)
Cheux	-	Plaque to Wing Commander Baker (D70)

Monsieur Bréhin also researched the crash site of Pilot Officer Donald William Mason, Royal Australian Air Force, died 18 June 1944, and in March 1993 his body was re-interred at St Charles de Percy. The intact engine of his plane is the museum at Tilly-sur-Seulles.

INTERNET

There is an increasing number of sites devoted to the Second World War. One of the best is at www.normandyallies.org, which has been established by the Normandy Allies Organisation, which is part of the World War Two Web Ring. Normandy Allies is a non-profit organisation created to commemorate the actions of the American Forces, together with the people of Normandy in their struggle against the Nazis in 1944.

TOURIST INFORMATION

[For more Tourist Information, in particular how to get to Normandy, see the Approach Routes at the beginning of the book.]

It would not be appropriate in this book, which is first and foremost a guide to the D-Day Landing Beaches, to include a comprehensive account of the province's rich history and culture. However, as the visitor will pass through areas redolent of its eventful past and productive present, he or she deserves at least a brief background to Normandy's culture, the better to enjoy the tour. It is also an area of outstanding natural beauty and delicious food - neither of which should be neglected.

Norman Architecture

The routes one must follow to visit the Landing Beaches and Dropping Zones of the D-Day Invasion take the visitor past some outstanding examples of ecclesiastical, agricultural and manorial architecture.

The predominating style (many superb examples of which, thankfully, survived the fearful battering of the invasion) is known as *Romanesque*. The Normans created their own brand of Romanesque, which in Britain is known as Norman, and which can still be seen in many churches in Southern England.

It was a harmonious, geometric style, with zigzag decoration, square towers and narrow windows, which retained the rounded Roman arch. William the Bastard's Abbeys at Caen (L'Abbaye aux Hommes and L'Abbaye aux Dames) are High Romanesque, but the style was modified when, as the Conqueror, he carried it over the Channel to England.

Yacht Basin, Courseulles.

On a simpler scale, the churches in many rural and littoral villages are fine examples of the style, e.g. at Secqueville-en-Bessin and Ouistreham. The distinctive, tall, wedge-shaped, tiled roof surmounting a square tower can be seen on old farmhouses and churches, throughout the Bessin. With their courtyards enclosed by high walls and turrets, the farms, still in daily use, seem like living pages from history books.

The restraint of the *Romanesque/Normand* period gave way to the exuberant, ornate Gothic era. Again, the Normans had their own version - Gothique Normand. The most glorious example in Calvados is the cathedral at Bayeux, but more modest churches are to be found at Bernières, Langrune and in many smaller towns.

The Renaissance left its architectural mark, principally on the church of St Pierre in Caen, with interesting examples of statuary and furniture scattered throughout the surrounding district.

Of the scores of picturesque châteaux in the areas covered by the Landing Beaches (most of which were used as German, then Allied, command posts) that of Fontaine-Henry, with its beautiful Renaissance wing and high, pointed slate roofs, is probably the most architecturally interesting. The local villagers sheltered in its cellars during the bombardments covering the invasion. Creullet Château, where General Montgomery pitched his caravan, is not open to the public, but is perfectly visible through the ironwork gates, and it is very close to Creully, whose sprawling, multi-period château was used by Allied broadcasters after the invasion. Their broadcasting tower can be visited by appointment with the town council, whose offices it now houses.

The beautiful creamy-coloured Normandy stone, quarried from the Caen area, and which was exported by the Normans to build their new castles and churches in England (notably Canterbury Cathedral and the Tower of London) is the building material used for many Norman towns and villages, even today. Some of the delightful villages bear a strong resemblance to Cotswold villages.

The most characteristic Normandy style, however, is the half-timbered, lath and plaster façade, akin to the English 'Elizabethan style'. It is much reproduced in modern pseudo-Norman buildings. It is the image that the visitor will most likely retain from his visit to Normandy.

The philosophical Normans approached the destruction of their buildings (an estimated 200,000 were damaged) in a practical way during the reconstruction. Many towns, in particular the devastated city of Caen, were rebuilt with wider roads more fitting to today's modern transport, better housing and office buildings and pleasant parks. Modern architects were able to leave their mark, too, on this ancient countryside. The new university building at Caen is considered an important example of modern style.

The most recent building of note in the area is the impressive new *Mémorial* Museum at Caen. It was designed by architects Jacques Millet and Philippe Kauffmann, with artistic designer Yves Devraine, and was inaugurated on 6 June 1988 by President Mittérand.

Geography and Economy

The old province of Normandy is divided into administrative *Départements*, two of which include the sites of the June 1944 Landings:

CALVADOS (bordered by the River Vire to the south, the Eure to the east and by the

Département of La Manche to the west). Its capital is Caen. It includes the area of the British action at Merville, the airborne landings near Ranville, GOLD, JUNO AND SWORD beaches, OMAHA Beach and Pointe du Hoc.

Calvados got its name in the 1790s, when the old provinces were divided into Départements. Resisting the description *Orne Inférieure*, the inhabitants preferred the suggestion of a Bayeux lady, who proposed that they should be named after the rocks lying off Arromanches - les Rochers du Calvados. They in turn had been named after one of Philip II of Spain's Armada ships, the *San Salvador*, which was wrecked on them.

Départements are further divided into *pays*, from the Gallo-Roman *pagi*. Those that concern our itineraries are:

Plaine de Caen. A rich agricultural plateau that grows sugar beet and grain, famous for its stone. Caen is now the eighth busiest port in France, especially since the new Portsmouth to Ouistreham Brittany Ferry route has been in service.

The Bessin. Bayeux (city of the Bacojasses) is its main town, Port-en-Bessin (where the British and American sectors met in June 1944) and Grandcamp are its main ports. Arromanches, on the tiny River Arro, is its most important resort, due now mainly to the remnants of its Mulberry Harbour and its museum. The ruggedly beautiful Pointe du Hoc, where the US Rangers landed, is its most picturesque site.

The Côte du Nâcre (The Mother of Pearl Coast). This runs from Ouistreham to Courseulles (SWORD and JUNO Beaches) with beautiful sandy beaches, where today it is difficult to imagine the terrible drama that was played out in June 1944. The small holiday resorts are very popular in the summer for their excellent seafood restaurants and water sports.

LA MANCHE (bordered by Calvados to the east - between Carentan and Isigny - and to the north and east by the English Channel, which gives it its name.) The area which interests us mostly comprises the near-island of the Cotentin Peninsula.

La Manche includes UTAH Beach, Ste Mère Eglise and the US Airborne drop zones and Cherbourg, its main town and port. Cherbourg was provided with a hospital and a church by William the Conqueror and was often of importance during the 100 Years' War. Vauban recognised its potential as a large port but the main port was not opened until 1853, seeing its first transatlantic ship as late as 1869. It was taken by the Americans on 26 June 1944 and in late August its PLUTO was in operation. The taking of Cherbourg had been crucial to Montgomery's plan. Today it has an attractive pleasure port and is an important ferry terminal. The *Département* is famous for its thoroughbred racing and trotting horses.

Gourmet Products and Specialities

Both *Départements* share a climate similar to the south coast of England, although somewhat milder and sunnier. Their moistness contributes to their fertility and to the lush pastureland which feeds the cattle, which are the *Départements'* greatest asset. There are some six million head of cattle in Normandy, whose pedigree is proudly guarded. Dairy products include milk, cream and fabulous cheeses like Camembert, Petite Ste Mère Eglise, Livarot and Pont l'Evèque. The cream forms the basis of the rich *sauce normande*, served on seafood, chicken and pork chops.

The apple is also important in Normandy as it is the basis for its scrumptious cider (look for *cidre bouché* [mature bottled] or *cidre fermière* [home-brewed on the farm]). To drive through Normandy in apple blossom time is a visual delight. Calvados, distilled apple brandy, is the famous *trou normand*. This sharp liqueur is drunk in gulps between rich courses to clear the palate and then as a *digestif* finale to a good meal. Make sure your Calvados has been aged for 15 years, or it will take the skin off your throat - as many an Allied soldier found to his cost, sometimes fatally, in 1944. Other local specialities are: *Tripes à la Mode de Caen* (tripe cooked in the Caen style) which is an acquired taste, Courseulles oysters, Isigny mussels and caramels.

Crêpes (pancakes) make a superb lunchtime snack. Savoury pancakes are called *galettes*, usually made with whole-wheat flour and come with a variety of delicious fillings: *Vallée d'Auge* (with cream and mushrooms), ham, cheese, onions, tomatoes, bacon etc. They are sold in Crêperies, often simple but attractive establishments. A *galette*, tossed green salad, crunchy *baguette* (long French loaf), Normandy cheese and a glass of *cidre bouché* make a perfect midday meal.

Attractions of the Area

Visitors to the Normandy Landing Beaches are coming to an area which is full of other attractions. There are safe, sandy beaches, casinos, tennis, horse-racing, fishing, sailing, wind-surfing, water-skiing, golf, horse-riding, delicious food and drink, fascinating history, culture, architecture from Romanesque to modern, handicrafts and beautiful, varied scenery - from the ever-changing coastline to the open wooded areas of the famous 'Bocage' (high hedges and ditches enclosing small fields, which were a great hazard to glider landings and tank progress in the battle for Normandy), the pretty villages, the colourful apple orchards. You may come to Normandy to study the D-Day Landings and fall in love with the country and its people.

'Piper Bill Millin' tee, OMAHA Golf Club.

BEFORE YOU COME

All these attractions add up to a very popular holiday area - not only with British and American veterans, but also with French holiday makers, especially from Paris, which is a short, easy journey away. It is, therefore, very important to book hotels or camping sites in advance during the busy summer season, which lasts from June to early September. These are the steps to take before travelling:

Contact the French Government Tourist Office

Obtain a copy of their current Reference Guide for the *Traveller in France* from them at 178 Piccadilly, London, W1V OAL, Tel: 0891 244123. It contains up-to-date practical advice on *everything* the visitor to France needs to know. A few vital points are summarised here:

Phoning to the UK from France: Dial 00 44, then drop the first 0 from your number

Phoning to Normandy from the UK: Dial 00 33 2 followed by the local number.
Phoning from one number to another in Normandy: Dial 02 followed by the local number.
Note that since 1 January 1999 prices are quoted in **Euros** as well as in Francs and in the year 2000 Euro notes and coins will be in general circulation.

Opening Hours

Banks: 0900-1200, 1400-1600 weekdays (some close Mondays or Saturdays).
Post Offices: 0800-1900 weekdays. 0800-1200 Saturdays. Currency may be exchanged at main Post Offices. You may need your passport at smaller ones. Stamps are also available at *Tabacs* (tobacconists).
Shops: 0800-1200/1230. 1400-1700/1800. Larger shops may close on Sunday and even Monday. Small food shops normally open Sunday morning. Supermarkets are open till late.
Restaurants: often have a weekly closing day (e.g. Sunday evening or an arbitrary day early in the week).
Churches: Normally not visitable by tourists during services.
Museums: Many shut on Mondays or Tuesday. Smaller museums have restricted opening hours from October to Easter. Generally open weekends.
Public Holidays: New Year's Day, Easter Monday, May Day (1 May), VE (8 May), Armistice Day (11 November), Christmas Day.
Electricity: Mostly 220-30 volts. Two pin, circular plugs. An international plug adapter is recommended.
Metric Measurements: 1 kilo = 2.2lb. 1 litre = $1^3/_4$ pints. 1 gallon = 4.5 litres. 1 kilometer = 0.6 miles.

Tourist Offices

Known as *Offices de Tourisme or Syndicats d'Initiative,* they are to be found in all towns of any size. Follow **'i'** for information signs. Most of the useful tourist offices for Landing Beaches tours are listed as they are passed on the itineraries. Important offices are:

Normandy Tourist Board: The Old Bakery, 44 Bath Hill, Keynsham, Bristol BS18 1HG, UK. Tel: 0117 986 0386. Fax: 0117 986 0379.

Remember that even Normandy can be wet and muddy off-season.

Calvados Departmental Office: Place du Canada, 14000 Caen. Tel: (0)2 31 27 90 30, Fax (0)2 31 27 90 35.

La Manche Departmental Office: *Maison du Département,* 50008 Saint-Lô. Tel: 02 33 05 98 70. Fax: 02 33 56 07 03.

These tourist offices will make hotel reservations, give information on local restaurants, events (e.g. festivals, sporting events, concerts, shows), places of interest (e.g. museums, markets, Calvados distilleries), guided tours and 'Routes'; *du Fromage* (cheese);

du Cidre (cider); *des Moulins* (mills); *des Trois Rivières* (three rivers - l'Aure, la Drôme and la Tortonne), etc, all with well-signed itineraries.
Note that tourist offices usually close during the French lunch hour.

Accommodation

Lists are obtainable from the national or local tourist offices (see above). Book well in advance for busy holiday periods and in September when the Caen International Fair (Foire de Caen) takes place - check the precise dates with the tourist office. Details of the Hotels that lie conveniently along the itineraries are given as they are passed. The area is rich in hotels, which are graded as follows:

* - plain and basic, often known as *Auberge or Pension;*

** - can be quite comfortable, especially if in modern chains like Ibis, Urbis, Campanile, Fimotel, which have private bathrooms, but small rooms;

*** - good quality hotel, with private bathrooms, often with lift, bar, swimming pool, restaurants (eg Novotel and Mercure groups);

**** - top class, very comfortable;

**** L - luxury class, with superbly equipped bedrooms, gracious public rooms, many facilities.

Logis de France. A grouping of small, normally family run hotels, with good regional and 'home' cooking. Head Office (which will supply their current brochure) 25 rue Jean Mermoz, 75008 Paris, France (or from French Government Tourist Office).

Gites de France. Self-catering cottages, apartments, farms, often in rural areas. All have running water, inside loo, shower. (List available from Tourist Offices.)

Chambres D'Hôte. Bed and breakfast often in farms or cottages, sometimes in small châteaux. (Lists available from Tourist Offices.)

Camping Sites. The area (especially along the coast and on inland farms) abounds with camping sites, from sophisticated (with showers and many other facilities) to basic. On some, caravans can be hired. Lists from national or local Tourist Offices.

Veterans/Entrance Fees

D-Day or Normandy battles veterans should not be required to pay entrance fees in official museums. They may, however, be asked to sign the museum's *Livre d'Or* (VIP Visitors' Book).

N.B: CHANGING INFORMATION

Tourism is a transient industry! The reader must be aware that all tourist information is subject to frequent change.

Road numbers change as improvements are made, some roads morphing alarmingly from beginning to end so that one may start on an 'A' road and finish on a 'C'. Hotels and restaurants change management and sometimes standards, or simply close down. Museums change their opening times, admission prices, exhibits, or they, too, simply close down. Sometimes they do not open according to their advertised opening times. Therefore the visitor must take any tourist information given here as a guide and appreciate that it is as correct as possible at the time of going to press. Phone numbers are given where available so that visitors can phone ahead to confirm details.

ACKNOWLEDGMENTS

Our sincere thanks for their help in preparing the original version of this book go to the following - some of whom are, sadly, no longer with us, some of whose jobs have changed: M Raymond Triboulet, OBE, President of the *Comité du Débarquement*; Roger Dalley of the CWGC for permission to reproduce their Normandy information; Régine Turgis and M du Gourmand, Comité Départemental de Tourisme du Calvados; Michael Poulain, Bureau de Tourisme de Bayeux; M Carpentier, Maire de Bayeux and M Green; Tony Watts, Commercial Attaché, la Manche; Isabelle Chollet, *l'Association Liberté 44*, St Lô; M Duhommet, Tourist Office, St Lô; Madame Bérot, Tourist Office, Cherbourg; Madame Bouvier-Muller, Franco-American 9th USAAF Association; M Bertrand Nourry, Souvenir JUNO Association; M. Michel Bréhin, Wings of Victory over Normandy Association; Mr Joseph P. Rivers, Superintendent, the American National Cemetery, St Laurent and Sylvie; M Noel, former curator of the Arromanches Museum and M Jacquinot of the old Bénouville Museum; Arlette Gondrée-Pritchet; Bob Slaughter, US 29th Div; the incomparable Major Strafford and those who have so kindly written to us with comments after the publication of the original Normandy Guide.

For their moving, vivid, sometimes amusing, sometimes sad 'Memories of D-Day', our heartfelt thanks to the following (with their 1944 ranks): Lieutenant Laurie Anderson, Paratrooper Les Cartwright, Sergeant John Clewlow, Gunfitter Harry Cooper, Lieutenant Commander Rupert Curtis, Major Tony Dyball, Aircraft Engineer John Ginter, Trooper 'Goody' Goodson, Major John Howard, Lance Corporal P. L. M. Hennessey, Piper Bill Millin, Brigadier Nigel Poett, Major Pat Porteous VC, Pte Lee Ratel, Lieutenant 'Tod' Sweeney, Lieutenant J. J. Whitmeyer, Captain John Winckworth, Lieutenant D. J. Wood.

For particular help in the preparation of the 55th Anniversary version our grateful thanks go - once again - to our good friends Michel Poulain of the Bayeux Tourist Office (and Chantal Cheer) and Joe (or Phil, as he is otherwise known) Rivers, Superintendent of the US Cemetery, St Laurent. Also of immense assistance were Françoise Marie of the Calvados Tourist Office and Isabelle Gardie of the Manche Tourist Office. We are grateful to Stephen Rogers and Lucy Walker of the Normandy Tourist Office; Matthew Little of the Royal Marines Museum; Major Jack Watson of the Airborne Trust; Neil McIntosh of RHQ The Green Howards; Mike Fry of MFH Foundry; M J. Tirard of the HMS Association, Hermanville; Ken Ewing of the Sherwood Rangers Yeomanry Regimental Association; Maurice Hillebrandt of the LST & Landing Craft Association; General Sir Robert Ford of the 4th/7th Royal Dragoon Guards; Mr Eddie Hannath of the Normandy Veterans' Association; Stephen Brooks of the Portsmouth Archives Department; Winston Ramsay, Publisher of *After the Battle*; Monsieur Benoit Noël of the UTAH Beach Museum; Monsieur Philippe Chapron of the *Bayeux Musée Mémorial de la Bataille de Normandie*.

For information for 2000 update: Sir Beville Stanier, Bt; Eddie Hannath and A.E. Innes of the NVA; Lt Col S.V. Peskett, RM and Eddy Spink, 'Big Red 1' expert.

And, finally, to Tom (who was at School) Hartman and to Elaine, for keeping us "on the road".

Picture Acknowledgements

The authors and publishers would like to thank the following for the use of illustrations:
Portsmouth Archives, page 27; *Musée Mémorial de la Bataille de Normandie*, page 134; UTAH Beach Museum, page 70; Ken Ewing, page 155.

INDEX

FORCES

These are listed in descending order, i.e. Armies, Corps, Divisions, Brigades, Regiments... numerically and then alphabetically.

General Index

MÉMORIALS BY TOWN/VILLAGE

In addition to those below, many streets, roads and squares are named as memorials to individuals and units who took part in the landings and the Battle for Normandy; a number are mentioned in the text.

MUSEUMS/PRESERVED BATTERIES

WAR CEMETERIES